Miscellanies

OF

the Fuller Worthies' Library

IN FOUR VOLUMES

VOLUME 1

EDITED BY THE REV. ALEXANDER B. GROSART

AMS PRESS
NEW YORK

Original pagination has been maintained in this reprint.

Reprinted from a copy in the collections of the Harvard College Library
From the edition of 1870–1876, Blackburn
First AMS EDITION published 1970
Manufactured in the United States of America

International Standard Book Number:
Complete Set: 0-404-02670-2

Volume 1: 0-404-02671-0

Library of Congress Card Catalog Number: 70-129362

AMS PRESS, INC.
NEW YORK, N.Y. 10003

Miscellanies

OF

The Fuller Worthies' Library.

IN FOUR VOLUMES.

VOL. I.

CONTAINING

THE POEMS OF LORD BACON—
THE POEMS OF BISHOP JEREMY TAYLOR—
THE 'TEMPTACYON', A SACRED PLAY, BY
BISHOP BALE—
THE POEMS OF WILLIAM HARBERT, OF
GLAMORGAN—
THE POEMS OF HUMPHREY GIFFORD—
AND
THE POEMS OF DR. WILLIAM LOE.

EDITED WITH

Memorial-Introductions and Notes:

BY THE

REV. ALEXANDER B. GROSART,

ST. GEORGE'S, BLACKBURN, LANCASHIRE.

PRINTED FOR PRIVATE CIRCULATION.
1871.
156 COPIES ONLY.

Miscellanies

OF

The Fuller Worthies' Library.

IN THREE VOLUMES.

VOL. I.

CONTAINING

THE POEMS OF LORD BACON—
THE POEMS OF BISHOP JEREMY TAYLOR—
THE 'TEMPTACYON,' A SACRED PLAY, BY
BISHOP BALE—
THE POEMS OF WILLIAM HARBERT, OF
GLAMORGAN—
THE POEMS OF HUMPHREY GIFFORD—
AND
THE POEMS OF DR. WILLIAM LOE.

EDITED WITH

Memorial-Introductions and Notes,

BY THE

REV. ALEXANDER B. GROSART,

ST. GEORGE'S, BLACKBURN, LANCASHIRE.

PRINTED FOR PRIVATE CIRCULATION.
1870.
156 COPIES ONLY.

TO

William Carew Hazlitt, Esq.,

OF THE INNER TEMPLE:

INHERITOR OF THE BLOOD AND NAME
OF A MAN OF FINE GENIUS—
—OF RARE CRITICAL INSIGHT—OF BURNING
ELOQUENCE—AND
WITH WHOM, IN HIS CASE, IN BOOK-LOVE AND LORE,
'COMPARISONS ARE' *NOT* 'ODIOUS':

This Volume is Inscribed

WITH HIGH REGARD AND THANKS BY

THE EDITOR.

Preface.

I INTEND to include in three volumes of Miscellanies, such lesser, though not less noticeable Worthies, as would not make volumes separately. Each is paged above by itself, beneath as part of the Collection. Pecuniarily, the Miscellanies of the present volume it would be impossible to purchase as a whole, at any price, as the 'Temptacion' of Bishop Bale and the 'Posie of Gilloflowers' of Gifford are preserved in single exemplars: and all the others are extremely rare.

It may be noted with reference to BACON that having followed his original and early editors and the ultimate one (Mr. Spedding), in calling him 'Baron *of* Verulam', an interesting and curious exchange of "Notes and Queries" thereupon, appeared in that well-known publication. One communication from my friend Mr. Spedding is of permanent value. Oddly enough, while pouncing down on the '*of*', neither the erudite Editor nor any one of his correspondents has a word on the popular title 'Lord Bacon', which of course is (technically) incorrect.

The Introductions and Notes to the several Miscellanies, furnish any additional information needed. Rich materials await Vols IId and IIId, as elsewhere announced in detail.

ALEXANDER B. GROSART.

St. George's Blackburn,
  Lancashire Novr. 5th. 1870.

MISCELLANIES

OF

𝕿𝖍𝖊 𝕱𝖚𝖑𝖑𝖊𝖗 𝖂𝖔𝖗𝖙𝖍𝖎𝖊𝖘' 𝕷𝖎𝖇𝖗𝖆𝖗𝖞.

THE

POEMS

OF

FRANCIS BACON,

BARON OF VERULAM, VISCOUNT ST. ALBAN,

AND

LORD HIGH CHANCELLOR OF ENGLAND.

FOR THE

FIRST TIME COLLECTED AND EDITED

AFTER THE ORIGINAL TEXTS.

WITH

INTRODUCTION.

BY THE

REV. ALEXANDER B. GROSART,

ST. GEORGE'S, BLACKBURN, LANCASHIRE.

PRINTED FOR PRIVATE CIRCULATION.

1870.

156 COPIES ONLY.

Francis Bacon,
Born January 22nd, 1561.
Died April 9th, 1629.

Contents.

✱*✱ Portrait (in large paper copies) to face title-page.

I. Introduction.

FEEL that it were a work of supereroga-
tion to do much more than transfer here
Mr. Spedding's preface to the "Psalmes",
in his ultimate edition of the Works. I take
the opportunity of returning him my very hearty
thanks for favouring me with the use of his own
private plate of the miniature-portrait of Bacon
—given in the large paper copies of our little
collection—and on which see onward—and I
know he will make me equally welcome to
appropriate his excellent criticism. I shall
occasionally intercalate a few words.

Mr. Spedding speaks first of the 'Psalmes'
as follows:[1] "The *translation of certaine Psalmes
into English verse*—the only verses certainly of
Bacon's making that have come down to us, and
probably with one or two slight exceptions the
only verses he ever attempted,—was made, as the

---

collection of Apophthegms also was, during a fit of sickness in 1624. Had it been merely composed, fairly copied, and presented with a grateful and graceful dedication to his friend George Herbert, there would have been nothing in the matter to call for explanation. A full mind, accustomed to work under the excitement of an eager temperament, and the consciousness of great purposes unaccomplished, and the time fast approaching when no man can work, cannot find rest in inaction; but only in some other mode of activity, which may occupy without exciting or too deeply engaging it. For this purpose no exercises can be better than the turning over and reviewing of the miscellaneous stores of the memory, and the mechanical process of arranging words in metre :

> But for the unquiet heart and brain
> A use in measured language lies :
> The sad mechanic exercise,
> Like dull narcotic, numbing pain.

Bacon however not only composed these two little works, but published them—in December, 1624 : see Court and Times of James I., ii, p 486 —: a fact which, considering how little he had cared to publish during the first sixty years of his life, and how many things of weightier character and more careful workmanship he had then by him

in his cabinet, (including the entire contents of the
Miscellany works and the *Resuscitatio*,) is somewhat
remarkable. My own conjecture is, that things
of more serious import he did not like to publish
in an imperfect shape as long as he could hope to
perfect them, but that he owed money to his printer and bookseller, and if such trifles as these
would help to pay it, he had no objection to their
being used for the purpose." The latter solution
with all respect, is surely most improbable, as the
imprint shews that the printer was *not* his usual
printer, neither the publisher his usual publisher,
besides the grotesqueness of a five or ten pound
note—all needed or likely to result—being a
'debt' to be met in this round-about way. To
my mind it is clear Bacon chose to bring out of
his treasures these "certaine Psalmes," and that
is noticeable, nay ought to quicken every reader
to remember the axiom 'The eye sees what it
brings', and so repress stupidities like this: "the
certaine Psalmes are beneath criticism".

Mr. Spedding continues, "In compositions upon
which a man would have thought it a culpable
waste of time to bestow any serious labour, it
would be idle to seek either for indications of
his taste or for a measure of his powers. And
yet as Bacon could not have gone on turning

as many of the Psalms into verse without
thinking a good deal about the way in which
it should be done, there is some interest in
watching his progress. At first he seems to have
tried to keep close to the text : adding no more
than the necessities of metre required. His two
first experiments appear to be done on this principle, and the effect is flat enough. I fancy too,
that he felt it to be so. For as he advances he
falls more and more into a kind of a paraphrase ;
in which the inevitable loss of lyric fire and force
is in some degree compensated by the development of meanings which are implied or suggested
by the original, but not so as to strike the imagination of a modern reader ; so that the translation
serves for a kind of poetical commentary ; and
though far from representing the effect of the
original in itself, holds up a light to read it by.
For myself at least, I may say that deeply pathetic
as the opening of the 137th psalm always seemed
to be, I have found it much more affecting, since
I read Bacon's paraphrase of it.

" By the waters of Babylon we sat down, and wept when
we remembered Sion. As for our harps, we hanged them
up, upon the trees that are therein. For they that
led us away captive required of us then a song, and
melod in our heaviness," &c.

When as we sate, all sad and desolate,
  By Babylon upon the river's side,
Eased from the tasks which in our captive state
  We were enforcéd daily to abide,
Our harps we had brought with us to the field,
Some solace to our heavy souls to yield.

But soon we found, we fail'd of our account :
  For *when our minds some freedom did obtain,*
Straightways the memory of Sion Mount
  Did cause afresh our wounds to bleed again ;
So that with present griefs and future fears
Our eyes burst forth into a stream of tears.

As for our harps, *since sorrow struck them dumb,*
  We hang'd them on the willow trees were near, &c.

To those who heard the psalm sung, a word was
enough to bring the whole scene with all its
pathetic circumstances to the mind ;—the short
respite from servile toil, the recurrence of the
thoughts to Sion, and the overpowering recollec-
tions awakened by the melody. But to us they
are not obvious enough to make description superfluous; and I doubt whether there are many
readers who fully realise the situation. All
poetry, but more especially lyrical poetry, requires
many things to be translated besides the words,
before it can bear flower and fruit in another
language and another age. And it is possible

that if an attempt were made to translate the
Psalms of David on this principle, it might not
end (as almost all attempts have ended hitherto) in
the degradation of them out of very rich prose into
very poor verse ". I may be permitted in passing to take these remarks *cum grano salis* and to
affirm that a wider knowledge of versification of
individual psalms by England's " sweet Singers "
would have spared us the too sweeping generalisa-
tion of un-success : besides the Psalms are in
the original, poetry not prose. Renderings of the
entire Psalms by one or two are comparative
failures but it were easy to gather from the fields
of our national Poetry, through one here and
another there—ancient and modern—a noble version. PHINEAS FLETCHER and GEORGE WITHER
and SANDYS earlier, furnish in their translations
excellent opportunity for comparison with Bacon's,
in above and others. But that by-the-bye : and so
I resume from Mr. Spedding. " Of these verses of
BACON's, it has been usual to speak not only as a
failure, but as a ridiculous failure : a censure in
which I cannot concur." Nor marvel : but I
suspect that the mis-judgement is here broadened
over-much. What competent Baconian student—
what critic of insight worth naming—has ever
spoken so foolishly and frivolously ? I trow none,

or in culpable and presumptuous hastiness. Our friend proceeds : "an unpractised versifier, who will not take time and trouble about the work, must of course leave many bad verses : for poetic feeling and imagination, though they will dislike a wrong word, will not of themselves suggest a right one that will suit metre and rhyme : and it would be easy to quote from the few pages that follow, not only many bad lines, but many poor stanzas. [Not ' *many* '] But in a work that is executed carelessly or hastily, we must look at the best parts, and not at the worst, for signs of what a man can do. And taking this test, I should myself infer from this sample that Bacon had all the natural faculty which a poet wants : a fine ear for metre, a fine feeling for imaginative effect in words, and a vein of poetic passion.

"Thou carriest man away as with a tide :
  Then down swim all his thoughts that mounted high ;
Much like a mocking dream, that will not bide,
  But flies before the sight of waking eye ;
Or as the grass, that cannot term obtain
To see the Summer come about again.

The thought in the second line could not well be fitted with imagery, words and rhyme more apt and imaginative ; and there is a tenderness of expression in the concluding couplet which comes

1

manifestly out of a heart in sensitive sympathy
with nature, and fully capable of the poet's faith

> " that every flower
> Enjoys the air it breathes."

Fine and finely put: and whoever really studies
reverentially and lovingly—as is due to so much as
the signature of a name so supreme as Bacon's—
any one of these " certaine Psalmes ", will find
thought or tremble of feeling or epithet like a
touch of autumnal colour, in the most apparently
tame. My experience in returning again and again
to these " certaine Psalmes " has been fresh dis-
coveries of beauty, ineffable scintillations of the
true " Promethean heat."   Indeed it is much with
these " Psalmes " and the slightest productions of
a great mind as with the works of the Greatest.
You fling yourself down on what seems no more
than a square foot of grass : but lo ! as you look
away through the innumerable spires, you have
myriad minute bloomings and insect life and the
shimmering gold of sunshine burnishing every
minutest particle, and elsewhere the play and
interlacing of soft shadows, and a quiet hum of
music everywhere.   Not figuratively but literally
have I found it so, and so have I found it when
thinking and feeling my way through these

" certaine Psalmes " and other kindred things. I would scarcely say that the above quotation is the best of Bacon's " Psalmes ". The whole of the 103rd Psalm seems to me grand in thought, auto-biographic in certain allusive-words, and sustained and sonorous in its versification. Psalm 90th is extremely plaintive and vivid, and has also the most pathetic auto-biographic allusions. Others will prefer other portions.

I return on Mr. Spedding : " Take again as a sample of versification, the opening of the 104th Psalm :

> " Father and King of Powers, both high and low,
> Whose sounding fame all creatures serve to blow :
> My voice shall with the rest strike up thy praise
> And carol of thy works and wondrous ways.
> But who can blaze thy beauties, Lord aright ?
> They turn the brittle beams of mortal sight :
> Upon thy head thou wearest a glorious crown,
> All set with virtues, polish'd with renown ;
> Thence round about a siluer veil doth fall
> Of crystal light, mother of colours all," &c.

The heroic couplet could hardly do its work better in the hand of Dryden. The truth is that Bacon was not without the " fine phrensy " of the poet ; but the world into which it transported him is one which, while it promised visions more glorious

than any poet could imagine, promised them upon
the express condition that fiction should be utterly
prohibited and excluded. Had it taken the ordinary direction, I have little doubt that it would
have carried him to a place among the great poets;
but it was the study of his life to refrain [restrain?]
his imagination, and keep it within the modesty
of truth; aspiring no higher than to be a faithful
interpreter of nature, waiting for the day when
the " Kingdom of Man should come."

I have only to add concerning these " certaine
Psalmes " that all the editors—not I am sorry to
say excepting Mr. Spedding—have modernized
the orthography, and changed the wording. I
reproduce the Author's own text exactly, *i.e.* I
retain all the original capitals and peculiar grammatical forms, as well as the (now) quaint orthography. It seems due in so small a work of
Bacon as this to give for once his own way of
putting it before the world. It will be noticed
that even so careful an editor as Mr. Spedding
has allowed a number of misreadings to pass.
These are marked at the end of the " Psalmes."
Prefixed to the " Psalmes " is a Latin Poem by
GEORGE HERBERT addressed to Bacon. This I
give *verbatim* from the Poet's own autograph
written in a copy of the first edition of the

"certaine Psalmes" now in the possession of a lady in Tunbridge Wells (Mrs. Seaman). The Verses are included in all the editions of HERBERT: but I am sure the Reader will agree with me that there is a special interest in this transcript from the original manuscript. I also give there a very interesting verse-tribute to Bacon in his retirement by Thomas Powell.

Following the "certaine Psalmes" are,

(*a*) Verses made by Mr. Fra. Bacon.

(*b*) Expansion of a Greek Epigram.

On these and another Mr. Spedding must again be allowed to speak : " Besides these translations, Bacon once wrote a sonnet : but we know no more of it than that it was meant in some way or other to assist in sweetening the Queen's temper towards the Earl of Essex : and it has either not been preserved at all, or not so as to be identified. There are also two other poems which have been ascribed to him, whether upon the authority of any one who had means of knowing, I cannot say ; but certainly upon external evidence which in the absence of internal evidence to the contrary, entitles them to a place somewhere in this edition : and there can be no place fitter than this. The first is to be found in a volume of manuscript collections now in the British Museum (Bibl.

Regia, 17, b. l.); but the hand is that of a copyist, and tells us only that *somebody* had said or thought that the verses were by Bacon :—a fact however which is rather more in this case than in many others; inasmuch as (verses being out of Bacon's line) a man merely guessing at the author is not likely to have thought of him. The internal evidence tells for little either way. They are such lines as might very well have been written by Bacon, or by a hundred other people."

The evidence for the Baconian-authorship is understated: for it is noteworthy that whoever the scribe of the Manuscript was he is admittedly correct in his assignment of other pieces to other noted names. None ever has disputed these other names. Therefore when this particular portion of the Manuscript is headed "Passages of the Earle of Essex when he was [in] the Tower and alsoe of Mr. Francis Bacon" and a second heading "2. Verses made by Mr. Fra. Bacon" you can't admit the authority in the one and refuse it in the other. As then the one is accepted it is useless incredulity or caution to reject its associate. Moreover Bacon's greatest books are from copyists also.

Mr. Spedding continues : " The other is a more remarkable performance ; and is ascribed to Bacon on the authority of Thomas Farnaby, a contemp-

orary and a scholar. It is a paraphrase of a
Greek epigram, attributed by some to Poseidippus,
by others to Plato the Comic poet, by others to
Crates the Cynic. In 1629, onely three years
after Bacon's death, Farnaby published a collection of Greek epigrams under the title Ἡ τῆς
ανθολογίας Ἀνθολογία: *Florilegium Epigram-
matum Græcorum, eorumque Latina versu a variis
redditorum.* After giving the epigram in question,
with its Latin translation on the opposite page,
he adds—*Huc elegantem V. C. L. Domini Veru-
lamii παρῳδίαν adjicere adlubuit;* and then prints
the English lines below (the only English in the
book) ; with a translation of his own opposite, in
rhyming Greek. A copy of the English lines was
also found among Sir Henry Wotton's papers with
the name *Francis Lord Bacon* at the bottom ; (See
Reliquiæ Wottonianæ p 513) a fact which would be
of weight, if one could infer from it that Wotton
believed them to be genuine ; for he was a man
likely enough to know. This however would be
too much to infer from the mere circumstance
that the paper had been in Wotton's possession,
for it may have been sent to him by a correspondent, he knowing nothing about it : and as the
case stands, he is not sufficiently connected with
it to be cited as a witness. But on the other

hand Farnaby's evidence is direct and strong. He speaks as if there were no doubt about the fact; nor has there ever, I believe, been a rival claim put in for anybody else. So that unless the supposition involves some improbability (and I do not myself see any) the natural conclusion is that the lines were really written by Bacon. And when I compare them with his translations of the 90th. and 137th. psalms, the metre of which, though not the same, has a kind of resemblance, which makes the comparison more easy,—especially in the rhymed couplet which closes each stanza,—I should myself say that the internal evidence is in favour of them being by the same hand." On all this his Grace the Archbishop of Dublin (Trench) in his "Household Book of English Poetry" observes (p389) " See Spedding's *Works of Lord Bacon*, Vol. VII. p 267 sqq., for the external evidence making it reasonably probable, but certainly not lifting above all doubt, that the ascription of these lines to Lord Bacon is a right one." This is I must think refinement of scrupulosity. Farnaby is certainly un-challengeable and indeed the Baconian authorship never has been challenged nor has any claim been put in for another.

I have also to adduce a second witness—hitherto

overlooked—between Farnaby and Wotton, and in all likelihood independent. This is found in Joshua Sylvester's "Panthea" 1630, or only about three years after Bacon's death. On the title-page after " Panthea " are these words " Where-unto is added an Appendix containing an excellent Elegy written by the L[ord] Viscount St. Albans, late Lord High Chancelour of England &c." and in the Epistle Dedicatory by the Editor of the volume " J. M. Master of Arts " are these further noticeable words to " the nobly-descended and vertuously accomplisht Sir Richard Gargrave, Knight "—" Being moued to adioyne to the prece-dent canzonets, the ensuing nectarines of the late excellent Viscount St. Albans—the Prince of English oratory—I presumed to inscribe them to your noble selfe.......,the subject ¡is ponderous and diuine, being a graphicall delineation of hu-mane misery."

It is clear that the Verses were the recognized production of Bacon in 1630.

On the poem itself Mr. Spedding concludes : " The English lines which follow [the Original : for which see onward]—described as " Lord Ve-rulan's elegant παρῳδία "—are not meant for a translation, and can hardly be called a paraphrase. They are rather another poem on the same subject and with the same sentiment; and though the topics are mostly the same, the treatment of them is very different. The merit of the original consists almost entirely in its compactness: there being no special felicity in the expression, or music of the metre. In the English, compactness is not aimed at, and a tone of plaintive melody is imparted, which is due chiefly to the metrical arrangement, and has something very pathetic in it to my ear."

Once more the Editors have modernized the orthography, and otherwise injured these two Poems, as well as the " certaine Psalmes." Even Mr. Spedding and Dr. Hannah have adopted the strange mis-reading in the second (line 21st.) of "moan" for " none"—spoiling the thought and the rhyme and correspondent with a flaw in a jewel-fascet. I reproduce the Manuscript of the one and of Farnaby of the other, save that in the latter I adopt the "Panthea" reading of 'none'.[1]

---

[1] I leave out Wotton's supposed testimony, because while the poem was among his papers, it seems to have been anonymous to him, inasmuch as in first edition of the " Reliquiæ" (1651) it had no name prefixed or affixed, but is signed "Ignoto". Dr. Hannah in his " Courtly Poets" has this note : " In MS. Rawl. Poet. 117, fol. 161,

I am disappointed that I cannot glean verse-renderings from Bacon's prose Works as with THOMAS FULLER and BISHOP JEREMY TAYLOR. We search in vain for such. I can't help anticipating that some of these days Bacon letters or other papers will turn up interpretative of his at present dark phrase to SIR JOHN DAVIES of "your *concealed* poet." We have noble contemporary poetry unhappily anonymous: and I should not be surprized to find Bacon the 'concealed' Singer of some of it. May I live to have my expectation verified! Turn the page for account of the exquisite portrait of Bacon prefixed to our large paper copies.

ALEXANDER B. GROSART.

ST. GEORGE'S BLACKBURN.

---

it was first entitled "The Bubble, by R. W." (? H. W.) altered to "by yᵉ Lord Bacon." In MS. Ashm. 38, p. 2, the first title was "On Man's Mortality, by Dr. Donn;" altered to "Sʳ Fran Bacon." In a MS, belonging to the late Mr. Pickering the title is "Upon the Misery of Man;" the first signature is "Henry Harrington", altered to "Lᵈ Verulam Viscount St. Alban's." p. 117.

ON THE PORTRAIT OF BACON, PREFIXED TO LARGE PAPER COPIES,

BY JAMES SPEDDING, ESQ.

"In the "History and Plan of the Editor" prefixed to the Philosophical Works, I told what I then knew about the Portraits of Bacon: at which time (January, 1857) I had not seen any likeness of him in mature life which did not appear traceable to one or other of two originals,— the full-length painting in Gorhambury by Van Somer, or the old engraving by Simon Pass. But among the miniatures lent to the South Kensington Museum for exhibition in 1865 there was a small one belonging to the Duke of Buccleugh, which though evidently representing not only the same man but the same *likeness* of the same man as Van Somer's picture, could not be taken for a copy of it. In all those points in which copies always agree and independent originals always differ,—the attitude, the arrangement of the dress, the light and shadow, etc,—the resemblance between the two is exact: in all those in which all copies fall short, and only the best come near,— the physiognomical character, the drawing of the more delicate features, the living look,—the differences were considerable, and the inferiority of the large picture manifest. All that was in the picture (as far as the head and shoulders) might easily have been got from the miniature:

23

but there was much in the miniature which could not have been got from the picture. And though, if we judge from modern practice, it may seem improbable that an artist of reputation like Van Somer would have painted a full-length portrait of a living subject from a miniature drawing by another man, I was told by the late Sir Charles Eastlake that it is not so. In those times it was the common practice (he said), when a portrait was wanted, to have in the first instance a careful drawing done in miniature, from which various copies would afterwards be made in any size that might be wished; " and therefore " (he added) " when you meet with two portraits of that period— miniature and a life-size painting—of which there is reason to believe that one has been copied from the other, the presumption is that the miniature is the one taken from the life." I am persuaded that there is no other way of explaining satisfactorily the peculiar relation between these two; and I look upon the Duke of Buccleugh's miniature as the undoubted head of that whole family of Bacon portraits.

That it has never been engraved before, I cannot assert positively : for it is evident to me that Houbraken's well-known engraving was taken, not from Van Somer's painting (as I formerly supposed), but from this,—either directly or through some other copy. The resemblance however which convinces me of that fact is only in the composition and the general effect. It does not extend to the features, which are treated as usual with so little care for the likeness that no one could guess from the copy what the character of the face in the original really is. Without saying, therefore, that it has never been engraved

before, I may at least say that another engraving was
wanted : and having by the Duke of Buccleugh's permission (for which I hope everybody will join me in
thanking him) had one made directly from the original,
I leave it to speak for itself, and make good its own title
to acceptance.

Of the history and adventures of this miniature before
it came into the Duke's possession, nothing I believe, is
known. It is said to be by Peter Oliver; though, if the
dates be correct, he must have been a very young man
when it was done. Isaac Oliver is said to have died in
1617, Peter to have been born in 1601. The picture is
dated 1620. If there is no better reason for ascribing it
to Peter than that his father was dead when the date was
inserted, it is obvious that the date represents the time
when it was *finished :* the face may have been painted
some years earlier. But whether it were a very early
work of the son's, or a very late one of the father's, or a
work left unfinished by the father, and finished by the
son, it is a masterly performance, and bears upon its face
the evidence of its value. The letters seen round the
margin, giving the year, date, and the age are in the
original painted with gold on the blue background of the
picture, round the inner border. In white or black it was
thought they would be scarcely visible. In all other
respects the engraving is as exact as it could be made.

There still remains to be discovered the original of
Pass's print; which is to be sought for, not (as I once
thought) among pictures by Cornelius Jansen, but among
miniatures by Hilliard and the Olivers. A miniature
undoubtedly representing the same portrait, and also

ascribed to Peter Oliver, was to be seen in another part of
the exhibition at South Kensington ; and though I cannot
think it was the same which Pass engraved, because the
engraving has so much more life and character in it, or
that it can have been the work of either Oliver's own hand
at any stage in the development of their powers, it affords
a fair presumption that such a miniature was once in
existence ".

(The Letters and the Life of Bacon : Vol. III.
[1865] : Preface pp.iii—v.)

III. George Herbert to Bacon.

In Honorem Illustrissimi Domini Francisci de
    Verulamio Vice-comitis S[anc]ti Albani,
    Post Editam ab Eo Instaaur: Magnam.

Qᴜɪs iste tandem ? non enim vultu ambulat
Quotidiano.   Nescis, ignare ? audies,
Dux Notionum ; Veritatis Pontifex ;
Inductionis Dominus : et Verulamij ;
Rerum Magister Unicus, at non Artium ;
Profunditatis Pinus atq. Elegantiæ,
Naturæ Aruspex intimus : Philosophiæ
Ærarium, Sequester Experientiæ,
Speculationisq : Æquitatis signifer :
Scientiarum sub pupillari statu
Degentium olim Emancipator : Luminis
Promus : Fugator Idolûm, atq. Nubium :
Collega solis : Quadra Certitudinis :
Sephismatum Mastix : Brutus Literarius,
Authoritatis exuens Tyrannidem :
Rationis et sensus stupendus Arbiter :
Repumicator mentis : Atlas Physicus,

27

Alcide succumbente Stagiritico :
Columba Noæ, quæ in vetustate Artibus
Nullum locum requiemq : cernens, præstitit
Ad se suumq : Matris Arcam regredi.
Subtilitatis terebra ; Temporis nepos
Ex Veritate Matre : Mellis Alveus ;
Mundiq : et Animarum Sacerdos Unicus ;
Securisq : Errorum : inq; Natalibus
Granum Sinapis, acre aliis, crescens sibi
O me prope lassum, Juvate Posteri.

> Geor. Herbert Orat. Pub.
> in Academ. Cantab.

(From Mrs. Seaman's copy of Bacon's " certaine
Psalmes" (1625)—probably the dedication-copy
to Herbert.)

This text agrees, save in its multiplied capitals
and its contractions, with that usually given in the
collective editions of the Poems of HERBERT.   In
a small volume forwarded to me by my excellent
correspondent Mr. W. T. Brooke of London,
entitled "Reverendi Patris Emanvelis Thesavri e
Societate Iesv, Cæsares ; et ejusdem varia carmina
etc . . . Oxon., 1637 ", the Lines form the
first in the little collection, and the following
slight variations it may be worth while recording :

line 14th., 'matrix' for 'mastix'; line 21st.,
'suamq;' line 25th., 'Securis . . . . Natura-
libus'; and line 27th., 'probe'. G.

IV 𝕿𝖍𝖔𝖒𝖆𝖘 𝕻𝖔𝖜𝖊𝖑𝖑 𝖙𝖔 𝕭𝖆𝖈𝖔𝖓.

To
Trve Nobility and Tryde Learning,
Beholden
To no Mountaine of Eminence, nor Supportment
for Height, Francis, Lord Verulam, and Viscount
St. Albanes.

O GIUE me leaue to pull the curtaine by,
  That clouds thy Worth in such obscurity ;
Good Seneca, stay but a while thy bleeding,
T'accept what I receiuèd at thy Reading :
  Here I present it in a solemne strayne :
  And thus I plucke this curtayne backe againe.
(From "The Attovrney's Academy" by Thomas
Powell: 3rd edition, 1630. These noticeable lines
to Bacon in his 'disgrace' have hitherto es-
caped notice). G.

𝕮𝖊𝖗𝖙𝖆𝖎𝖓𝖊 𝕻𝖘𝖆𝖑𝖒𝖊𝖘.

The following is the original title-page :

THE

TRANSLATION

OF

CERTAINE PSALMES

INTO ENGLISH

VERSE:

BY

THE] RIGHT HO-
NOVRABLE,

Francis

Lo. VERVLAM,

Viscount

ST. ALBAN.

LONDON,

Printed for *Hanna Barret*, and *Richard Whittaker*, and
are to be sold at the signe of the Kings Head
in Pauls Church-yard. 1625. (4o)

[Collation : Title-page-Epistle Dedicatory and pp 1—21
apparently ; but as page 11 is numbered by mistake 15,
and the pagination continued on, the real number of pages
is 1—17—in all, 11 leaves. G.]

31

Dedication.

TO HIS VERY GOOD FREND, MR. GEORGE HERBERT.

THE paines that it pleased you to take about some of my Writings, I cannot forget : which did put me in minde, to dedicate to you, this poore Exercise of my sicknesse. Besides, it being my manner for Dedications, to choose those that I hold most fit for the Argument, I thought that in respect of Diuinitie, and Poesie, met, (whereof the one is the Matter, the other the Stile of this little Writing) I could not make better choice. So with signification of my Loue and Acknowledgement, I euer rest

Your affectionate Frend,

FR. ST. ALBAN.

IV. Certaine Psalmes.

THE TRANSLATION OF THE FIRST PSALM.

WHO neuer gaue to wicked read,
    A yeelding and attentiue eare :
    Who neuer Sinners paths did tread,
Nor sate him downe in Scorners chaire :
But maketh it his whole delight,
On Law of God to meditate,
And therein spendeth day and Night;
That man is in a happie State.

He shall be like the fruitfull Tree,
Planted along a running Spring,
Which, in due season, constantly,
A goodly yeeld of Fruit doth bring.
Whose leaues continue alwayes greene,
And are no prey to Winters power :
So shall that Man not once be seene
Surprizèd with an euill Hower.

With wicked Men it is not so,
Their Lot is of another kinde :
All as the Chaffe, which too and fro,
Is tost at Mercie of the winde.
And when he shall in Judgment plead,
A casting Sentence bide he must :
So shall he not lift vp his Head,
In the Assembly of the Just.

For why ? the Lord hath speciall eye,
To be the godlie's stay at call :
And hath giuen ouer, righteously,
The wicked Man to take his fall.

THE TRANSLATION OF THE
12. PSALME.

ELP Lord, for godly Men haue took their
flight,
And left the Earth to be the Wickeds
Den :
Not one that standeth fast to Truth and Right,
But feares, or seekes to please, the Eies of Men.
When one with other fall's in talke apart,
Their meaning goeth not with their words, in
proofe ;

But faire they flatter, with a clouen Heart,
By pleasing words, to worke their owne behoofe.

But God cut off the Lips, that are all set,
To trap the harmlesse Soule, that peace hath
    vow'd ;
And pierce the Tongues, that seeke to counterfet
The Confidence of Truth, by lying loud :
Yet so they thinke to raigne, and worke their will,
By subtill speech, which enter's euery where :
And say, Our Tongues are ours, to helpe vs still,
What need we any Higher Power to feare ?

Now for the bitter sighing of the Poore,
The lord hath said, I will no more forbeare,
The Wicked's Kingdome to inuade and scoure,
And set at large the men restrain'd in feare.
And sure, the Word of God is pure, and fine,
And in the triall neuer looseth waight ;
Like Noble Gold, which, since it left the Mine,
Hath seuen times passed through the fiery straight.

And now thou wilt not first thy Word forsake,
Nor yet the Righteous man, that leanes theretoo ;
But will't his safe Protection vndertake,
In spight of all, their force and wiles can doe.
And time it is, ô Lord, thou didst draw nigh,

The Wicked daily doe enlarge their Bands;
And that, which makes them follow ill a vie,
Rule is betaken to vnworthy Hands.

THE TRANSLATION OF
THE 90. PSALME.

 LORD, thou art our Home, to whom we
       fly,
       And so hast alwaies beene from Age to
       Age.
Before-the Hills did intercept the Eye,
Or that the Frame was vp of Earthly Stage,
One God thou wert, and art, and still shalt bee;
The Line of Time, it doth not measure thee.

Both Death and Life obey thy holy lore,
And visit in their turnes, as they are sent.
A Thousand yeares with thee, they are no more,
Then yesterday, which, ere it is, is spent:
    Or as a Watch by night, that course doth keepe,
    And goes, and comes, vnwares to them that
       sleepe.

Thou carriest Man away as with a Tide:
Then downe swim all his Thoughts, that mounted
       high;

Much like a mocking Dreame, that will not bide,
But flies before the sight of waking eye;
  Or as the Grasse, that cannot terme obtaine,
  To see the Summer come about aga ne.

At Morning, faire it musters, on the Ground,
At Euen, it is cut downe, and laid along:
And though it sparèd were and fauour found,
The wether would performe the Mowers wrong:
  Thus hast thou hang'd our Life on brittle Pins,
  To let us know, it will not beare our Sins.

Thou buriest not within obliuious Tombe
Our Trespasses, but entrest them aright:
Euen those that are conceiu'd in Darkenesse
    Wombe,
To thee appeare, as done at broad day light.
  As a Tale told, which sometimes men attend,
  And sometimes not, our Life steales to an end.

The Life of Man is threescore yeares and ten,
Or if that he be strong, perhaps fourescore,
Yet all things are but labour to him then,
New sorrowes still come on, Pleasures no more:
  Why should there be such turmoile and such
    strife,
  To spin in length this feeble Line of Life?

But who consider's duely of thine Ire ?
Or doth the thoughts thereof wisely embrace ?
For thou, O God, art a consuming Fire,
Fraile Man, how can he stand before thy face ?
    If thy displeasure thou do'st not refraine,
    A Moment brings all backe to Dust againe.

Teach vs, O Lord, to number well our Daies,
Thereby our Hearts to Wisdome to apply ;
For that, which guides Man best in all his waies,
Is Meditation of Mortality.
    This bubble light, this vapour of our Breath,
    Teach vs to consecrate to Howre of Death.

Returne vnto vs Lord, and ballance now
With daies of Joy, our daies of Misery ;
Helpe vs right soone, our knees to thee we bow,
Depending wholy on thy Clemency :
    Then shall thy Seruants both with heart and
        voice
    All the daies of their Life, in thee reioyce.

Begin thy worke O Lord, in this ovr Age,
Shew it vnto thy Seruants that now liue ;
But to our Children raise it many a Stage
That all the World to thee may glory giue.
    Our Handy worke likewise, as fruitfull Tree,
    Let it, O Lord, blessed not blasted be.

THE TRANSLATION OF THE 104.
PSALME.

FATHER and King of Powers, both high
    and low
    Whose sounding Fame all creatures serue
      to blow;
My Soule shall with the rest strike vp thy praise,
And Caroll of thy workes and wondrous waies.
But who can blaze thy Beauties, Lord, aright?
They turne the brittle Beames of mortall sight.
Vpon thy head thou wear'st a glorious Crowne,
All set with vertues, polisht with renowne:
Thence round about a Siluer Vaile doth fall
Of Chrystall Light, Mother of Colours all.
The Compasse heauen, smooth without grain, or
    fold,
All set with Spangs of glitt'ring Stars vntold,
And strip't with golden Beames of power vnpent,
Is raisèd vp for a remouing Tent.
Vaulted and archèd are his Chamber Beames,
Vpon the Seas, the Waters, and the streames:
The Clouds as Chariots swift doe scoure the sky;
The stormy Winds vpon their wings doe fly.
His Angels Spirits are that wait his Will,
As flames of Fire his anger they fulfill.
In the Beginning with a mighty Hand,

He made the Earth by Counterpoyse to stand ;
Neuer to moue, but to be fixèd still ;
Yet hath no Pillars but his Sacred Will.
This Earth as with a vaile, once couered was,
The Waters ouerflowèd all the Masse :
But vpon his rebuke away they fled,
And then the Hills began to shew their Head ;
The Vales their hollow Bosomes opened plaine,
The Streames ran trembling down the vales
    again :
And that the Earth no more might drownèd be
He set the Sea his Bounds of Liberty ;
And though his Waues resound, and beat the shore,
Yet is it brideled by his holy lore.
Then did the Riuers seek their proper places
And found their Heads, their Issues, and their
    Races :
The Springs doe feed the Riuers all the way
And so the Tribute to the Sea repay :
Running along through many a pleasant field,
Much fruitfulnesse vnto the Earth they yeeld :
That know the Beasts and Cattell feeding by,
Which for to slake their Thirst doe thither hie.
Nay Desert Grounds the Streames doe not forsake,
But through the vnknown waies their iourney
    take :
The Asses wilde that bide in Wildernesse,

Doe thither come, their Thirst for to refresh.
The shady Trees along their Bankes doe spring
In which the Birds doe build, and sit, and sing ;
Stroking the gentle Ayre with pleasant notes,
Plaining or Chirping through their warbling
    throtes.
The higher Grounds where Waters cannot rise,
By raine and Deawes are watred from the Skies ;
Causing the Earth put forth the Grasse for Beasts,
And garden Herbs, seru'd at the greatest Feasts ;
And Bread that is all Viands Firmament,
And giues a firme and solid Nourishment ;
And Wine Mans Spirits for to recreate ;
And Oyle his Face for to exhilarate.
The sappy Cedars tall like stately Towers,
High flying Birds doe harbour in their Bowers :
The holy Storkes that are the Trauellers,
Choose for to dwell and build among the Firs :
The climing Goats hang on steep Mountaines
    side ;
The digging Conies in the Rocks doe bide.
The Moone, so constant in Inconstancy,
Doth rule the Monethly seasons orderly :
The Sunne, Eye of the World, doth know his race,
And when to shew, and when to hide his face.
Thou makest Darknesse that it may be Night,
When as the Sauage Beasts, that fly the Light,

(As conscious of Mans hatred) leaue their Den,
And range abroad, secur'd from Sight of Men.
Then doe the Forrests ring of Lions roaring,
That aske their meat of God, their strength re-
    storing:
But when the Day appeares, they backe doe flye,
And in their Dens againe doe lurking lye,
Then Man goes forth to labour in the Field,
Whereby his Grounds more rich encrease may
    yeeld.
O Lord, thy Prouidence sufficeth all,
Thy Goodnesse not restrain'd, but generall
Ouer thy creatures; the whole Earth doth flow
With thy great Largesse pour'd forth here below.
Nor is it Earth alone exalts thy Name,
But Seas and streames likewise doe spread the
    same.
The rowling Seas unto the Lot doe fall,
Of Beasts innumerable, great and small:
There doe the stately Ships plow vp the Flouds,
The greater Nauies looke like walking woods:
The Fishes there farre voyages doe make,
To diuers shores their Journey they doe take:
There hast thou set the great Leuiathan,
That makes the Seas to seeth like boyling Pan:
All these doe aske of thee their Meat to liue,
Which in due season thou to them dost giue.

Ope thou thy Hand, and then they haue good fare,
Shut thou thy Hand, and then they troubled are.
All Life, and Spirit, from thy Breath proceed,
Thy word doth all things generate and feed ;
If thou withdraw'st it, then they cease to be,
And straight returne to Dust and Vanitie :
But when thy Breath do'st send forth againe,
Then all things doe renew, and spring amaine ;
So that the Earth but lately desolate
Doth now returne vnto the former State.
The glorious Maiesty of God aboue,
Shall euer raigne, in Mercy, and in Loue :
God shall reioyce all his faire workes to see,
For, as they came from him, all perfect bee.
The Earth shall quake if ought his wrath prouoke,
Let him but touch the Mountains, they shall smoke.
As long as Life doth last, I Hymnes will sing,
With chearful voice to the eternall King :
As long as I have beeing, I will praise
The works of God, and all his wondrous waies.
I know that he my words will not despise ;
Thanksgiuing is to him a Sacrifice.
But as for Sinners, they shall be destroi'd
From off the Earth, their places shall be void,
Let all his Works praise him with one accord ;
Oh praise the Lord, my Soule ; praise ye the
    Lord.

THE TRANSLATION OF THE
126. PSALME.

WHEN God return'd vs graciously
    Vnto our Natiue Land,
    We seem'd as in a Dreame to be
And in a Maze to stand.

The Heathen likewise they could say,
    The God, that these men serue,
Hath done great Things for them this Day,
    Their Nation to preserue.

Tis true, God hath pour'd out his grace
    On vs abundantly,
For which we yeeld him Psalmes, and Praise,
    And thanks, with Jubilee.

O Lord, turne our Captiuity,
    As Winds that blow at South,
Doe poure the Tides with violence
    Back to the Riuers Mouth.

Who sowes in Teares, shall reape in ioy,
    The Lord doth so ordaine :
So that his Seed be pure and good,
    His Haruest shall be gaine.

THE TRANSLATION OF THE
137. PSALME.

WHEN as we sate all sad and desolate,
 By Babylon, vpon the Riuers side,
 Eas'd from the Taskes, which in our
  captiue state,
We were enforcèd daily to abide :
 Our Harps we had brought with vs to the field,
 Some solace to our heauy Soules to yeeld.

But soone we found, we fail'd of our account,
For when our Mindes some freedome did obtaine,
Straight-waies the memory of Sion Mount,
Did cause afresh our wounds to bleed againe ;
 So that with present griefs, and future feares,
 Our Eyes burst forth into a streame of Teares.

As for our Harps, since Sorrow strooke them
  dumbe,
We hang'd them on the Willow Trees were neare ;
Yet did our cruell Masters to vs come,
Asking of vs some Hebrew Songs to heare ;
 Taunting vs rather in our Misery,
 Then much delighting in our Melody.

Alas (said we) who can once force or frame,
His grieuèd and oppressèd Heart to sing,

The Prayses of Jehoua's glorious Name,
In banishment, vnder a forraine King?
  In Sion is his Seat, and dwelling place,
  Thence doth he shew the brightnesse of his face.

Hierusalem, where God his Throne hath set,
Shall any Hower absent thee from my minde?
Then let my right Hand quite her skill forget,
Then let my voice, and words, no passage finde;
  Nay if I doe not thee prefer in all,
  That in the compasse of my thoughts can fall.

Remember thou, ô Lord, the cruell cry
Of Edoms Children, which did ring and sound,
Inciting the Chaldœan's Cruelty,
"Downe with it, downe with it, euen vnto the
    ground."
  In that good day, repay it vnto them,
  When thou shalt visit thy Hierusalem.

And thou, o Babylon, shalt haue thy turne
By iust Reuenge; and happy shall he bee,
That thy proud Walls and Towers shall wast and
    burne,
And as thou did'st by vs, so doe by thee.
  Yea happy he, that takes thy childrens Bones,
  And dasheth them against the pauement Stones.

THE TRANSLATION OF THE
149. PSALME.

 SING a new Song, to our God aboue,
Auoid profane ones, 'tis for holy Quire :
Let Israel sing Songs of holy Loue
To him that made them, with their Hearts on fire :
  Let Sions Sonnes lift vp their Voice, and sing
  Carolls and Anthems to their Heauenly King.

Let not your voice alone his praise forth tell,
But moue withall, and praise him in the Dance ;
Cymbals and Harps let them be tunèd well,
'Tis he that doth the Poore's estate aduance :
  Doe this not onely on the solemne daies,
  But on your secret Beds your Spirits raise.

O let the Saints beare in their Mouth his Praise,
And a two-edgèd Sword drawne in their Hand,
Therewith for to reuenge the former Daies,
Vpon all Nations, that their Zeale withstand ;
  To binde their Kings in chaines of Iron strong,
  And manacle their Nobles for their wrong.

Expect the time, for 'tis decreed in Heauen,
Such Honour shall vnto his Saints be giuen.

Finis.

V. ΠΟΣΕΙΔΙΠΠΟΥ, οἱ δὲ ΠΛΑΤΩΝΟΣ ΚΩΜΙΚΟΥ.

Ποίην τις βιότοιο τάμοι τρίβον; εἰν ἀγορῇ μὲν
  Νείκεα καὶ χαλεπαὶ πρήζιες· ἐν δὲ δόμοις
Φροντίδες· ἐν δ᾽ ἀγροῖς καμάτων ἅλις· ἐν δὲ θαλάσσῃ
  Τάρβος· ἐπὶ ξείνης δ,᾽ ἢν μὲν ἔχῃς τι, δέος·
Ἢν δ᾽ ἀπορῇς, ἀνιηρόν. ἔχεις γάμον; οὐκ ἀμέριμνος
  Ἔσσεαι· οὐ γαμέεις; ξῆς ἐτ᾽ ἐρημότερος.
Τέκνα πόνοι. πηρωσις ἄπαις βίος· αἱ νεότητες
  Ἄφρονες· αἱ πολιαὶ δ᾽ ἔμπαλιν ἀδρανέες.
Ἢν ἄρα τοῖνδε δυοῖν ἑνὸς αἵρεσις, ἢ τὸ γενέσθαι
  Μηδέποτ᾽, ἢ τὸ θανεῖν αὐτίκα τικτόμενον.

The World's a bubble; and the life of man
        Lesse then a span.
In his conception wretched; from the wombe,
        so to the tombe :
Curst from the cradle, and brought vp to yeares,
        With cares and feares.
Who then to fraile Mortality shall trust,
But limmes the water, or but writes in dust.

Yet, since with sorrow here we liue opprest,
   What life is best ?
Courts are but onely superficial Scholes
   to dandle fooles :
The rurall parts are turn'd into a den
   of sauage men :
And where's a city from all vice so free,
But may be term'd the worst of all the three ?

Domesticke cares afflict the husband's bed,
   or paines, his head :
Those that liue single, take it for a curse,
   or doe things worse :
Some would haue children ; those that haue them
 none ;
   or wish them gone.
What is it then to haue or haue no wife,
But single thraldome or a double strife ?

Our own affections still at home to please,
   is a disease :
To crosse the sea to any foreine soyle,
   perills and toyle :
Warres with their noyse affright vs : when they
 cease,
   W' are worse in peace :
What then remaines, but that we still should cry,
Not to be borne, or being borne, to dye.

(From Farnaby's "Florilegium Epig. as *ante* : pp 8 and 10 : save 'none' from "Panthea" for 'mone'. See our Introduction. G.)

Mr. Spedding has thus rendered the original (*supra*) :

What life shall a man choose ? in court and mart
Are quarrels and hard dealing ; cares at home ;
Labours by land ; terrors at sea ; abroad,
Either the fear of losing what thou hast
Or worse, nought left to lose ; if wedded, much
Discomfort ; comfortless unwed : a life
With children troubled, incomplete without :
Youth foolish, age outworn. Of these two choose
  then ;
Or never to be born, or straight to die.

Compare Sir John Beaumont's paraphrase in our edition of his Poems (pp 238-239). I take the following note from Dr. Hannah's " Courtly Poets" [1870 : pp 235-6] " The lines bear some resemblance to a well-known epigram ascribed to Posidippus, which had been very frequently translated ; *e.g.* in Tottels' "Songs and Sonnets," 1557 ; in Puttenham's "Art of Poesy," 1589 ; by Sir John Beaumont, and by others. Possibly from this circumstance, the last line frequently occurs in almost exactly the same shape among the minor poems of the time; *e. g.* Bacon as here :

" What then remains, but that we still should cry
For being born, and, being born, to die " ?

Drummond of Hawthornden, " Works " 1711 : Poems, p 44 :

" Who would not one of those two offers try,—
Not to be born, or being born, to die ?"

Bishop King, " Poems," &c. 1657, p 145 :

" At least with that Greek sage still make us cry,
Not to be born, or, being born to die."

The mythical author of the phrase was Silenus,

who is said to have bestowed it on his captor, King Midas."   G.

VI. Verses made by Mr. Fra. Bacon.

The man of life upright, whose giltless heart is
    free
From all dishonest deeds and thoughts of vanitie:
The man whose silent daies in harmles ioyes are
    spent,
Whom hopes cannot delude, nor fortune discontent;
That man needs neither Towers nor Armor for
    defence,
Nor secret vaults to flie from Thunder's violence:
He onlie can behold with unaffrighted eyes
The horrors of the deepe and terrors of the skies;
Thus scorning all the care that fate or fortune
    bring[s],
Hee makes the heauen his booke, his wisdome
    heavenlie things;
Good thoughts his only freinds, his welth a well-
    spent Age,
The earth his sober inne and quiet pilgramage.

[From Bibl. Regia 17. B. L. in British Museum,
as *ante*: See our Introduction.   In the Chetham
MS., in Chetham Library, Manchester, 8012, p
79, there is another copy altogether anonymous.
It is entitled "Who lives well": and furnishes
a few slight variations as follows :

Line 1st ' guiltles '.
  „   2nd ' vanitye '.
  „   3rd 'joyes'
  „   4th ' sorrowes ' for ' fortune'.
  „   5th 'needes neyther tower.'
  „   6th ' vault,' ' fly '.
  „   7th and 8th lines omitted.
  „   9th ' But' for 'Thus,' and ' chance ' for ' care,'
        and ' yt' and ' bringes '.
  ,.   10th ' He,' ' heavens', ' bookes', ' wisedome',
        eavenly thinges'.
  „   11th ' friendes ', ' welth ' for 'life '.
  „   12th, ' and ' for ' a'.

I have accepted as very superior to the B. M. MS., in
line 11th, the reading of 'wealth' for ' life', and in line
12th 'and' for 'a'.   G.

Notes and Illustrations.

I. " Certaine Psalmes " :

(1) Psalm Ist., line 1st. : **Mr** Spedding has ' reed ' for
' read '. Rede or reed is ' counsel ', from A. S.
ræd, speech, counsel.

(2) Psalm XIIth., line 5th. : Note the apostrophe 'fall's '
here and in other words, as in line 14th. ' cnter's '.

(3) Psalm XIIth., line 26th. : Note ' theretoo ' as elsewhere ' too ' for ' to '.

(4) Psalm XIIth., line 31st. : ' a-vie '   This occurs in
Holland's Pliny (xxxxi. 5). Speaking of Agor-
acritus and Alcamenes the pupils of Phidias, he
says : " Now these two apprentices of his strove
a-vie, whether of them could make the statue of
Venus better " *i. e.* they *vied* with each other &c.

(5) Psalm XC., line 3rd. : Note ' Before-the '.

(6) Psalm XC., line 5th. : Mr. Spedding has ' shall ' for
' shalt '.

(7) Psalm CIVth., line 34th. : **Mr.** Spedding mis-reads
" it is " for " is it ".

(8) Psalm CIVth., line 45th. : Mr. Spedding unfortunately mis-reads ' hide ' for ' bide '.

(9) Psalm CIVth., line 52nd. : ' deaw ' is the contemporary spelling, as earlier in Sir John Davies, the
Fletchers &c. Mr. Spedding reads ' water'd ' for
' watred '.

(10) Psalm CIVth., line 82nd. : Mr. Spedding again unfortunately mis-reads ' largenesse ' for ' largesse '.

(11) Psalm CIVth., line 109th. : **Mr.** Spedding reads
' aught ' for ' ought '.

II.   Expansion of Epigram :

 (1) Line 15th : Mr. Spedding mis-reads ' ' the for ' *a*
       City '.

 (2) Line 21st. : J. M. in " Panthea ", &c. in his edn.
       changes the orthography and capitals consider-
       ably : and in this line reads—as adopted by us—
       .... " those that haue them *none* " :
       which must surely have been Bacon's word. This
       and the differing orthography and abundant cap-
       itals, as in " certaine Psalmes " disposes me to
       accredit J. M. with an independent MS.   He has
       entitled the Lines "Humane Life characterized :
       By the Right noble Peere, Francis Viscount St.
       Albans, late High Chancelour of England."   See
       our Introduction.   G.

The End.

MISCELLANIES

OF

𝕿𝖍𝖊 𝕱𝖚𝖑𝖑𝖊𝖗 𝖂𝖔𝖗𝖙𝖍𝖎𝖊𝖘' 𝕷𝖎𝖇𝖗𝖆𝖗𝖞.

THE

POEMS

AND

VERSE-TRANSLATIONS

OF THE

RIGHT REV. JEREMY TAYLOR, D.D.

LORD BISHOP OF DOWN, CONNOR, AND DROMORE.

FOR THE

FIRST TIME COLLECTED AND EDITED

AFTER THE AUTHOR'S OWN TEXT:

WITH

INTRODUCTION.

BY THE

REV. ALEXANDER B. GROSART,

ST. GEORGE'S, BLACKBURN, LANCASHIRE.

PRINTED FOR PRIVATE CIRCULATION.

1870.

156 COPIES ONLY.

Jeremy Taylor:

Born August, 1613.
Died August 13th, 1667.

Contents.

CONTENTS.

I. Introduction.

WILLMOTT, Heber, and Bonney—the order being a descending scale of worth —have written the Life in full, of Jeremy Taylor—and since her martyr-days, the Church of England has had few more lovely in their lives, few more intrinsically apostolic. A beautiful, modestly-heroic, pathetic, memorable Life it was: none the less Christly that it has inscribed over its academic commencement '*pauper scholaris*'—like unto the Lord's poor pair of turtle doves offered for Him.

I am not called upon to estimate our Worthy as a Theologian or Polemic. Briefly—if his thought must be pronounced beneath his eloquence, and his eloquence more resonant than illuminative, and his multifarious reading cumbersome to him as a Preacher as was Saul's armour to David—so that one yearns o'times for the simple ' sling and pebble' of a direct simple statement of "The

Way, the Truth and the Life" and would prefer
a beechen cup or homeliest ware full of "living
water" to the richest goblet surcharged with
perfumed distillations, even when the fragrance
comes from Roses of Sharon—on the other hand,
he stands supreme in English Theological literature as a pulpit-orator. "If, remarks Dr. George
Macdonald, "he had written verse equal to his
prose, he would have had a lofty place amongst
poets as well as amongst preachers."* This will
be universally conceded. As it is, what of verse-
proper he has left, deserves, if I err not, higher
recognition than it has hitherto met. I grant
there are conceits and quibbles—the smoke
rather than the flame of Fancy : but even his
conceits are rich as the gems that encrust an
Eastern nargilly. The thinking generally appears
to me more substantive and compacted than in his
prose, wide, and grand, and potent, the march of it
radiant and solemn, the music and involute rhyme
and rhythm stately, with occasional felicities alike
of idea and wording, glancing out of the Cowley-
Pindaric stanzas like the scarlet of the cactus from
its fantastic lobes of prickles. I may here continue my quotation from "Antiphon" : "They

---

* "Antiphon" p. 217.

[the Festival Hymns] bear marks, observes Dr. Macdonald further, " of the careless impatience of rhythm and rhyme of one who though ever bursting into a natural trill of song, sometimes with more rhymes apparently than he intended, would yet rather let his thoughts pour themselves out in that unmeasured chant, that " poetry in solution ", which is the natural speech of the prophet orator. He is like a full river that must flow, which rejoices in a flood, and rebels against the constraint of mole or conduit. He exults in utterance itself, caring little for the mode, which however, the law of his indwelling melody guides though never compels. Charmingly diffuse in his prose, his verse ever sounds as if it would overflow the banks of its self-imposed restraints ". * The examples chosen by the Critic are " The second hymn for Advent ", the second " for Christmas " and the prayers " My soul doth pant toward Thee " and " for Charity." In the first he notes " a little confusion of imagery ; and in others of them . . . . a little obscurity ". Of the first prayer he remarks, " This last is quite regular, that is, the second stanza is arranged precisely as the first, though such will not appear to be the

---

* " Antiphon " p. 218.

case without examination : the disposition of the
lines, so various in length, is confusing though
not confused." Then summarily, " In these
poems will be found that love of homeliness
which is characteristic of all true poets. The
meeting of the homely and the grand is heaven."*

The following is the original title-page of the
volume in which all the Festival Hyms, save one
—of which anon—first appeared, and which is our
text.

The

GOLDEN GROVE

or

A MANUALL

of

Daily Prayers and Letanies,
Fitted to the dayes of the Week.
Containing a short Summary of
What is to be ⎰ Believed,
⎱ Practised,
⎱ Desired.

also

FESTIVAL HYMNS

According to the manner of
The Ancient Church.

* Antiphon, pp. 221, 222.

Composed for the Use of the Devout, especially
of Younger Persons; By the Author of
The Great Exemplar.

London, Printed by J. F. for R. Royston, at the
Angel in Ivie Lane, 1655. [12mo.]

A second edition appeared in 1657 with the
Author's name thus "By Jer: Taylor, D.D.
Chaplain in Ordinary to his late Majesty"—a
valiant announcement in the circumstances. The
third edition I have not succeeded in tracing: but
the 4th appeared in 1659: and from it I take the
second Christmas Hymn, "Awake my Soul"
which was not in the 1st or 2nd edition. Curiously and blameably neither Bishop Heber and
Pitman earlier, nor Eden more recently, in their
collective editions of Taylor's Works, observed
this precious addition to the "Festival Hymns,"
and hence it is not included by either.

In a long and sharp Epistle "to the pious and
devout Reader" explanation is given of the
motive and purpose of the treatise of the "Golden
Grove"—name recalling VAUGHAN—and I take
these closing references to the Hymns from it:
"Christian religion is admirable for its wisdome,
for its simplicity, and he that presents these
papers to thee, designs to teach thee as the

Church was taught in the early days of the
Apostles.   To believe the Christian Faith, and to
represent plain rules of good life; to describe
easie forms of prayer ; to bring into your Assemblies hymnes of glorification and thanksgiving, and
psalms of prayer.   By these easie paths they lead
Christ's little ones into the Fold of their great
Bishop; and if by this way service be done to
God, any ministry to the soule of a childe or an
ignorant woman, it is hoped that God will accept
it ; and it is reward enough, if by my ministery
God will bring it to pass, that any soul shall be
instructed and brought into that state of good
things that it shall rejoyce for ever."

Published in 1655 it is no great marvel that the
" still small voice " of these Hymns and Songs
for the " simple ones "—in a good tender sense—
of the Church, went unheard or at least unheeded
by the majority.   No more a marvel that when
the tempestuous season was past, listeners were
found—much as after the Winter, grown men
pause to catch the vernal singing of the lowliest
bird.   Beyond the successive editions of the
" Golden Grove " and related treatises, the Hymns
passed into various collections—as the Hymnolo-
gies and bibliography of Hymns shew.   Thither
the student will turn.   JAMES MONTGOMERY called

attention in fitting words to the Hymns in his "Christian Poet" (1825) where he quotes several and remarks, " his verse, as might be expected is crude, but rich in noble thoughts ". Heber followed, by inserting in his Collection—published posthumously in 1827—the second Hymn for Advent and the Prayer for Charity, altered. More recently and representing Nonconformity, the Hymn for Advent is found in the Leeds Congregational Collection : and in the Sarum 'Hymnal' edited by Earl Nelson and others. It appears also in its original text in Sir Roundell Palmer's " Book of Praise ".

I would only notice one flagrant misappropriation viz. by SAMUEL SPEED in his " Prison Piety : or Meditations divine and moral. Digested into poetical heads on mixt and various subjects . .
. . . by Samuel Speed, Prisoner in Ludgate, London " (1677). Without name or marking this unworthy scion of quaint and venerable JOHN SPEED, has incorporated substantially the whole of Taylor's Hymns—with such changes as take the gipsy-form of defacing in order to conceal the larceny. I note below the pages in " Prison-Piety " where the several Hymns will be found :*

---

* Pages 102, 103 (2), 104, 110, 131, 137, 141 (2) 142,

and were it worth-while—which it is not—I
might go over the whole collection, and convict of
like felonies against other poets and singers of
Zion's songs, leaving nothing of any value the
lawful property of SPEED. I had intended re-
printing " Prison-Piety ", and had spent no little
time and labour in searching out facts of the
obscure and worthless life. But I need hardly
say that I have now no intention of reviving the
book or the memory. I must ask pardon of the
shade of our Worthy for having momentarily
forgotten him in my quotation " of Death " in
PHINEAS FLETCHER (I., cclxxxiv—v.) I owe
thanks to my friendly correspondent, Mr. W. T.
Brooke, London, for much help in bringing
together super-abundant proofs of the appropria-
tions, that is, misappropriations of SPEED. I
suppose he satisfied what fragment of conscience
he had by these words in his Epistle " to the
devout "—"I have *compiled* and composed this
Manual of Meditations."

Hitherto these Hymns have been either
mangled as by Speed or modernized and otherwise
altered, as by the best editors of Taylor, *e.g.*,

---

143. See examples of Speed's Readings in our notes at
close of the Hymns.

Heber and Pitman, and Eden and the Collections. I for the first time, in later days, return to the original text and orthography, and as already pointed out, restore the fine Christmas hymn "Awake my soul", so culpably overlooked by Heber and Eden. In Notes and Illustrations a few variations from the 1657 edition are added.

Besides the Festival Hymns in the "Golden Grove" I have the pleasure to give Taylor's rendering of Job's curse, *not* in the bewildering form WILLMOTT has presented it from Playford's "Harmonia Sacra"—as exhibited in our Note in its place—but from "Miscellanea Sacra: or Poems on Divine and Moral Subjects. Collected by N. Tate, Servant to his Majesty. London: Printed for Hen. Playford in the Temple-Change in Fleet-street" (1696)—2nd edition, 1698. The text of "Miscellanea Sacra" vindicates itself as opposed to the same Publisher's "Harmonia Sacra."

Further, it is no common satisfaction to me to embody in this little gathering certain utterly neglected verse-renderings of quotations from the Classics in our illustrious prelate's works. Throughout his numerous Writings—sermons included—Bishop Taylor is fond of working into the web of his own thinking, the cloth-of-gold of lines

69

from the ancient Poets of Greece and Rome, and
later : and with reference to the Sermons more
especially, one wonders if he really delivered *ore
rotundo*, the abundant Greek and Latin that
speckle his pages. Most are left in the original.
Occasionally he renders into musical prose, also
occasionally into rhymed verse. These latter
which I designate *Aurea Grana* I have carefully
gleaned from his " Deus Justificatus " and " Discourse of the Nature and Offices of Friendship ".
I do not think that any other of his books con-
tain in text so much as one couplet more : but
below I invite attention to Lines from the Engrav-
ings of the " Great Exemplar." It is extremely
interesting to come on these additional proofs of
the poetic yearning if it may not be called " the
vision and the faculty divine". Those in
" Friendship " are extremely noticeable as having
been addressed to " the matchless Orinda "—a
lady egregiously over-lauded in her brief day.
Perhaps her (imagined) poetical gifts may have
stimulated Taylor to emulation. At any rate he
translates into verse all his quotations in the
"Discourse of Friendship ". He had a sufficiently
humble estimate of his success in so far as these
minor things went : witness these words in " Deus
Justificatus, " which anticipate Dr. Macdonald's

criticism (*supra*)—" I could translate these also
[from Horace] into bad English verse as I do the
others ; but that now I am earnest for my liberty,
I will not so much as confine myself to the measures of feet ". I have given the original in each
instance, and as much of the context—the quartz
wherein the golden grains glitter—as seemed necessary for the elucidation of the translations. There
is not always closeness but there is almost invari-
ably smoothness and harmony in advance of the
Hymns, though by the nature of the quotations,
none of their largeness and opulence of thought.
I owe thanks to Eden's collective edition of the
Works for verification of some of the references :
" Deus Justificatus " in Vol. VII. pp 493—538
and " Friendship " in Vol. I. pp 69—98 : but I
reproduce the genuine orthography from the 1656
edition of the former, and that of 1657 of the
latter. I must also ask it to be kept in mind that
the prose context given, follows, as do the verse-
renderings, Taylor's own text, not Heber-Pitman
or Eden, who modernize and blunder sorrowfully.
Finally, there will be found four verse-portraits of
the four Evangelists. These are engraved under
their respective portraits in the 1657 edition of the
" Great Exemplar ", and are not included in any
of the modern collective or separate editions of

this noble book, though they were continued until the plates were worn out.   There seem to me true poetic touches, if only touches, in some of these Lines, and the traditional symbols of the Evang- elists are well described.

So I put into the hands for the lips and hearts of the select Readers of our Worthies, these Poems of Bishop Jeremy Taylor, saying of him with Wordsworth,

> " Thanks to his pure imaginative soul,
> Capacious and serene, his blameless life,
> His knowledge, wisdom, love of truth, and love
> Of human-kind."

ALEXANDER   B.   GROSART.

St. George's, Blackburn.

II. Festival Hymns.

*"I will sing with the spirit, und I will sing with
the understanding also."*

[1 Corinthians xiv. 15.   G.]

HYMNS

CELEBRATING THE MYSTERIES AND CHIEF FESTIVALS
OF THE YEAR, ACCORDING TO THE MANNER OF THE
ANCIENT CHURCH: FITTED TO THE FANCY AND
DEVOTION OF THE YOUNGER AND PIOUS PERSONS,

Apt for memory, and to be joyned to their other PRAYERS.

Hymns for Advent, or the weeks immediately before the Birth of our blessed Saviour.

I.

WHEN Lord, O when shall we
   Our dear salvation see?
   Arise, arise,
     Our fainting eyes
Have long'd all night; and 'twas a long one too.
Man never yet could say

He saw more then one day,
　　One day of Eden's seven :
The guilty hours there blasted with the breath
　　　　　　　Of Sin and Death,
Have ever since worn a nocturnal hue.
But Thou hast given us hopes that we
At length another day shall see,
　　Wherein each vile neglected place,
　　Gilt with the aspect of Thy face,
Shall be like that, the porch and gate of Heaven.
　　How long, dear God, how long !
　　See how the nations throng :
　　All humane kinde
　　Knit and combin'd
Into one body, look for Thee their Head.
　　Pity our multitude ;
　　Lord we are vile and rude,
Headless and sensless without Thee,
Of all things but the want of Thy blest face ;
　　　　　　　O haste apace !
And Thy bright Self to this our body wed,
　　That through the influx of Thy power,
　　Each part that er'st confusion wore
　　May put on order, and appear
　　Spruce as the childhood of the year,
When Thou to it shalt so united be.

　　　　　　　　　　Amen.

The Second Hymn for Advent; or Christ's coming
to Jerusalem in Triumph.

LORD come away,
    Why dost Thou stay?
Thy rode is ready; and Thy paths,
        made strait,
With longing expectation, wait
The consecration of Thy beauteous feet.
Ride on triumphantly; behold we lay
Our lusts and proud wills in Thy way.
Hosanna! welcome to our hearts! Lord, here
Thou hast a temple too, and full as dear
As that of Sion, and as full of sin:
Nothing but thieves and robbers dwel therein,
Enter, and chase them forth, and cleanse the
        floore;
Crucifie them, that they may never more
            Profane that holy place
        Where Thou hast chose to set Thy face.
And then if our stiff tongues shall be
Mute in the praises of Thy Deity;
        The stones out of the Temple-wall
        Shall cry aloud and call
Hosanna! and Thy glorious footsteps greet.
                                    Amen.

Hymns for Christmas-day.

I.

YSTERIOUS truth! that the self-same
should be
A Lamb, a Shepherd, and a Lion too!
        Yet such was He
   Whom first the shepherds knew,
   When they themselves became
   Sheep to the Shepherd-Lamb.
Shepherd of men and angels, Lamb of God,
  Lion of Judah, by these titles keep
  The wolf from Thy indangered sheep.
    Bring all the world unto Thy fold,
      Let Jews and Gentiles hither come
    In numbers great that can't be told,
      And call Thy lambs that wander, home.
    Glory be to God on high,
  All glories be to th'glorious Deity.

The Second Hymn; being a Dialogue between Three Shepherds.

HERE is this blessed Babe
      That hath made
  All the world so full of joy
   And expectation;

That glorious Boy
That crowns each nation
With a triumphant wreath of blessedness?

Where should He be but in the throng,
And among
His angel-ministers, that sing
And take wing
Just as may echo to His voyce,
And rejoyce
When wing and tongue and all
May so procure their happiness?

But He hath other waiters now ;
A poor cow,
An ox and mule stand and behold,
And wonder,
That a stable should enfold
Him that can thunder.
CHORUS.   O what a gracious God have we !
How good ? how great ? Even as our misery.

The Third Hymn: of Christ's Birth in an Inne.

HE blessed virgin travail'd without pain,
And lodgèd in an inne ;
A glorious star the sign,
But of a greater guest then ever came that way ;

For there He lay
That is the God of night and day,
And over all the pow'rs of heaven doth reign.
It was the time of great Augustus tax,
And then He comes
That pays all sums,
Even the whole price of lost humanity ;
And set us free
From the ungodly emperie
Of sin, and Satan, and of death.
O make our hearts, blest God, Thy lodging-place,
And in our brest
Be pleas'd to rest,
For thou lov'st temples better then an inne,
And cause that sin
May not profane the Deity within,
And sully o're the ornaments of grace.   Amen.

[The fourth] Hymn for Christmas Day.

WAKE, my soul, and come away !
Put on thy best array;
Least if thou longer stay,
Thou lose some minitts of so blest a day.
Goe run,
And bid good morrow to the sun :

Welcome his safe return,
    to Capricorn;
  And that great morne
  Wherein a God was borne,
  Whose story none can tell
But He Whose every word's a miracle.
  To-day Almightiness grew weak;
The Worde itself was mute, and could not speak.
  That Jacob's star Which made the sun
  To dazle if he durst look on,
  Now mantled ore in Beth'lem's night,
  Borrowed a star to shew Him light.
   He that begirt each zone,
   To Whom both poles are one,
   Who grasp't the Zodiack in's hand
   And made it move or stand,
   Is now by nature MAN,
   By stature but a span;
   Eternitie is now grown short;
   A King is borne without a court;
   The water thirsts; the fountain's dry;
  And Life being borne, made apt to dye.
Chorus.   Then let our prayers emulate and vie
    With His humilitie:
   Since Hee's exil'd from skeyes
    That we might rise,—
   From low estate of men

Let's sing Him up agen!
Each man winde up's heart
        To bear a part
In that angelick quire, and show
His glory high as He was low!
Let's sing t'wards men good wil and charity,
Peace upon Earth, glory to God on high
                Hallelujah, Hallelujah!

A Hymn upon St John's day.

HIS day
        We sing
        The friend of our eternal King :
Who in His bosome lay.
And kept the keys
Of His profound and glorious mysteries :
Which to the world dispensèd by his hand,
                Made it stand
Fix'd in amazement to behold that light
                Which came
From the throne of the Lamb,
                To invite
Our wretched eyes—which nothing else could see
But fire, and sword, hunger and miserie—
        To anticipate by their ravish'd sight
        The beauty of celestial delight.

Mysterious God, regard me when I pray :
    And when this load of clay
              Shall fall away,
O let Thy gracious hand conduct me up,
Where on the Lamb's rich viands I may sup :
        And in this last Supper I
May with Thy friend in Thy sweet bosome lie
      For ever in Eternity.
                  Allelujah.

Upon the Day of the Holy Innocents.

MOURNFUL Iudah shreeks and cries
      At the obsequies
      Of their babes, that cry
More that they lose the paps, then that they die.
    He that came with life to all,
      Brings the babes a funeral,
      To redeem from slaughter Him
      Who did redeem us all from sin.
      They like Himself went spotless hence,
      A sacrifice to Innocence ;
        Which now does ride
      Trampling upon Herod's pride :
Passing from their fontinels of clay
To heaven, a milky and a bloody way.

All their tears and groans are dead
And they to rest and glory fled.
Lord, Who wert pleased so many babes should fall
Whil'st each sword hop'd that every of the all
Was the desirèd king : make us to be
In innocence like them, in glory, Thee.

Amen.

Upon the Epiphany, and the Three Wise Men of the East coming to Worship Jesus.

COMET dangling in the aire,
Presag'd the ruine both of Death and
Sin ;
And told the wise-men of a King,
The King of Glory, and the Sun
Of Righteousness, Who then begun
To draw towards that blesed Hemisphere.
They from the furthest East this new
And unknown light pursue,
Till they appeare
In this blest Infant-King's propitious eye ;
And pay their homage to His Royalty.
Persia might then the rising Sun adore,
It was idolatry no more :
Great God they gave to Thee,

Myrrhe, frankincense, and gold ;
But Lord, with what shall we
Present our selves before Thy majesty,
Whom Thou redeem'st when we were sold ?
W'have nothing but our selves, and scarce that
neither,
Vile dirt and clay :
Yet it is soft, and may
Impression take :
Accept it, Lord, and say, this Thou had'st rather;
Stamp it, and on this sordid metal make
Thy holy image, and it shall out-shine
The beauty of the golden myne.
Amen.

| *A Meditation of the* *Four last things* | Death,
Judgment,
Heaven,
Hell | *For the* *time of* Lent *e-* *specially.* |

A Meditation of Death.

EATH, the old serpent's son,
Thou had'st a sting once like thy
sire,
That carried Hell, and ever-burning fire :
But those black dayes are done ;

83

Thy foolish spite buried thy sting
   In the profound and wide
    Wound of our Saviour's side.
And now thou art become a tame and harmless
  thing,
    A thing we dare not fear
     Since we hear
That our triumphant God to punish thee
For the affront thou didst Him on the tree,
Hath snatcht the keyes of Hell out of thy hand,
    And made thee stand
A porter to the gate of Life, thy mortal enemie.
O Thou who art that gate, command that he
    May when we die
    And thither flie,
Let us into the courts of Heaven through Thee.
        Allelujah.

The Prayer.

Y soul doth pant tow'rds Thee
 My God, source of eternal life:
 Flesh fights with me;
  Oh end the strife
And part us, that in peace I may
    Unclay

My wearied spirit, and take
My flight to Thy eternal spring ;
  Where for His sake
  Who is my King,
I may wash all my tears away
    That day.
  Thou conqueror of Death,
Glorious triumpher o're the grave,
  Whose holy breath
  Was spent to save
Lost mankinde ; make me to be stil'd,
    Thy child,
  And take me when I dye
And go unto the dust ; my soul
  Above the sky
  With saints enroll,
That in Thy arms for ever I
    May lie.
      Amen.

Of the Day of Judgement.

GREAT Judge of all, how we vile wretches
  quake !
  Our guilty bones do ake,
 Our marrow freezes, when we think

Of the consuming fire
      Of Thine ire ;
And horrid phials thou shalt make
      The wicked drink,
When Thou the wine press of Thy wrath shalt
    tread
        With feet of lead.
Sinfull rebellious clay ! what unknown place
      Shall hide it from Thy face!
When Earth shall vanish from Thy sight,
    The heavens that never err'd,
      But observ'd
Thy laws, shal from Thy presence take their flight,
And kil'd with glory, their bright eyes, stark dead
    Start from their head :
    Lord, how shall we
Thy enemies, endure to see
      So bright, so killing majesty ?
Mercy dear Saviour : Thy judgement-seat
    We dare not, Lord, intreat ;
    We are condemn'd already, there.
    Mercy : vouchsafe one look
      On Thy book
Of life ; Lord we can read the saving Jesus, here,
And in His name our own salvation see :
    Lord set us free :

The book of sin
Is cross'd within,
Our debts are paid by Thee.
                    Mercy !

Of Heaven.

BEAUTEOUS God, uncircumscribèd
        treasure
    Of an eternal pleasure,
    Thy throne is seated far
    Above the highest star,
Where Thou prepar'st a glorious place
Within the brightness of Thy face
            For every spirit
            To inherit
That builds his hopes on Thy merit,
And loves Thee with a holy charity.
What ravish't heart, seraphick tongue or eyes,
        Clear as the Morning's rise,
        Can speak, or think, or see
        That bright eternity ?
Where the great King's transparent throne,
Is of an intire jaspar stone :
            There the eye
            O'th'chrysolite,
            And a sky
87

Of diamonds, rubies, chrysoprase,
And above all, Thy holy face
Makes an eternal clarity,
When Thou thy jewels up dost binde; that day
    Remember us, we pray.
    That where the beryl lies
    And the crystal, 'bove the skyes,
There thou may'st appoint us place
Within the brightness of Thy face;
    And our soul
    In the scrowl
Of life and blissfulness enrowl,
That we may praise Thee to eternity.
        Allelujah.

Of Hell.

ORRID darkness, sad and sore,
    And an eternal night,
Groanes and shrieks, and thousands more
    In the want of glorious light:
    Every corner hath a snake
    In the accursèd lake:
Seas of fire, beds of snow
Are the best delights below,
    A viper from the fire
      Is his hire

That knows not moments from eternity.
Glorious God of day and night,
            Spring of eternall light,
Allelujahs, hymns and psalms
            And coronets of palms
Fill Thy temple evermore.
            O mighty God
            Let not thy bruising rod
Crush our loins with an eternal pressure;
O let Thy mercy be the measure,
For if Thou keepest wrath in store
            We all shall die,
            And none be left to glorifie
            Thy name, and tell
How Thou hast sav'd our souls from Hell.
                              Mercy.

On the Conversion of St. Paul.

FULL of wrath, his threatning breath
    Belching nought, but chains and death :
        Saul was arrested in his way
            By a voice and a light,
    That if a thousand dayes
    Should joyn rayes
    To beautifie one day,
It would not show so glorious and so bright.

89

On his amazèd eyes it night did fling,
That day might break within :
And by those beams of faith
Make him of a childe of wrath
Become a vessel full of glory.
Lord, curb us in our dark and sinful way,
We humbly pray,
When we down horrid precipices run
With feet that thirst to be undone,
That this may be our story.
Allelujah.

On the Purification of the blessed Virgin.

URE and spotless was the maid
That to the Temple came,
A pair of turtle-doves she paid,
Although she brought the Lamb.
Pure and spotless though she were,
Her body chaste, and her soul faire,
She to the Temple went
To be purifi'd
And try'd,
That she was spotless and obedient ;
O make us follow so blest precedent,
And purifie our souls, for we

90

Are cloth'd with sin and misery.
From our conception
One imperfection,
And a continued state of sin,
Hath sullied all our faculties within.
We present our souls to Thee
Full of need and misery:
And for redemption a Lamb
The purest, whitest that e're came
A sacrifice to Thee,
Even He that bled upon the Tree.

On Good-Friday.

THE Lamb is eaten, and is yet again
Preparing to be slain;
The cup is full and mixt,
And must be drunk:
Wormwood and gall
To this, are draughts to beguile care withall,
Yet the decree is fixt.
Doubled knees, and groans, and cries,
Prayers and sighs, and flowing eyes
Could not intreat
His sad soul, sunk

Under the heavy preasure of our sin :
   The pains of Death and Hell
    About Him dwell.
His Father's burning wrath did make
His very heart, like melting wax, to sweat
    Rivers of blood,
  Through the pure strainer of his skin,
   His boiling body stood
    Bubling all o're
As if the wretched whole were but one dore
   To let in pain and grief,
   And turn out all relief.
O Thou, Who for our sake
  Dids't drink up
  This bitter cup :
Remember us, we pray,
  In Thy day,
  When down
The strugling throats of wicked men
The dregs of Thy just fury shall be thrown.
      Oh then
Let Thy unbounded mercy think
   On us, for whom
  Thou underwent'st this heavy doom,
And give us of the well of life to drink.
      Amen.

On the Annunciation of the Blessed Virgin.

 Wingèd harbinger from bright heav'n
flown
  Bespeaks a lodging-room
   For the mighty King of Love.
 The spotless structure of a virgin womb,
O'reshadow'd with the wings of the blest Dove:
  For He was travelling to Earth,
    But did desire to lay
    By the way
  That He might shift his clothes, and be
  A perfect Man as well as we.
How good a God have we! Who for our sake,
  To save us from the burning lake,
Did change the order of creation:
    At first He made
Man like Himself in His own Image; now
  In the more blessed reparation
    The heavens bow:
Eternity took the measure of a span,
     And said
Let us make our self like Man,
  And not from man the woman take
  But from the woman, Man.
Allelujah: we adore
His name, whose goodness hath no store.
     Allelujah.

Easter Day.

HAT glorious light!
How bright a sun after so sad a night
Does now begin to dawn! Bless'd were
those eyes
That did behold
This sun when He did first unfold
His glorious beams, and now begin to rise:
It was the holy tender sex
That saw the first ray:
Saint Peter and the other, had the reflex,
The second glimpse o'th'day.
Innocence had the first, and he
That fled, and then did penance, next did see
The glorious Sun of Righteousness
In His new dress
Of triumph, immortality, and bliss.
O dearest God, preserve our souls
In holy innocence;
Or if we do amiss
Make us to rise again to th'life of grace
That we may live with Thee, and see Thy glorious
face,
The crown of holy penitence.
Allelujah.

On the day of Ascension.

H E is risen higher, not set :
　　　　Indeed a cloud
　　Did with His leave make bold to shroud
The Sun of Glory, from Mount Olivet.
At Pentecost He'll shew Himself again,
　When every ray shall be a tongue
To speak all comforts, and inspire
Our souls with their celestial fire ;
　　　That we the saints among
　　　May sing, and love, and reign.
　　　　　　　　Amen.

On the Feast of Pentecost, or Whitsunday.

T ONGUES of fire from heaven descend,
　　With a mighty rushing wind
　　　To blow it up, and make
　　　　A living fire
Of heavenly charity, and pure desire,
Where they their residence should take :
On the Apostles sacred heads they sit,
Who now like beacons do proclaim and tell
Th'invasion of the host of Hell ;
　　And give men warning to defend
Themselves from the inragèd brunt of it.

Lord, let the flames of holy charity,
      And all her gifts and graces slide
      Into our hearts, and there abide;
That thus refinèd, we may soar above
With it unto the element of love,
      Even unto Thee, dear Spirit,
And there eternal peace and rest inherit.

                Amen.

Penitentiall Hymns.

I.

LORD, I have sinn'd, and the black number
    swells
      To such a dismal sum,
That should my stony heart and eyes,
And this whole sinful trunk a flood become,
And run to tears, their drops could not suffice
      To count my score,
      Much less to pay:
But Thou, my God, hast blood in store,
And art the patron of the poore.
  Yet since the balsam of Thy blood,
    Although it can, will do no good,
Unless the wounds be cleans'd with tears before;
Thou in Whose sweet but pensive face

Laughter could never steal a place,
  Teach but my heart and eyes
    To melt away,
And then one drop of balsam will suffice.

       Amen.

II.

REAT God, and just! how canst Thou see,
    Dear God, our miserie,
   And not in mercy set us free?
Poor miserable man! how wert thou born,
Week as the dewy jewels of the morn,
   Rapt up in tender dust,
    Guarded with sins and lust,
  Who like Court-flatterers waite
  To serve themselves in thy unhappy fate.
Wealth is a snare, and poverty brings in
Inlets of theft, paving the way for sin:
Each perfum'd vanity doth gently breath
Sin in thy Soul, and whispers it to Death.
Our faults like ulcerated sores do go
O're the sound flesh, and do corrupt that too:
   Lord, we are sick, spotted with sin:
   Thick as a crusty leaper's skin;
  Like Naaman, bid us wash, yet let it be

In streams of blood that flow from Thee :
Then will we sing.
Touch'd by the heavenly Dove's bright wing,
Hallelujahs, psalms and praise
To God the Lord of night and dayes ;
Ever good, and ever just,
Ever high, Who ever must
Thus be sung ; is still the same ;
Eternal praises crown His name.
Amen.

A prayer for Charity.

ULL of mercy, full of love,
Look upon us from above ;
Thou who taught'st the blinde man's
night
To entertain a double light,
Thine and the dayes—and that Thine too—
The lame away his crutches threw,
The parchèd crust of Leprosie
Return'd unto its infancy :
The dumb amazèd was to hear
His own unchain'd tongue strike his ear ;
Thy powerful mercy did even chase
The devil from his usurp'd place,

Where Thou Thy self shouldst dwell, not he,
O let Thy love our pattern be ;
Let Thy mercy teach one brother
To forgive and love another,
That copying Thy mercy here,
Thy goodness may hereafter reare
Our souls unto Thy glory, when
Our dust shall cease to be with men.

III. Job's Curse.

LET the night perish, cursèd be the morn
Wherein 'twas said there is a man-child
born !
Let not the Lord regard that day, but shroud
It's fatal glory in some sullen cloud.
May the dark shades of an eternal night
Exclude the least kind beam of dawning light ;
Let unknown babes as in the womb they lye,
If it be mention'd, give a groan and dye.
No sounds of joy therein shall charm the ear,
No sun, no moon, no twilight star appear,
But a thick vale of gloomy darkness wear.
Why did I not, when first my mother's womb
Discharg'd me thence, drop down into my tomb ?
Then had I been as quiet : and mine eyes
Had slept and seen no sorrow ; there the wise
And subtil councillor, the potentate,
Who for themselves built palaces of state,
Lie hush't in silence ; there's no midnight cry
Caus'd by oppressive tyranny

Of wicked rulers; there the weary cease
From labour, there the prisoner sleeps in peace,
The rich, the poor, the monarch, and the slave,
Rest undisturb'd, and no distinction have
Within the silent chambers of the grave.

[From "Miscellanea Sacra" (pp 11-12), as
described in Introduction, page 13 : in the Preface
(2nd edition, 1698) Tate specially refers to above:
"Some of 'em carry their sanction in the names
of their authors : such as Dr. Jeremy Taylor"..]

NOTE.

The text in Playford's " Harmonia Sacra " presents these variations :

Line 7th, " unborn " for " unknown."

" 11th, " veil " for " vale ".

" 19th, " oppression and the. "

" 20th, " here, here the weary".

" 21st, " here, the pris'ner".

and at end chorus " Here, here, the weary cease ". But the most extraordinary blundering of the " Harmonia Sacra " is the chaos of prose and verse at the close— repeated singularly enough by WILLMOTT in his Life of Taylor (2nd edition, 1848 : p. 231) without detection or remark. As a " Curiosity of Literature " and an addit- ional proof of how perfunctorily the Poems of our Prelate have been hitherto edited even by scholarly men, I subjoin the lines in question from WILLMOTT literally :

" Then had I been at quiet, and mine eyes had
slept and seen no sorrow ;
there, there the Wise and Subtile Counsellor,
the Potentate, who for themselves build Palaces of
    State,
lye hushed in Silence ; there's no Midnight cry
caus'd by Oppression, and the Tyranny of wicked
    Rulers.
Here, here the Weary cease from Labour,
here the pris'ner sleeps in Peace ;
the Rich, the Poor, the Monarch, and the Slave,
rest undisturbed and no distinction have,
within the silent Chambers of the Grave.
                   Chorus.
        Here, here, the weary cease, &c.   G.

IV.

Verse-portraits of the Four Evangelists;

FROM THE "GREAT EXEMPLAR" (1657).

1 St. Matthew.

HIS Mathew and that angel doth implie
Christe's roial ligne in His humanitie :
Mankinde Himself, deriving downe the same
To Joseph's tribe, from faithfull Abraham.

2 St. Marke.

Marke's lion—as his gospell—doth beginne
A crier's voice the wilderness within,
Make straight His pathes : the same is onely Hee
Of Judah's tribe who was foretold to bee.

3. St. Luke.

This holy artist with inspirèd pen
The great Messiah pourtrayes, and to men
Whose sin ore-loaded soules to death encline
Att once becomes physician and devine.[1]

---

[1] " Luke, the beloved physician " Colossians iv. 11. G.

4. St. John.

Looke how the quick-sight eagle mounts on
 high
Beholds the sunne with her all-piercing eie :
So unto Christe's diuinitie I soare
Beyond the straine of these that are before.

V.

𝔄𝔲𝔯𝔢𝔞 𝔊𝔯𝔞𝔫𝔞.

𝔙𝔢𝔯𝔰𝔢 𝔗𝔯𝔞𝔫𝔰𝔩𝔞𝔱𝔦𝔬𝔫𝔰.

I. From " Deus Justificatus or a Vindication of the Glory of the Divine Attributes in the Question of Original Sin: in a Letter to a Person of Quality." 1656 (12º) and 1657 (folio).

I. THE FALL.

" THE main thing is this : when God was angry with Adam, the man fell from the state of grace ; for God withdrew His grace, and we returned to the state of meer nature, of our prime creation. And although I am not of Petrus Diaconus, his mind, who said that when we all fell in Adam, we fell into the dirt, and not only so, but we fell also upon a heap of stones ; so that we not onely were made naked, but defiled also, and broken all in pieces : yet this I believe to be certain, that we by his fall received evill enough to undoe us,

105

and ruine us all; but yet the evil did so descend
upon us, that we were left in powers and capaci-
ties to serve and glorifie God; God's service was
made much harder, but not impossible; mankind
was made miserable, but not desperate; we con-
tracted an actuall mortality, but we were redeem-
able from the power of Death; sinne was easie
and ready at the door, but it was resistable; our
Will was abused, but yet not destroyed; our
Understanding was cozened, but still capable of
the best instructions; and though the Devill had
wounded us, yet God sent His Son, Who like the
good Samaritan poured oyll and wine into our
wounds, and we were cured before we felt the
hurt, that might have ruined us upon that occasion. It is sad enough, but not altogether so
intolerable and decretory [as some would make
it] which the Sibylline oracle describes to be the
effect of Adam's sin :

Ἄνθρωπον πέπλασθαι θεοῦ παλαμαῖς ἐνὶ αὐταῖς
Ὅν τε πλάνησεν ὄφις δολίως ἐπὶ μοῖραν ἀνέλθειν
Τοῦ θανατοῦ, γνῶσιν τε λαβεῖν ἀγαθοῦ τε κακοῦ τε.

Man was the worke of God, fram'd by His hands;
Him did the Serpent cheat, that to death's bands
He was subjected for his sin : for this was all :
He tasted good and evill by his Fall.

[Sic apud Lactant. ii. 13 : fol. Cæsenæ, 1646.
Aliter in edd-recent.]

2. GUILT AND DESTINY.

" To say that our actual sins should any more proceed from Adam's fall, then Adam's fall should should proceed from itself, is not to be imagined ; for what made Adam sin when he fell ? If a fatal decree made him sin, then he was nothing to blame :

> Fati ista culpa est,
> Nemo fit fato nocens.
> No guilt upon Mankinde can lie
> For what's the fault of Destiny.
>
> [Seneca Œdip, line 1019.]

3. ORIGINAL SIN.

" Because I have proved it cannot infer damnation, I can safely conclude it is not formally, properly and inherently a sin in us.
Nec placet, O superi, cum vobis vertere cuncta
Propositum, nostris erroribus addere crimen.
Nor did it please our God, when that our state
Was chang'd, to adde a crime unto our fate.

> [' Hoc placet ', &c.—Lucan vii., 58.]

4. NO MASTERS: ONE MASTER.

" ' They that taught of this article before me are good guides, but no lords and masters;' for I must acknowledge none upon Earth; for so I am

107

commanded by my Master that is in Heaven ; and
I remember what we are taught in Palingenius,
when wee were boyes.

Quicquid Aristoteles vel quivis dicat, eorum
Dicta nihil moror a vero cum forte recedunt :
Sæpe graves magnosque famaque verendos
Errare et labi continget, plurima secum
Ingenia in tenebras consueti nominis alti
Authores, ubi connivent, deducere easdem.
If Aristotle be deceiv'd, and say that's true
What nor himself nor others ever knew,
I leave his text, and let his schollers talke
Till they be hoarse or weary in their walke :
When wise men erre, though their fame ring like
    bells,
I scape a danger when I leave their spells.

   ⌊In Poemate cui nomen ' Zodiacus vitæ ', lib.
      viii. sive ' scorpio', p. 187.—Basil 1563.
      8vo.—(It is something to know one of the
      school-books of Taylor. Barnabe Googe
      quaintly translated the ' Zodiake of Life ' :
      various editions. G.)⌉

5. THE SOFT ANSWER.

" If any man is of my opinion, I confesse I love
him the better, but if he refutes it, I will not love
him lesse after than I did before; but he that

dissents, and reviles me, must expect from me no other kindness but that I forgive him, and pray for him, and offer to reclaim him, and that I resolve nothing shall ever make me either hate him or reproach him. And that still in the greatest of his difference, I refuse not to give him the communion of a brother; I believe I shall be chidden by some or other for my easinesse and want of fierceness, which they call zeal; but it is a fault of my nature, a part of my original sin :

Unicuique dedit vitium natura creato,

Mi natura aliquid semper amare dedit.

Some weaknesse to each man by birth descends,
To me too great a kindnesse Nature lends.

[Propertius : lib. ii. el. 22.17. Be it noted that the ascription of his ' charity ' to his original sin is a playful gibe against his adversaries from the topic of his book ; and also, that Eden &c. misread ' refuses ' for ' refutes ' in 2nd. *supra*—one of swarming errors in the edition of the Works current. G.]

6. HINDRANCES.

Qui serere ingenuum volet agrum,
Liberet arva prius fructibus,
Falce rubos filicemque resecet

Ut novâ fruge gravis Ceres eat.

He that will sow his field with hopefull seed,
Must every bramble, every thistle weed ;
And when each hindrance to the graine is gone,
A fruitfull crop shall rise of corn alone.

      [al. 'liberat,' 'resecat.' Boethius, lib. iii.
      metr. 1.]

7.   CONSCIENCE.

Extemplo quodcunque malum committitur, ipsi
Displicet authori ;—
He that is guilty of a sin
Shal rue the crime that he lies in.

      [Lege ' Exemplo......malo' :   Juvenal,
      Sat. xiii. I.]

8.   TRUE IF NEW.

" I end with the words of Lucretius,
Desine quâpropter novitate exterritus ipsa
Expuere eo animo rationem, sed magis acri
Judicio perpende, et si tibi vera videtur,
Dede manus, aut si falsa est, accingere contra.
Fear not to own what's said because 'tis new ;
Weigh well and wisely if the thing be true.
Truth and not conquest is the best reward ;
'Gainst falsehood onely stand upon thy guard.

      [Lib. ii. lines 1039 et seqq.]

II. From "A Discourse of the Nature, Offices, and
Measures of Friendship" 1657 and 1673 (folio)
and 1678 (12o.)

9. FRIENDSHIPS.

" A Good man is the best friend, and therefore
soonest to be chosen, longer to be retain'd; and
indeed never to be parted with; unless he cease
to be that for which he was chosen :

Τῶν δ' ἄλλων ἀρετῇ ποειῶ φίλον ὅστις ἄριστοσ.*
Μήποτε τὸν κακόν ἄνδρα φίλον ποιεῖσθαι ἑταῖρον†

Where Vertue dwells there friendships make,
But evil neighbourhoods forsake.

[* Pythag. carm. aur. 5 : † Theogn. lin.
113.]

10. LOVE FOR LOVE.

" That was the commendation of the bravest
friendship in Theocritus : "

They lov'd each other with a love
That did in all things equal prove.

. . . . ῎Η ῥα τότ' ἦσαν
χρύσειοι πάλαι ἄνδρες ὅκ' ἀντεφίλασ' ὁ φιλαθεῖσ·

The world was under Saturn's reign
When he that lov'd was lov'd again.

[Idyll xii. 15.]

111

11. MUTUAL FRIENDS.

Ζεύς μοι τῶν τε φίλων δοίη τίσιν οἵ με φιλεῦσι·*
"Ολβιοι οἱ φιλέοντες, ἐπὴν ἴσον 'αντεράωνται.‡

Let God give friends to me for my reward,
Who shall my love with equal love regard ;
Happy are they, who when they give their heart
Find such as in exchange their own impart.

[* Theogn. line 337 : ‡ Bion, ap. Stob. floril,
tit. lxiii. (de Venere, &c.) 28.]

12. A FRIEND NOT MONEY.

'Εν τοῖς δὲ δεινοῖς χρημάτων κρείττων φίλος.

When Fortune frowns upon a man,
A friend does more than money can.

[Auct. incert. ap. Grot. excerpt. ex trag. et
com. p. 945. Paris 1626. 4o.]

13. A NOBLE FRIENDSHIP.

" I confess it is possible to be a friend to
one that is ignorant, and pitiable, handsome and
good for nothing, that eats well, and drinks deep ;
but he cannot be a friend to me : and I love him
with a fondness or a pity, but it cannot be a
noble friendship.

Οὐκ ἐᾷ πότων καὶ τῆς καθ' ἡμέραν τρυφῆς
ζητοῦμεν ᾧ πιστεύσομεν τὰ τοῦ βίου

πάτερ; οὐ τεριττὸν οἶσι τ᾽ ἐξευηκεναι
αγαθὸν ἕκαστος ἐὰν ἔχῃ φίλου σκίαν·

said Menander;

By wine and mirth and every daye's delight
We choose our friends to whom we think we might
Our souls intrust; but fools are they that lend
Their bosome to the shadow of a friend.

> [Line 3rd πάτερ . . ὀίετ᾽, edd. recentt: ap.
> Plutarch de frat. am. t vii. p. 872.]

14. UNSELFISHNESS IN FRIENDSHIP.

" I account that one of the greatest demonstra-
tions of real friendship is that a friend can really
endeavour to have his friend advanced in honour,
in reputation, in the opinion of wit or learning,
before himself :

Aurum, et opes, et rura frequens donabit amicus :
    Qui velit ingenio cedere, rarus erit.*
Sed tibi tantus inest veteris respectus amici,
    Carior ut mea sit quam tua fama tibi.†
Lands, gold, and trifles many give or lend :
But he that stoops in fame is a rare friend ;
In friendship's orbe thou art the brightest starre,
Before thy fame mine thou preferrest far.

> [* Martial, lib. viii, ep. 18 : † *Ibid*, lin. 3.]

15.   BROTHERS.

" It is observable that ' brother ' is indeed a
word of friendship and charity and of mutual
endearment, and so is a title of the bravest society;
yet in all the Scripture there are no precepts given
of any duty and comport which brothers, that is,
the decendants of the same parents, are to have
one towards another in that capacity; and it is
not because their nearness is such that they need
none : for parents and children are nearer, and yet
need tables of duty to be described; and for
brothers, certainly they need it infinitely if there
be any peculiar duty. Cain and Abel are the
great probation of that, and you know who said,

...... fratrum quoque gratia rara est :
       It is not often you shall see
       Two brothers live in amity.
                        [Ovid, Met. i., 145.]

16.   FRIENDSHIP IMMORTAL.

" We may do any thing or suffer any thing, that
is wise or necessary, or greatly beneficial to my
friend, and that in any thing in which I am perfect master of my person and fortunes. But I
would not in bravery visit my friend when he is
sick of the plague, unless I can do him good

114

equall at least to my danger ; but I will procure him physicians and prayers, all the assistances
that he can receive, and that he can desire, if
they be in my power : and when he is dead I will
not run into his grave and be stifled with his
earth ; but I will mourn for him, and perform his
will and take care of his relatives, and doe for
him as if he were alive ; and I think that is the
meaning of that hard saying of a Greek Poet,

Ἄνθρωπ' ἀλλήλοισιν ἀπόπροθεν ὦμεν ἑταῖροι·

πλὴν τούτου, πάντος χρήματός ἐστι κόρος.

To me though distant let thy friendship fly ;
Though men be mortal, friendships must not die ;
Of all things else ther's great satiety.

[Theogn lin. 595.]

17. HELP IN ADVERSITY.

" He that chooses a worthy friend that himself
in the dayes of sorrow and need might receive the
advantage, hath no excuse, no pardon, unless himself be as certain to do assistances when evil
fortune shall require them. The summe of this
answer to this enquiry I give you in a pair of
Greek verses :

ἴσον θεῷ σου τοὺς φίλους τιμᾶν θέλε.

ἐν τοῖς κακοῖς δὲ τοὺς φίλους εὐεργέτει·

Friends are to friends as lesser gods, while they
Honour and service to each other pay :
But when a dark cloud comes, grudge not to lend
Thy head, thy heart, thy fortune to thy friend.

[Poet incert .—Grot. excerpt. p. 945.]

Notes and Illustrations.

----

1. See close of Job's curse, page 46th for various readings and corrections.

2. Hymn for Advent, page 18th, line 24th. Some of the Collections if I do not err in my recollection read 'heedless': but the sequel shews that it is Christ as the Head of His body the Church that is meant. In line 11th, in 1680 (12o.) edn., a misprint ' hath' is repeated in Parker's reprint, as below.

3. *Ibid*, line 31st, 'spruce' = lively. So Milton in Comus, line 985 :

4. 2nd Hymn for Advent, page 19th, line 3rd., 'strait' — straight *i. e.* plain, ready. Cf. Isaiah xl. 3. and Mr. W. A Wright's Bible Word-Book in its place.

5. *Ibid*. Speed, as before, thus begins this Hymn,
> " Behold, we stay
> Lord, come away :
> Thy road is ready, and thy paths made strait
> With languishing expect and wait &c.

6. *Ibid*, lines 9-15 : cf St. John II. 13—17.

7. The 2nd. Christmas Hymn, page 21st, st. 3rd. lines 5—6. SPEED, as before, besides various other mischanges, here reads,
> " The ox and mule do all behold
> With wonder,
> An homely stable should unfold
> The thunder."

117

8. *Ibid.* See Sir John Beaumont's priceless "Of the Epiphany": our edition of his Poems pp 69-70.

9. The 3rd. Christmas Hymn, page 22nd, line 12th: in 1657 edition 'sets'.

10. *Ibid,* line 13th, 'emperie' = sovereignty or dominion In 1657 edition spelled 'empire' which conceals the rhyme with 'free.' Speed, as before sadly mars this Hymn.

11. The 4th Christmas Hymn, pages 22-24. As in Job's Curse from "Harmonia Sacra" and Willmott, the somewhat eccentric measure and rhythm of the opening of this Hymn are made more so by mis-printing. In the 1659 and other texts, lines 5-6 read thus:

> "Goe run, and bid good-morrow to the sun,
> Welcome his safe return to Capricorn".

I have had no hesitation in adopting the reading given, for which I am indebted to Dr Macdonald in "Antiphon" p 220. So in 1659, and other texts, line 14th is divided at 'mute' and thus fails to rhyme. The paradoxes of lines 19-28 recal Giles Fletcher and Herbert Palmer.

12. Lines 24th—25th: Taylor here remembered Crashaw's Hymn of the Nativity, in the full Chorus:

> "Welcome all wonders in one sight!
> Eternity shut in a span".

13. Hymn on St. John's day, page 24th, line 7th: in 1657 edition the reading is 'to' for 'by his hand'— a misprint.

14. Upon the day of the Holy Innocents, page 25th, line 13th, fontinels = little fountaines, *i e*, the breasts. So faithful Teate in his "Ter Tria",

" these *fontinels* thus dri'd." (p. 107.)

15. Lines 13th and 14th: Crashaw's own rendering of
his Epigram " to the Infant Martyrs" probably
suggested this couplet. It is as follows:

" Go smiling soules, your new built cages breake,
In heaven you'l learne to sing, ere here to speake :
Nor let the milkie fonts that bath your thirst
Be your delay,
The place that calls you hence, is at the worst
Milke all the way."

16. *Ibid*, line 19th: I have ventured to alter " desir'd"
into "desirèd."

17. *Ibid*. Under this Hymn cf. Nahum Tate in his
" Slaughter of the Innocents " :

" Early, but not untimely, dead :
Who to preserve the World's great Saviour bled ;

.   .   .   .   .

If then 'tis glorious to pursue
His great example, what must be your due,
Who dy'd for Him before He dy'd for you " ?

(Misc. Sacra p 39, as before)—One does sometimes in
books as in Nature chance on a primrose glittering
with   celestial dew upon a heap of sand.   Earlier
than either is John Davies of Hereford—an unequal
Poet, nevertheless the undoubted possessor of *the*
true gift—in his " Muses Sacrifice," as follows :

..... " to a Nation, most idolatrous.

Thou wast constrain'd, from his pursuite to flye :
So Innocence' life preservèd thus :
for which deare innocents were forc'd to dye.
Then Innocence, Innocencie slew :

119

how then could it therein be innocent ?
For both are innocent ; yet both is true ;
   the first indeede ; the other, in event.
They lost their bloud for Him ; He His for them :
   so both did bleede : and for each other bled :
And both as innocent, their blouds did streame,
   He as their Head : they, members of that Head.
O had I beene so blest, ere sinne I knew,
   t'have di'd for Thee, among those innocents :
Or, that I could my sinne, to death, pursue ;
   or make them liue like banish'd male-contents.
Then would I dye for Thee, an innocent
   if curst Herodian hands would blesse me so ;
O let me trie this deare experiment,
   —although it cost my heart-bloud—ere I goe.
(A Meditation gratulating for our Redemption : 1612
   pp 41—42.)
The Earl of Stirling has pathetic verses also on
   " Those guiltless babes of Bethel, slain by guess."

18. Upon the Epiphany, page 26th, line 10th, misprinted
   " Infant's King's " and line 18th, redeem'st, is =
   redeemd'st.

19. Meditation of Death, pages 27-28. See Speed's version
   of this in our Phineas Fletcher, Vol. I. cclxxxiv-v :
   and context, concerning Death as degraded into a
   'porter', with relation to Fletcher and Milton,
   Davies of Hereford puts the idea in another way and
   very wonderfully :

   How oft haue I beene at the gates of Hell
     and could not enter though I went about :

Thou did'st the diuell from his charge compell;
so Porter wast Thy selfe to keepe me out.
"Muses Sacrifice" 1612 p 21.

20. *Ibid*, line 2nd, from end, in 1680 edition, has 'flee' for 'flie' in error.

21. The Prayer, page 28th, line 6th, "un-clay" = disembody. So Phineas Fletcher has "un-hide" (II. 289, 331 ; III. 84) and "unshade". (IV. 337.)

22. Of the day of Judgement, page 30th, line 6th phials = vials as in Revelations xvi. 1. *et alibi*.

23. *Ibid*, line 25th, is inadvertently dropped in Parker's reprint of the "Golden Grove".

24. On the purification of the blessed virgin, page 34th, line 11th, on authority of 10th edition (1680) I have dropped the superfluous 'to' before 'follow'.

25. On Good Friday, page 36th, line 34th : 1657 edition misreads 'from' for 'for', and next line "underwent's" for "underwent'st."

26. On the Annunciation......page 37th, line 24th, "no store" = no limitation. Cf. on "Good Friday", line 4th from end.

27. Penitential Hymns, I, page 40th, line 10th. Dr. Thomas Washbourne, who preceded Taylor, in his very fine "Wounded spirit" thus sings,

"......if that favour be too high :
Yet this I pray Thee not deny :
That soveraign balsom, though it cost Thee deer,
Thy blood I mean,
To wash me clean,
A cleansèd spirit I can bear". (our edition p 105).

121

28. Conversion of St. Paul, page 33rd.   Cf. here also
    Crashaw's fine Epigram on the same subject, and
    with the same antitheses.   G.

The End.

MISCELLANIES

OF

The Fuller Worthies' Library.

" The Temptacyon of our Lorde :"

BY

JOHN BALE

BISHOP OF OSSORY :

NOW FIRST RE-PRINTED, AND EDITED

BY THE

REV. ALEXANDER B. GROSART,

ST. GEORGE'S, BLACKBURN, LANCASHIRE.

PRINTED FOR PRIVATE CIRCULATION.

1870.

156 COPIES ONLY.

John Bale:

Born 1495 : Died 1563.

Note.

IT were out of place to prefix a Memoir of BISHOP BALE to so slender a performance—relative to his numerous Writings—as the present. I refer the Reader for abundant sources of information concerning him, to the inestimable *Athenæ Cantabrigienses* of Charles Henry Cooper, Esq. F.S.A., and Thompson Cooper, Esq. (Vol. I., pp. 225—230). For details on his 'Plays'—if they may be so called—Mr. Collier's "Annals of the Stage" (I., 133, 137 : II., 124, 237, 238) and valuable Introduction to "Kynge Johan" (Camden Society, 1838), may be consulted. The Memoir introductory to the Selection of our Worthy's Works, issued by the Parker Society, is empty as the Selection is inadequate.

The only known copy of the ecclesiastical 'Comedy' *now for the first time re-printed* is that preserved in the Douce collection, Oxford. I have taken considerable pains to re-produce the original accurately. My transcript had the advantage of a vigilant collation by my excellent friend Colonel Chester.

It seemed to me a pity to risk the loss of such a curiosity of our Reformation-literature by leaving it extant in only a single exemplar. I don't claim for it much literary merit or dramatic reality or vividness. But it has a noticeable quaint outspokenness and an equally noticeable, quaint and sarcastic simplicity : while behind the most stammering words you have a vision in the 'Prolocutor' of a man in right dead earnest to have the very Evangel free to all England, and beyond, a man

A   125

consecrate to his " Lorde and Sauer" for the " common
people." Thus curious in itself, this antique and uniquely
preserved ' Comedy' has the additional value of furnishing
another contribution to the growing study of the formative
elements of our language and literature. It is of more
human interest, I opine, than many of the Miracle and
Boy-Bishop ' Plays' that have been re-published. A very
few slight notes are added at close.

ALEXANDER B. GROSART.

A brefe Comedy or enter

lude concernynge the temptacyon of our
lorde and sauer Jesus Christ by Sathan in the desart.   Compyled by Johan Bale, *Anno*
M.D. XXXVIII.

Jesus was led from thens of the spre-
te into the wyldernes, to be tempted of the deuyll.
And whan
he had fasted fourty dayes and fourty nyghtes, he
was at last an hungered.
Mathei iiij.

Interlocutores.

Jesus Christus.   *Satan tentator :*

Angelvs primus.   *Angelus alter.*

Baleus Prolocutor.

[Small 4o.]

---

[1] ' And whan ' is at end of preceding line, not a separate line by itself.   G.

Præfatio.

Baleus Prolocutor.

FTER hys baptyme, Christ was Gods sonne
    declared.
   By the fathers voyce, as ye before haue
    hearde,
Whych sygnyfyeth to vs, that we ones baptysed
Are the sonnes of God, by hys gift & rewarde,
And bycause that we, should haue Christ in
    regarde,
He gaue vnto hym, the myghtye autoryte,
Of hys heauenlye worde, our only teacher to be.

Now is he gone fourth, into the desart place,
With the holy Ghost, hys offyce to begynne.
Where Sathan the deuyll, with hys assaultes apace,
With colours of craft, and manye a subtyle gynne,
Wyll vndermynede hym, yet nothynge shall he
    wynne,
But shame and rebuke, in the conclusyon fynall,
Thys tokenneth our rayse, and hys vnrecurable
    fall.

Lerne first in thys acte, that we whom Christe
    doth call,
Ought not to folowe, the fantasyes of Man,
But the holy Ghost, as our gyde specyall,

Whych to defende vs, is he that wyll and can,
To persecucyon, lete vs prepare vs than,
For that wyll folowe, in them that seke the truth.
Marke in thys processe, what trubles to Christ
     ensuth.

  Sathan assaulteth hym, with manye a subtyle
     dryft,
So wyll he do vs, if we take Christes part.
And whan that helpeth not, he seketh an other
     shyft,
The rulers amonge, to put Christ vnto smart,
With so manye els, as beare hym their good hart.
Be ye sure of thys, as ye are of dayly meate,
If ye folowe Christ, with hym ye must be beate.

  For assaultes of Sathan, lerne here the remedye,
Take the worde of God, lete tnat be your defence.
So wyll Christ teach yow, in our next Comedye,
Ernestly prent it, in your quyck intellygence.
Resyst not the worlde, but with meke-pacyence,
If ye be of Christ. Of thys herafter ye shall,
Perceyue more at large, by the story as it fall.

Incipit Commœdia.

Jesus Christus.

INTO thys desart the holy Ghost hath
  brought me,
  After my baptyme, of Sathan to be temp-
   ted.
Therby to instruct, of Man the imbecyllyte,
That after he hath, Gods holy sprete receyued,
Dyuersely he must, of Sathan be impugned,
Least he for Gods gyft, shuld fall into a
  pryde.
And that in parell, he take me for hys gyde.
 Thynke not me to fast, bycause I wolde yow to
  fast,
For than ye thynke wronge, and haue vayne iudge-
  ment,
But of my fastynge, thynke rather thys my cast,
Sathan to prouoke, to worke hys cursed intent,
And to teache yow wayes, hys myschefes to pre-
  uent,
By the worde of God, whych must be your defence,
Rather than fastynges, to withstande hys vyolence.
 I have fasted here, the space of forty dayes,
Perfourmynge that fast, whych Moses had in
  fygure,

130

To stoppe their mouthes with, whych bable &
    prate alwayes
Thus ded our fathers, My name and fame to dys [f]
    uygure.
Therfor now I tast, of fastynge here the rygure,
And am ryght hungrye, after longe abstynence.
Thys mortall bodye, complayneth of indygence.

Satan tentator.

No where I fourther, but euery where I noye,
For I am Sathan, the commen aduersarye,
An enemy to Man, hym sekyinge to destroye
And to brynge to nought, by my assaultes most
    craftye.
I watche euery where, wantynge no polycye,
To trappe hym in snare, and make hym the chylde
    of hell.
What nombre I wynne, it were very longe to tell.

I hearde a great noyse, in Jordane now of late,
Vpon one Jesus, soundynge from heauen aboue.
Thys is myne owne sonne, whych hath withdrawne
    al hate,
And he that doth stande, most hyghly in my loue.
My wyttes the same sounde, doth not a lyttle moue.
He cometh to redeme, the kynde of Man I feare,
Hygh tyme is it than, for me the cooles to steare.

131

I wyll not leaue hym, tyll I knowe what he **ys**,
And what he entendeth, in tl.ys same border heare
Subtyltie must helpe, els all wyll be amys,
A godlye pretence, outwardly must I beare,
Semynge relygyouse, deuoute and sad in my geare,
If he be come now, for the redempcyon of Man,
As I feare he is, I wyll stoppe hym if I can.

Hic simulata religione Christum aggreditur.

It is a great ioye, by my holydome to se,
So vertuouse a lyfe, in a yonge man as yow be.
As here thus to wander, in godly contemplacyon.
And to lyue alone, in the desart solytarye.

Iesus Christus.

Your pleasure is it, to vtter your fantasye.

Satan tentator.

A brother am I, of thys desart wyldernesse,
And full glad wolde be, to talke with yow of
goodnesse,
If ye wolde accept, my symple cumpanye.

Iesus Christus.

I dysdane nothynge, whych is of God trulye.

Satan tentator.

Than wyll I be bolde, a lyttle with yow to walke.

Iesus Christus.

Do so if ye lyst, and your mynde frely talke.

Satan tentator.

Now forsoth and God, it is ioye of your lyfe,

132

That ye take soch paynes, and are in vertu so ryfe.
Where so small ioyes are, to recreate the hart.

Iesus Christus.

Here are for pastyme, the wylde beastes of the
 desart,
With whom moch better, it is to be conuersaunt,
Than with soch people, as are to God repugnaunt.

Satan tentator.

Ye speake it full well, it is euen as ye saye,
But tell me how longe, ye haue bene here, I yow
 praye.

Iesus Christus.

Fourty dayes and nyghtes, without any sustenaunce.

Satan Tentator.

So moch I iudged, by your pale countenaunce
Then it is no maruele, I trowe, though ye hungrye.

Jesus Christus.

My stomack declareth, the weakenesse of my bodye.

Satan tentator.

Well, to be pleyne with yow, abroade the rumour
 doth rōne
Amonge the people, that ye shuld be Gods sonne.
If ye be Gods sonne, as it hath great lykelyhode,
Make of these stones breade, and geue your bodye
 hys fode.

Jesus Christus.

No offence is it, to eate whan men be hungrye,

But to make stones breade, it is vnnecessarye.
He whych in thys fast, hath bene my specyall
    gyde,
Fode for my bodye, is able to prouyde.
I thanke my lorde God, I am at no soche nede,
As to make stones breade, my bodye so to fede.

    Whā I come in place, where God hath appoynt-
        ed meate,
Geuynge him hygh thankes, I shall not spare to
        eate.

Satan tentator.

Not only for that, thys symylytude I brynge,
But my purpose is, to conclude an other thynge.
At the fathers voyce, ye toke thys lyfe in hande,
Myndynge now to preache, as I do vnderstande.
In case ye do so, ye shall fynde the offyce harde.
My mynde is in thys, ye shuld your body regarde.

    And not vndyscretelye, to cast your selfe awaye.
Rather take som ease, than ye shuld so decaye.
I put case ye be, Gods sonne, what can that
        further,
Preache ye ones the truth, the byshoppes wyll ye
        murther.
Therfor beleue not, the voyce that ye ded heare,
Though it came from God, for it is unsauery geare.

Beyonde your cumpas, rather than ye so ronne,
Forsake the offyce, and denye yourself Gods sonne.

Jesus Christus.

Ye speake in that poynt, very vnaduysedlye,
For it is written, in the eyt of Deutronomye,
Man lyueth not by breade, or corporall fedynge
    onlye,
But by Gods promyse, and by hys scriptures
    heauenlye.
Here ye persuade me, to recreate my bodye,
And neglected Gods worde, whych is great blas-
    phemye.

Thys caused Adam, from innocencye to fall,
And all hys ofsprynge, made myserable and mortall.
Where as in Gods worde, there is both sprete and
    lyfe,
And where that is not, death and dampnacyon is
    ryfe.
The strength of Gods worde, myghtyly sustayned
    Moses,
For fourty days space, therof soch is the goodnes.

It fortyfyed Helias, it preserued Daniel,
And holpe in the desart, the chyldren of Israel.
Sore plages do folowe, where Gods worde is reiect,
For no persuasyon, wyll I therfor neglect,
That offyce to do, whych God hath me commaund-
    ed,

But in all mekenesse, it shall be accomplyshed.

Satan tentator.

I had rather naye, consyderynge your feble-
nesse,

For ye are but tuly, ye are no stronge persone
doughtlesse.

Iesus Christus.

Well, it is not the breade, that doth a man
vpholde,

But the lorde of heauen, with hys graces many-
folde,

He that Man create, is able hym to norysh,

And after weakenesse, cause hym agayne to florysh.

Gods worde is a rule, for all that man shuld do,

And out of that rule, no creature ought to go.

He that it foloweth, can not out of the waye,

In meate nor in drynke, in sadnesse nor in playe.

Satan tentator.

Ye are styfnecked, ye wyll folowe no good
counsell.

Iesus Christus.

Yes, whan it is soch, as the holye scripture tell.

Satan tentator.

Scriptures I knowe non, for I am but an her-
myte I,

I maye saye to yow, it is no part of our stody.

We relygyouse men, lyue all in contemplacyon,

Scriptures to stodye, is not our occupacyon.

It longeth to doctours. Howbeyt I maye saye to
    yow,

As blynde are they as we, in the vnderstandynge
    now.

  Well shall it please ye, any farther, with me to
    walke,

Though I lyttle profyght, yet doth it me good to
    talke.

Iesus Christus.

  To tarry or go, it is all one to me.

Satan tentator.

  Lete vs than wander, into the holye cyte,

Of Hierusalem, to se what is there a do.

Iesus Christus.

  I shall not saye naye, but am agreable ther to.

Satan tentator.

  My purpose is thys, A voyce in your eare ded
    rynge,

That ye were Gods sone, and welbeloued darlynge,

And yow beleue it, but ye are the more vnwyse,

For to deceyue yow, it was some subtyle practyse.

Well, vpon that voyce, ye are geuen to perfyght-
    nesse,

Not els regardynge, but to lyue in ghostlynesse.

  Ye watche, fast and praye, ye shyne in contem-
    placyon,

Leadynge here a life, beyonde all estimacyon,
No meate wyll ye eate, but lyue by Gods worde
 onlye,
So good are ye wext, so perfyght and so holye.
I wyll brynge ye (I trowe) to the welle of ghost-
 lynesse,
Where I shall fyll ye, and glutt ye with holynesse.

 What, holy, quoth he? Naye, ye were neuer so
 holye,
As I wyll make ye, if ye folowe hansomlye.
Here is all holy, here is the holy cytie,
The holy temple and the holye prestes here be.
Ye wyll be holy: wel, ye shall be aboue them all,
Bycause ye are Gods sonne, it doth ye so befall.
 Come here, on the pynnacle, we wyll be by
 and by.
 Iesus Christus.
 What meane ye by that? shewe fourth your
 fantasy.
 Satan tentator.
 Whan ye were hungrye, I ded ye first persuade,
Of stones to make breade, but ye wolde non of that
 trade.
Ye layed for yourself, that scripture wolde not
 serue it,
That was your bucklar, but now I am for ye fyt.

For the suggestyon, that I now shall to ye laye,
I haue scripture at hande, ye shall it not denaye.
Iesus Christus.
Kepe it not secrete, but lete it than be hod.
Satan tentator.
If ye do beleue, that ye are the sonne of God,
Beleue thys also, if ye leape downe here in scoff,
From thys hygh pynnacle, ye can take no harme
 thereoff.
And therfor be bolde, thys enterpryse to ieoparde.
If ye be Gods sonne, cast downe your self here
 backwarde.
Iesus Christus.
Truly that nede not, here is other remedye,
To the grounde to go, than to fall downe folyshlye.
Here are gresynges made, to go vp and downe
 therby,
What nede I than leape, to the earthe presumpt-
 uously.
Satan tentator.
Saye that ye ded it, vpon a good intent.
Iesus Christus.
That were neyther good, nor yet conuenyent.
Daungers are doubtfull, where soch presumpcyon
 is.
Satan tentator.
Tush, scripture is with it, ye can not fare amys.

For it is written, how God hath geuen a charge,
Unto hys Angels, that if ye leape at large,
They shall receyue ye, in their handes tenderly
Least ye dashe your fote, agaynst a stone therby.

If ye do take scath, beleue God is not trewe,
Nor iust of hys worde, And than byd hym adewe.

Iesus Christus.

In no wyse ye ought, the scriptures to de-
praue,
But as they lye whole, so ought ye them to haue.
Nomore take ye here, than serue for your vayne
purpose
Leauynge out the best, as ye shuld tryfle or glose.
Ye mynde not by thys, towardes God to edyfye,
But of syncere faythe, to corrupt the innocencye.

Satan tentaior.

Whye, is it not true that soch a text there is?

Iesus Christus.

Yes, there is soch a text, but ye wrast it all
amys.
As the Psalme doth saye, God hath commaunded
Angels,
To preserue the iust, from daungerouse plages
and parels.

Satan tentator.

Well than I sayd true, and as it lyeth in the
text.

Iesus Christus.

Yea, but ye omytted, foure wordes whych
    foloweth next,

As (in all thy wayes) whych if ye put out of syght,

Ye shall neuer take, that place of scripture a
    ryght.

Their wayes are soch rules, as God hath them
    commaunded,

By hys lyuynge worde, iustlye to be obserued.

    If they passe those rules, the Angels are not
    bounde,

To be their sauegarde, but rather them to con-
    founde.

To fall downe backwarde, of a wanton peuyshnes,

Is non of those wayes, that God euer taught
    doughtles.

Then if I ded it, I shuld tempt God very sore,

And deserue to haue, hys anger euermore.

    I wyll not so do, for their fathers in the desart,

Ded so tempt hym ones, and had the hate of hys
    hart.

The clause that ye had, maketh for nō outwarde
    workynge.

If ye marke the Psalme, throughly from hys
    begynninge.

But what is the cause, ye wēt not fourth with the
                    next verse?

Satan tentator.

It made not for me, if ye wyll, ye maye it
reherse.

Iesus Christus.

Thu shalt (sayth the Psalme) subdue the
cruell serpent,
And treade vndre fote, the lyon and dragon
pestylent.

Satan tentator.

No nyghar (I saye) for there ye touche freholde.

Iesus Christus.

Some loue in no wyse, to haue their rudenesse
tolde.
To walke in Gods wayes, it becometh mortall man,
And therfor I wyll, obeye them if I can.
For it is written, in the sext of Deutronomy,
Thu shalt in no wyse, tempt God presumptuousely.

Satan tentator.

What is it to tempt God? after your iudgement.

Iesus Christus.

To take of hys worde, an outwarde experyment,
Of an ydle brayne, whych God neyther
thought nor ment.

Satan tentator.

What persones do so? Make that more euydent

Iesus Christus.

All soch as forsake, anye grace or remedye,
14

Appoynted of God, for their owne polycye.

As they that do thynke that God shuld fyll their
bellye,

Without their labours, whan hys lawes are con-
trarye.

And they that wyll saye, the scripture of God doth
slee,

They neuer serchynge, therof the veryte.

Those also tempt God, that vowe presumptuouslye,

Not hauinge hys gyft, to kepe their contynencye.

With so manye els, as folowe their good intentes

Not groūded on God, nor yet on hys commaunde-
mentes.

These throwe themselues downe, into most depe
dāpnacyon.

Satan tentator.

Lyttle good get I, by thys communycacyon.

Wyll ye walke farther, and lete thys pratlynge be?

A mountayne here is, whych I wolde yow to se,

Trust me and ye wyll, it is a commodyouse thynge.

Iesus Christus.

If it be so good, lete vs by thydre goynge.

Satan tentator.

Lo, how saye ye now, is not here a plesaunt syght?

If ye wyll ye maye, haue here all the worldes
delyght.

Here is to be seane, the kyngedome of Arabye,

With all the regyons, of Affryck, Europe, and
Asye,

And their whole delyghtes, their pompe, their
magnyfycēce,

Their ryches, their honour, their welth, their
concupyscece.

Here is golde and syluer, in wonderfull habun-
daunce,

Sylkes, veluetes, tyssues, with wynes and spyces
of plesaunce.

Hǝre are fayre women, of countenaunce ameable,

With all kyndes of meates to the body dylectable.

Here are camels, stoute horses and mules that neuer
wyll tyre,

With so manye pleasures, as your hart can desyre.

Iesus Christus.

Well, he be praysed, whych is of them the
geuer.

Satan tentator.

Alas it greueth me, that ye are soch a beleuer.

Nothynge can I laye, but euer ye auoyde me,

By the worde of God, Leaue that poynt ones I
pray ye.

If I byd ye make, of stones breade for your bodye,

Ye saye man lyueth not, in temporall feadynge
onlye.

As I byd ye leape, downe from the pynnacle aboue,
Ye wyll not tempt God, otherwyse than yow
  behoue.
Thus are ye styll poore, thus are ye styll weake
    and nedye.

Iesus Christus.

And what suppose ye, wyll that nede remedye?

Satan tentator.

Forsake the beleue, that ye haue in Gods worde,
That ye are hys sonne, for it is not worth a torde,
Is he a father, that se hys sonne thus famysh?
If ye beleue it, I saye ye are to folysh.
Ye se these pleasures. If yow be ruled by me,
I shall make ye a man. To my wordes therfor
  agre.
Loke on these kyngedomes, and incomparable
  treasure,
I the lorde of them, may geue them at my pleasure.
Forsake that father, whych leaueth the without
  confort,
In thys desolacyon, and hens fourth to me resort.
Knowledge me for head, of thys worlde vnyuersall,
And I wyll make the, possessor of them all.
Thu shalt no longar, be desolate and hungrye,
But haue all the worlde to do the obsequye.
Therfor knele downe here, and worshypp me
    thys houre,

145

And thu shalt haue all, with their whole strenth
    and poure.

Iesus Christus.

Auoyde thu Sathan, Thu deuyll, thu aduer-
    sarye,

For now thu perswadest, most damnable blas-
    phemye.

As thu art wycked, so is thy promyse wycked,

Not thyne is the worlde, but hys that it created,

Thu cannyst not geue it, for it is not thyne to
    geue,

Thus dedyst thu corrupt, the fayth of Adam and
    Eue,

Thus dedyst thu deceyue both Moses and
    Aaron,

Causynge them to doubt, at the lake of contra-
    dyccyon.

Get the hens thu fyende, and cruell aduersarye,

For it is written, in the tenth of Deutronomye.

God thu shalt worshypp, and magnyfye alone,

Holde hym for thy lorde, and make to hym thy
    mone.

He is the true God, he is the lorde of all,

Not only of thys, but the worlde celestyall.

Thy perswasyon is, I shuld not hys worde regarde,

A venemouse serpent, dampnacyon is thy rewarde.

Prouyde wyll I so, that thy kyngedome shall de-
    caye
Gods worde shall be hearde, of the worlde though
    thu saye naye.

Satan tentator.

  Wel, than it helpeth not, to tarry here any
    longar,
Aduauntage to haue, I se I must go farther.
So longe as thu lyuest, I am lyke to haue no
    profyght,
If all come to passe, I maye syt as moch in your
    lyght,
If ye preach Gods worde, as me thynke ye do
    intende,
Ere foure years be past, I shall yow to your father
    sende,
  If pharysees and scrybes can do any thynge
    therto,
False prestes and byshoppes, with my other ser-
    uantes mo.
Though I haue hynderaunce, it wyll be but for a
    season,
I dought not, thyne owne, herafter wyll worke
    some treason,
Thy vycar at Rome I thynke wyll be my frynde,
I defye the therfor, and take thy wordes but as
    wynde.

147

He shall me worshypp, and haue the worlde to
rewarde,

That thu here forsakest, he wyll most hyghlye
regarde.

Gods worde wyll he treade, vnderneth hys fote
for euer,

And the hartes of men from the truth therof
dysseuer,

Thy fayth wyll he hate, and slee thy flocke in
conclusyon.

All thys wyll I worke, to do the vtter confusyon.

Iesus Christus.

Thy cruell assaultes, shall hurt neyther me nor
myne,

Though we suffer both, by the prouydence dyuyne.

Soch strength is ours, that we wyll haue vyctorye,

Of synne death and helle, and of the in thy most
furye.

For God hath promysed, that hys shall treade the
dragon,

Vnderneth their fete, with the fearce roarynge
lyon.

Hic angeli accedunt, solacium administraturi.

Angelus primus.

The father of confort and heauenly consolacyon,

Hath sent vs hyther, to do our admynystracyon.

We come not to helpe, but to do our obsequye,

As seruauntes becometh, to their lorde and mastre
    mekelye.
If our offyce be, to wayte on creatures mortall,
Why should we not serue, the mastre and lorde
    of all ?

Angelus alter.

It is our confort, it is our whole felycyte,
To do our seruyce, and in your presence to be.
We haue brought ye fode, to confort your weake
    bodye,
After your great fast, and notable vyctorye.
Vnto all the worlde, your byrth we first declared,
And now these vytayles, we haue for yow prepared.

Iesus Christus.

Come nyghar to me, Swete father thankes to the,
For these gracyouse gyftes, of thy lyberaltyte.

Hie coram angelis ex appositis comedet.

Angelus primus.

How meke art thu lorde, to take that nature
    on the,
Whych is so tendre, and full of infyrmyte.
As Mannys nature is, both feble faynt and werye,
Weake after laboure, and after fastynge hungrye.
Forsoth heauen and earth, yea, helle maye be
    astoyned,
The Godhede to se, to so frayle nature ioyned.

149

Angelus alter.

In hys owne he is, for he the worlde firste create,
Yet semeth the worlde, to haue hym in great hate.
Aboute thirty yeares, hath he bene here amonge
   them,
Some tyme in Jewrye, and some tyme in Hieru-
   salem.
But fewe to thys daye, haue done hym reuerence.
Or as to their lorde, shewed their obedyence.

Iesus Christus.

My commynge hyther, is for to seke no glorye,
But the hygh pleasure, and wyll of my father
   heauenlye.
He wyll requyre it, at a certayne daye, no dought,
And shall reuenge it, loke they not wele abought.

Angelus primus.   Plebem alloquitur.

The lorde here for yow, was borne and
   cirnumcysed,
For yow here also, he was latelye baptysed.
In the wyldernesse, thys lorde for yow hath fasted.
And hath ouertomen, for yow the deuyll that
   tempted.
For yow fryndes for yow thys heauenly lorde doth all,
Only for your sake, he is become man mortall.

Angelus alter.

Take the shyelde of fayth, and lerne to resyst the
   deuyll,

150

After hys teachynges, that he do yow non euyll.
Full sure shall ye be, to haue vs on your syde,
If ye be faythfull, and holde hym for your gyde.

Iesus Christus.

If they folowe me, they shall not walke in
    darkenes.
But in the clere lyght, and haue felycyte endles,
For I am the waye, the lyfe and the veryte.
No man maye attayne, to the father but by me.

Angelus Primus.

In mannys frayle nature, ye haue conquerred
    the enemye.
That man ouer hym, should alwayes haue vyctorye

Angelus alter.

Our maner is it, most hyghlye to reioyce,
Whan Man hath confort, whych we now declare in
    voyce.

Hic dulce canticum coram Christo depromunt.

Baleus Prolocutor.

Let it not greue you, in thys worlde to be
    tempted,
Consyderynge your lorde, and your hygh byshopp
    Jesus,
Was here without synne, in euery purpose prouèd,
In all our weakenesse, to helpe and socor vs,
Farthermore to beare, with our fragylyte thus.
He is vnworthye, of hym to he a member,

That wyll not with hym, some persecucyon suffer.

The lyfe of Man is a profe or harde temptacyon,
As Job doth report, and Paule confirmeth the same.
Busye is the deuyll, and laboureth hys dampnatyon,
Yet haue no dyspayre, for Christ hath gote the
    game.
Now is it easye, hys cruelnessse to tame.
For Christes victorye, is theirs that do beleue.
Where fayth take rotynge, the deuyll can neuer
    greue.
Resyst (sayth Peter) resyst that roarynge lyon,
Not with your fastynges, Christ neuer taught ye so.
But with a stronge fayth, withstande hys false
    suggestyon,
And with the scriptures, vpon hym euer go.
Then shall he no harm, be able yow to do.
Now maye ye be bolde, ye haue Christe on your
    syde,
So longe as ye haue, hys veryte for your gyde.

What enemyes are they, that from the people
    wyll hyde,
The scriptures of God, whych are the myghty
    weapon,
That Christ left them here, their sowles from helle
    to saue
And throwe theme headlondes, into the deuyls
    domynyon.

If they be no deuyls, I say there are deuyles non,
They brynge in fastynge, but they leaue out, Scrip-
    tum est,
Chalke they geue for gold, soch fryndes are they
    to the Beest.
  Lete non report vs, that here we condempne
    fastynge.
For it is not true, we are of no soch mynde.
But thys we couete, that ye do take the thynge,
For a frute of fayth, as it is done in kynde,
Ane onlye Gods worde, to subdue the cruell fynde.
Folowe Christ alone, for he is the true sheparde,
Tne voyce of straungers, do neuer more regarde.

Thus endeth thys brefe Comedy concer-
nyinge the temptacyon of Jesus Christ in the
wylderness.
Compyled by Johan Bale, Anno M.D.XXXVIII.

Notes.

1. *Præfatio*, page 7th, line 32nd., quyck = quick. See Leviticus xiii. 10; Numbers xvi. 30; Psalm lv. 15; cxxiv. 3. = alive, living. Consult Mr. W. Aldis Wright's Bible Word-Book *s. v.* for interesting examples and illustrations.

2. *Iesus Christus*, page 8th, line 7th, parell =peril. So too onward.

3. *Ibid.* page 8th, line 10th, cast = contrivance.

4. *Satan tentator*, page 9th, line 7th, fourther = further, advance.

5. *Ibid*, page 9th, line 20th, cooles to steare = coals to stir *i. e.* to be awake and active.

6. *Ibid*, page 10th, line 5th, sad = serious. Cf. our Phineas Fletcher, Glossary, *s.v.*

7. *Iesus Christus*, page 13th, line 9th, for 'neglected' read 'neglecte' and line 12th, for 'is' I read 'in'—evident misprints.

8. *Satan tentator*, page 14th, line 4th: tuly = weak. Query—Is this the transition-form of *tulle*, a thin net or lace, and hence = weak, frail.

9. *Ibid*, page 15th, line 2nd., longeth = belongeth.

10. *Ibid*, page 16th, line 7th, hansomlye = Dutch *handzaam*, tractable or docile.

11. *Iesus Christus*, page 17th, line 4th, hod = had, *i. e.* communicated or spoken.

12. *Ibid*, page 17th, line 14th, gresynges = steps.

13. *Ibid*, page 10th, line 8th, saue garde = safe guard. Consult Mr. W. A. Wright's Bible Word-Book, as before, *s. v.*

14. *Satan tentator*, page 20th, line 7th, fre holde = held in fee-simple, fee-tail or for life.

154

15. *Iesus Christus*, page 20th, line 17th, experyment = experience, personal trial.

16. *Ibid*, page 21st, line 4th, slee = slay or kill.

17. *Satan tentator*, page 23rd., line 8th, torde = turd *i.e.* filth or ordure.

18. *Ibid*, page 23rd, line 20th, obsequye = honour or respect as at a funeral.

19. *Angelus primus*, page 26th, line 16th, confort, and several times : note the transition-form retained still in *con*solation &c.

20. *Ibid*, page 28th, line 17th, ouertomen : *sic*: but misprint for overcomen.

21. *Baleus prolocutor*, page 30th, line 5th, rotynge = rooting or root.

22. *Ibid*, page 30th, line 16th, headlones = head-a-long or headlong.

23. On the subject of this Enterlude, I take the liberty to name my own treatise, as follows: "The Prince of Light and the Prince of Darkness in Conflict or The Temptation of Christ Newly Translated, Explained, Illustrated and Applied. London [Nisbet & Co.] 1864 cr. 8vo. pp xxxiv and 360". G.

The End.

MISCELLANIES

OF

The Fuller Worthies' Library.

THE

POEMS

OF

WILLIAM HARBERT,

(USUALLY CALLED SIR WILLIAM HERBERT)
GLAMORGAN:

FOR THE

FIRST TIME COLLECTED AND EDITED:

WITH

Introduction:

BY THE

REV. ALEXANDER B. GROSART,

ST. GEORGE'S, BLACKBURN, LANCASHIRE.

PRINTED FOR PRIVATE CIRCULATION.
1870.
156 COPIES ONLY.

Memorial-Introduction.

———

HE original title-page of the exceedingly rare volume now for the first time reprinted, bears no name : but to the two Epistles-Dedicatory,—at commencement and toward the close—to Sir Philip Herbert, is subscribed " William Harbert." He is usually called ' Sir ' William Harbert or Herbert : but I believe without authority. So far as I have been able to trace, the first to employ it was RITSON in his " Bibliographica Poetica " (1802 : page 234). But he furnishes a corrective and solution of his blunder. He has confounded this " William Harbert " with a Sir William Herbert, to whom is given (*a*) " **A** letter to a pretended Roman Catholic " (1585) and (*b*) Some wretched doggrel or cat-rel, entitled " Sidney or Baripenthes, briefly shadowing out the rare and neuer-ending lauds of........Sir Philip Sidney, knight " (1586).

I can very well suppose that it may have been

to shield himself—alas! in vain—from being confounded with this rhymster-contemporary, that
our youthful Singer spelled his name ' Harbert '
as pronounced — much as Lord Derby sounds
Darby, Verney as Varney, Hertford as Hartford,
and the like, and much as my venerable friend
JAMES MONTGOMERY used ruefully to wish that he
could somehow protect himself from the humiliation
of the notoriety (*not* fame) of ' Satan ' ROBERT
MONTGOMERY. Perchance we soothed him by
reminding him of another poet Montgomery in
the author of the " Cherry and the Slae " : and
there were noble and nobly-gifted as well as saw-
dust brained Herberts, and onward saintly George
Herbert.   I have called our Poet ' youthful '.
This lies on the surface of " Cadwallader ", in its
speaking more than once of his " *infant* Muse ,"
and " fruites of youth " " and unripened yeeres ",
and in the boy-like lavishness of classical names and
references.   But besides this internal evidence I
have been guided by a tribute to " Christ College,
Oxford " as follows :

" Chiefe benefactor of what ere is mine" (page 84, l 19)

to his matriculation at the University, which thus
stands :

1600. Oct. 17. Gulielmus Harbert. 17. Arm. fil. Glamorg.

162

The age given in these Registers always means age at last birthday: so that Harbert may have been just over seventeen or a little under eighteen, i.e., in 1604, when " Cadwallader " was published, twenty-one or thereby. In the Register of Christ Church College, Dean Liddell informs me his age appears to be entered as ' 13 ': but he adds that it is probably a hasty (and erroneous) transcript from the Matriculation-Book. As the latter has ' 17 ', it is plain the former is incorrect; and indeed this might be suspected, albeit names as few-yeared and fewer, are found.

The date and age of our " William Harbert " settles that the author of " Baripenthes " and the author of " Cadwallader " were two, not one. For if the Singer of " Cadwallader " had previously published " Baripenthes ", he couldn't in 1604 have told us of his " *infant* Muse ", seeing " Baripenthes " was in print eighteen years before, viz. in 1586 as compared with 1604, by which date its author must have been thirty at least. Moreover in 1586 by the Matriculation-entry our ' William Harbert ' was only in his 3rd year,—an age somewhat premature for versifying, even of the type of " Baripenthes ". The same date leads me to assign to Sir William Herbert of Baripenthes, and not as Ritson and others have done to our Poet—who *is* a Poet—the verses in the 'Phœnix Nest' (1593) and those given to him by Sir Egerton Brydges in *Restituta* having ' W. Har. ' appended—the date being 1594. But there seems little doubt that our Worthy contributed the little poem prefixed to Peter Erondell's " French Garden " (1605). It is signed " William Harbert" as in " Cadwallader ". Here it is:

IN LAUDEM AUTHORIS.

Doth not the coward hardinesse admire?
and sencelesse ignorance the arts embrace?
Embrace they doe, and with a great desire,
Desire those gifts (those noble gifts of grace)
which they doe want, and others doe embrace:
　So I embrace, admire, applause thy skill,
　　As wanting knowledge, though not wanting will.

Will and good will which I did euer beare
To thee and those which learning doe professe,
Hath made me bolde, that euer wont to feare :
But feare not thou, whose labours doe expresse
thy carefull loue aud louing carefulnesse.
　with praise begin, so thus with thee I end :
　Praying for those that doe thy praise extend.
　　Non multa sed mea
　　　　　　WILLIAM HARBERT.

I incline to think that though spelled 'Herbert' our Poet also wrote the two copies of Verses

prefixed to Browne's " Britannia Pastorals" (1625),
and hence they must appear here :

TO HIS WORTHILY-AFFECTED FRIEND
Mr. W. BROWNE.

Awake sad Muse, and thou my sadder spright,
Made so by Time, but more by Fortune's spight,
 Awake, and hie us to the Greene,
  There shall be seene
 The quaintest Lad of all the time
  For neater Rime :
 Whose free and unaffected straines
  Take all the Swaines
That are not rude and ignorant,
  Or Enuy want.

And Enuy lest it's hate discouered be
A Courtly Loue and Friendship offers thee :
 The Shepherdesses blithe and faire
  For thee despaire.
 And whosoe'er depends on Pan,
  Holds him a man
 Beyond themselues, (if not compare,)
  He is so rare,
 So innocent in all his wayes
  As in his Layes
He masters no low soule who hopes to please
The Nephew of the braue Philisides.

Another to the same.

Were all men's enuies fixt in one man's lookes,
The monster that would prey on safest Fame,

165

> Durst not once checke at thine, nor at thy Name:
> So he who men can reade as well as Bookes
>   Attest thy Line: thus tride, they show to vs
>   As Scæua's shield, thy Selfe Emeritus.
> W. Herbert.[1]

Further—That the author of "Cadwallader" was no 'Sir' is additionally confirmed by the sorry epigram of William Gamage in his "Linsi Woolsie", so late as 1613. It is as empty as need be: but it is headed "To the ingenious poet Mr. William Herbert, of his booke intituled the Prophesie of Cadwallader." We give it the small space needed for it:

> "Thy royall prophesie doth blaze thy name
>   So poets must, if they will merit fame."
> (2nd. Century: Epigr. 92.)

These facts—slight though they be—correct Ritson, Mr. Collier, Mr. Hazlitt and others, as to the 'Sir' and supposed relationship or identity with Baripenthes' Sir William Herbert. Such *'knighting'* is a kind of literary *læsa majestatis*— eh?

The Verse of our Harbert reveals that he was a native of Wales ['Glamorgan'] —and in some

---

[1] Browne's Works. ed. Hazlitt, Vol. I. pp 157-8: slightly corrected from 1625 text. G.

way advanced by the Pembroke (Herbert) family; while Mr. Hunter in his Chorus Vatum surmises, that he was probably placed near the person of Prince Henry, soon after James became king of England. The 'Arm fil.' of the Matriculation, indicates much what the modern 'Esquire' is supposed to mean. In the Matriculation-Registers of Oxford, sons of baronets are described as 'Bart. fil.': sons of knights as 'Eq. Aur. fil.' Hence 'Arm. fil.' meant that the father was not a titled person but of social rank above that of a gentleman or 'gen. fil.' These terms were doubtless used all the more exactly in that they regulated the fees paid by the students matriculating.

Such is all that considerable research has yielded. A 'William Harbert' occurs in the Parish-Register of St. George's, Southwark, among the buried: 'prisoner in King's Bench, 20th Nov., 1628' —likely for debt. I am reluctant to know this was our Poet.

It is to be deplored that Welshmen, who spend their strength and enthusiasm without stint, over mythic-names and merely antiquarian, and as Lord Brooke puts it, 'life-forsaken' verse—leave such a name as this un-illumined, as they continue to their opprobrium to do a greater—Henry Vaughan the Silurist.

167

There is intellectual if exuberant force, and no little melody and good workmanship in 'Cadwallader' and related poems. His versification is usually harmonious: occasionally an epithet gleams out like a poppy in a cornfield or an old woman's red cloak or hood in a landscape, and now and then you come on aphoristic sayings that only need to be known to keep quick. His incense— stale and rank—to the king, was the *mode* of the day—an explanation if no apology. Then, young imagination is purpled, and purples, as the setting (or rising) sun transfigures a bit of broken glass into diamond-brilliance.

As before, our text reproduces the whole with strict fidelity. Most of the names that occur are trite: only a few brief notes are furnished.

The following is the original title-page:

A

PROPHESIE
of Cadwallader, last king
of the Britaines :
Containing a Comparison of the English
Kings, with many worthy Romanes, from
William Rufus, till Henry the fift.
Henry the fift, his life and death.
Foure Battels betweene the two Houses of
Yorke and *Lancanster*.

168

The Field of *Banbery*.
The losse of *Elizabeth*.
The praise of King Iames.
And lastly a Poeme to the yong
Prince.

LONDON

Printed by Thomas Creede, for Roger Iackson, and are to
be solde at his shop in Fleet streete, ouer against the
Conduit, 1604. [8vo.]
Title—Verse-dedication—to his Poem—to the Reader
[3 leaves] and 32 leaves—

As a book ' Cadwallader &c. is of the rarest—
being valued in the open market at treble the cost
of a complete set in large paper of our Worthies!
The copy in the Bodleian as that in the British
Museum, is imperfect.

Colonel Chester, my accomplished and indefati-
gable Anglo-American friend—curiously enough
the foremost living authority on all matters geneal-
ogical in English ' Registers ' — has obligingly
furnished me from his opulent stores, with a considerable number of ' Harberts ' and ' Herberts ':
but Christ Church fixes our Poet. To him I am
indebted for these memoranda on Sir Philip Herbert to whom our Poet dedicates his book—" Sir
Philip Herbert I suppose to have been afterwards
4th earl of Pembroke and 1st earl of Montgomery.
He was then (1604) quite a young man, having

169

matriculated at New College, Oxon, 9 Mch.
1592/3 at the early age of 9 years, (one of the few
instances of this sort). He was younger son of
Henry, 2nd earl, by his 3rd wife Lady Mary,
daughter of Sir Henry Sidney, K. G.—to her Sir
Philip Sidney dedicated his Arcadia. I find him
mentioned as Sir Philip in 1604 : and I know of
no other of that name at the period. He was no
doubt one of the knights of the Bath created on
the coronation of King James I, 25th July, 1603."

ALEXANDER B. GROSART.

St. George's, Blackburn, Lancashire,
October 11th, 1870.

NOTE.—It is an ungracious task to criticise a fellow-
editor's work: and therefore I prefer silence on the
(relatively) numerous misprints in title-page and (few)
quotations from our Harbert, in Mr. Collier's "Bibliographical Account" (I., pp. 361—363). But it is necessary to state that Mr Collier is wrong as to the name
being signed by the Author in his book indifferently
Harbert and Herbert. It is signed Harbert only. So
too it is Lancanster not Lancaster, and Banbery, not
Banbury in title-page. See foot-note (page 108) for
supposed *errata* pointed out by Mr. Collier. I must also
notice here that in the same place, Mr Collier singularly
enough mistakes prince Charles (afterwards Charles Ist)
for the 'yong Prince'. Plainly, Henry, prince of Wales,
is addressed : born 1594 : died 1612. I add that the
opening of the " Poeme to the yong Prince" (page 105,
lines 1—4) warrants Mr. Hunter's supposition that the
Author had been in personal attendance on the lamented
Prince Henry. G.

TO THE NO LESSE VERTUOUS THEN HONOURABLE GENTLEMAN SIR PHILIP HERBERT, KNIGHT OF THE MOST NOBLE ORDER OF THE BATHE.

RIGHT worthy Sir, the honor which I beare,
    And euer will vnto your worthy line,
Makes me presume—presumption cannot feare—
To tender you this little booke of mine:
  Whose substance if your honor will approue,
  My lines shall limits want; so doth my loue.

That man of men[1] whose fatall name you beare,
Of his vnnumbred worthes, the chiefe were these:
Three glorious wreathes, vpō his brow to weare,[2]
Which said, he loued learning, warre, and peace.
  O æmulate this man, the sonne of Fame,
  Haue all his vertues, though but halfe his name.

Pursue thy first designments—noble Knight—

---

[1] The initials S. P. S. on the margin are intended for Sir Philip Sidney. G.

[2] Baye, olive, and oake. H.

Affect[1] thy Country, and admire thy king :
Be as thou art, sincere in all men's sight,
Do this, and I thy praise will euer sing.
   I smoothe, not I, nor do I hope for gaine ;
   Accept my loue, and so requite my paine.[2]
     The admirer of your vertues, whose
        life is deuoted to your loue,
             WILLIAM HARBERT.

---

[1] = Love, choose. G.   [2] = painstaking. G.

The Author to his Poeme.

RACE the wide stage of spight and proud
    disdaine,
    And mount the steps of scornefull Enuie's
      staire,
Imperfect embrion of an idle braine;
Soare not aloft, vse meane, do not despaire,
The best way is betweene the sea and ayre :
    Be like thy selfe, be neither proud nor base,
    One enuy gets, the other gaynes disgrace.

Be not too huge in shew, in strength a childe,
These imateriall epithites eschew ;
Be to the scornfull proud, the humble milde,
Put not thy censure to an open view ;
Speech enuy oft, but Silence neuer knew.
    When thou seest good then prayse, when bad be
      blinde,
    Then wit will beare with thee, and fooles be
      kinde.

To The Reader.

WHICH in Silence' nest so many dayes,
Smoothered the flight of my vnfeathered
    quill,
Because I knew it could not merit prayse
Here, where the muses sang and shewd their skill,
For this did seeme to be Parnassus hill :
  But this amazd my minde, and grieu'd mine
    eye
  To see the buzards with the eagles flye.

To see a troupe of souldiers, neuer tride,
Besiege a fort by Nature fenc'd on high ;
I was asham'd to see the heires of pride,
Debase in vnexpirèd Poetry,
The immortall vertues of great maiestie :
  I,[1] these are they that do the Muses staine ;
  One wanton pen makes all be iudgèd vaine.

I which securely on these errours gaz'd,
And safely stood vpon the silent shore,
When others ships by Enuie's rockes were craz'd :

---

[1] = Ay. G.

Loue me constrain'd, as pride did them before,
To trust the rockes, and leaue the silent shore :
　The loue of friends, not prayse did me perswade,
　Against my will, against the streames to wade.

Therefore to you whose iudgement is sincere,
If any fault, as many faults there be,
Seeme harsh aud iarring to a tunèd eare,
Impute the blame to those, and not to me,
Who made my pen shew his infirmitie :
　If any good, as small there is you see,
　Reape you the profit, yeeld but thankes to me.
　　　　　　　　　Thine if he find thee his.[1]

---

[1] Cf. the sentiment and wording of these lines with
those quoted from Erondell's "Garden" and Browne, in
our Memorial-Introduction. As here 'silent shore' is
repeated in the same stanza, so there is ' embrace ' : and
similarly in the verses to Browne, Envy is dwelt upon. G.

Prophesie

OF

Cadwallader,

&c.

A Prophesie of Cadwallader, last king of the Britaines.

ITTING with Clio by the gliding Thame,[1]
    Neere to her siluer girt,[2] the verdant
    strand,
I saw Rhamusis so adornd by fame :
Dauncing in measures, on the farther sand,
Holding a ball of gold within her hand :
   She stood on that, that neuer stood but went :
   So must all those that trust her gouernment.

Then did this Queene, her wandring coach ascend,
Whose wheeles were more inconstant then the
    winde;
A mighty troope this Empresse did attend ;
There might you Caius Marius caruing find,
And martiall Scylla courting Venus kind :
   Times alter, and in times we chang̀ed bee ;
   Chaunce onely constant is in leuitie.

---

[1] Here on margin is the note " Description of Fortune."
Throughout I transfer these margin-notes to the bottom.
They bear the initial H, to distinguish from my own. G.
  [2] Girdle. G.

There might you see how Archimides' art,
As a strong bulwarke guarded Syracuse[1] :
How Scipio fought and Cato stabd his hart,
How Anthony did wrong the sacred muse,
And Cleopatra's body did abuse,
  How Mago fell in Spaine, and Hanniball
  Did pitch his tents before Saturnia's wall.

His stratagems, his snares, vnequall fightes,
Scipio, Sempronius, and Flaminius slaine :
Aemilius dead amidst his wounded knights,
How chance his youth with praise did entertaine,
And in his age how Fortune wrought his paine :
  All this shee did : oh man her fraude perceiue,
  And trust her not, for shee will thee deceiue.

How Alexander rose at Darius' fall,
Lysimachus within the lyon's den :
How Scipio did besiedge Numantia's wall,
And many thousands more which scape my pen :
Amongst this fatall troope of Fortune's men,
  I saw an agèd king, except I erre,
  That cleapèd[2] was, the high CADWALLADER.

He was the last, saue three of Fortune's trayne ;
Those were a Dane, a Saxon, and a Norman king :

---

[1] Geometry. H.   [2] Named, as ' y'clept ' G.

Hengist the first, next was Denmarke's Swayne;
The last was Normane's bastard, which did bring
Plenty of ioy; whose praise the English sing:
   William whose valure mixt with happy fate,
   Brought bondage to the Iuthes and Angles state.[1]

The Britaine monarch[2] ware a simple crowne,
Hauing small beades of amber, by his side,
A siluer crosse, a frier's white frize gowne;
Vpon an humble asse this king did ride,
As white as snow, or as the siluer tide.
   One hand a staffe, the other held a booke,
   On which his eyes continually did looke.

Wherein were charactred in lines of gold,
Locrinus' warres, and Humber's tragedy:
The king himselfe by Gwendoline controld,
The Scythian's paramour of Germany,
Estrilda drownd, the praise of Hungary:
   Sabrina thrust in Seuern's flowing maine,
   Poore Madan by the curres[3] of Ireland slaine.

The Britaine Manlius, not the Romane knight,

---

   [1] William the Conquerour. H.

   [2] Cadwallader, last King of the Britaines; his land being vexed with the scourge of Pestilence, [he] went to Rome, where he vndertooke the habit of a friar. H.

   [3] Wolues. H.

Thinking to slay Mempricius,[1] Madan's sonne
Himselfe was by his brother slaine in fight,
And he by wolues—as Madan was—vndone ;
For Sodome's gilt to lust his mind had wonne.
 The foremost booke did Britaine's raigne relate,
 The next of Swayne, the third of Saxons' state.

The fourth and last did write on William's raigne,
In which there was an ancient prophesie :
Written of yore, confirmed by Merlin's twaine ;
What should ensue to William's progeny,
Was there at large explainde in poetry :
 The Warres of England for the crowne of France,
 There many battels with their mournfull
  chance.

The Ciuill Warres of Yorke and Lancaster,
The Cambrian helmet changde for England's
  crowne :
How true discent and Tudor's blood preferre,
The brow of peace dispearcèd Mars, his frowne,
The land of Warre is rulde by Iustice gowne.
 These shall haue end, then shall arise a King
 Which plenty shall conduct, in Concord's string.

He with vnnumbred linkes of Reason's chaine,
Shall three in one, and one in three vnite :

---

[1] Madan's second sonne. H.

Britaine should be the name, for Brute doth raigne,
A king commands, no prince's fauorite;
This he intreates, for this his penne doth write :
   Cease to command, learn subiects to obay,
   Reason where Iustice rules, beares greatest sway.

Is it not peerlesse praise with peace to gaine,
That for the which our fathers spent their blood :
And neuer age but ours could reobtaine ?
O happy men if that you saw such good,
But Will is maskèd still with Error's hood.
   Let true obeisans vp this diet breake,
   So Cæsar wils, so Cicero doth speake.

The fect[1] was this, the prophesie was such
Which he had read with carefull industry,
And quoted every line with Iudgement's touch ;
Amidst his study casting vp his eye,
Seeing his mistresse Fortune was not nye.
   His booke he sleightly set into his gowne,
   Which on the yellow sand fell quickly downe.

Thence posted he on his maiestique asse,
Like some slow rider pacing to the race :
Then Isis' siluer channell did I passe,
And thither went, where as mine eyes might gaze,

---

[1] Fact. G.

On that faire booke, clad in a golden case,
  I past the Annales; for it pleasde mine eye,
  To muse vpon that sacred prophesie.

When I had read vnto the latter lyne,
I saw the agèd king returne with speede :
Kind Syr—quoth he—saw you a booke of mine?
I[1] Syr—quoth I—if this be he indeed :
I gaue it him ; he gaue me thankes for meed.
  He posted thence, I to my study went,
  Where on this matter many houres I spent.

At last I was resolu'd for to relate
In Poetry, the things mine eyes did see :
Which was the vncertainety of humane state :
To paint the things aright with equitie,
I did implore the ayde of Memorie ;
  Which she denide ; O worthies ! pardon mee,
  If ought I write amisse, which you shall see.

Not Orpheus' trees, and birds inchanting quill,
Nor Homer's art heere—Reader—shalt thou see :
Expect not Ouid's verse, nor Maroe's skill,
For if you doe, you shall deceiuèd bee :
If bad it is, pray gentles beare with mee.
  Say it is meane, thou dost mee much commend
  I'de haue it meane, because I meane to mend.

---

[1] = Ay, as before.

Mistake mee not, I liue in hope to please :
Dispraise mee not, before thou knowest mee well :
Maugre sweete, not reuenge, my lines loue peace,
Doe not my shame, before thou seest it, tell :
Marke euery line, and each worde's nature spell.
    Ere thou begin'st to reade, looke, beare in minde
    Of whom I write, yea how, and in what kind.

Faire England's peeres with Romanes I compare,
Their warres, their spoiles, their fightes and
        victory,
Their filthy vices, with their vertues rare :
Their laud, dispraise, their praise and infamy,
Their conquests' triumphes, with their treachery.
    Then doth our Muse declare intestine Warres,
    Kings' conquering fields, and princes' wounding
        iarres.

Then doth she mount the ayre with eagle's winges,
Then to the North shee goes, and passeth Twide[1]
And sings his praise, which endles glory bringes,
Who like a pilot doth this Island guide ;
Which like a barke, within the Sea doth ride.
    This land is seated like to Venice state,
    The waues the walles, and euery ship a gate.

---

[1] Tweed. **G.**

Least that my gates be wider then my towne,
And that Diogines my folly see :
My proem's[1] prologue Ile set quickly downe,
And bend my Muse vnto the Prophesie :
Where you may reade art mixt with industry.
　　Needs must I erre ; to erre all men are bent,
　　To perseuere, is a bad beast's intent.　[*sic.*]

The Comparison.

WHAT a sea of blood shall England spill
　　When Norman's prince and Palastina's
　　friend.[2]
With burgonets of steele our fieldes doth fill ;
Brothers must striue as did Seuerus' kind,
Enuious ambition makes iust Nature blind :
　　Arunce and Brutus dead, alarums cease,
　　Publicola doth liue, and loueth peace.

When Brutus dide,[3] Valerius then did raigne,
When Arunce fell, the Tuscan emperour fled :
When Tirroll's shaft shall enter Rufus' braine,
When Henrie's life with Roberts lightes are fled,

---

[1] Qy—poems ? G.
[2] So called for assisting Godfrey of Bullion in his
expedition to Juddæa, Bassianus, and Geta. H.
[3] = died. G.

When all these sleepe in Nature's earthly bed:
  Norfolke shall giue to Stephen, Henrie's due,
  Peace then shall be, but Warre shall soone
     ensue.[1]

Flora is fled, stout Hiems weares her crowne,
Attir'd like Mars in furniture of steele:
Aniou and Blois striue for the imperiall crowne;
A griefe surpassing griefe doth England feele,
Whilst doubtfull Fortune turns her doubtfull
     wheele:
  Camillus comes, the Frenchmen feare his voice,
  Alba is freed, and Albion hath her choice.

When Rome was sackt, Camillus ended strife,
And made Bellinus' brother to dispaire:[2]
When Germanes' empresse Mawd, shall end her
     life,
Henry shall claime the crowne, as lawfull heire;
His eame[3] in graue, but he in regall chaire
  Is plac't, and rules his princely peeres with
     peace,
  His sonnes rebell, and concord gins to cease.

---

[1] Henry the 2. sonne of Mawd the Empresse, and Stephen Earle of Blois, nephew to Henry the first. H.

[2] Brennus. H.

[3] Sometimes *eme* = uncle. G.

Now springs the plant,[1] from hence our ioy shall
    spring:
Victorious Aniow crown'd in regall state,
Liuing, adopts an heire, inuests a king:
Vngratefull child, spurd by a woman's hate,
Sturd[2] forrain foes the land to ruinate.[3]
    Rome's sword[4] is consul; foe-men tribute paies,
    Both Henries dead, Christ's friend the septer
    swaies.

Marcellus, which did Syracusa burne,
Made Affrick's praise, to praise his matchles minde,
And place his ashes in a golden vrne :
So Albion's lyon sprung from lyon's kinde,
When death the king and prince in cords shall
    binde,
    Hee'le spend his treasure, for Jehoua's good :
    But woe alas, a slaue shall spill his blood.

Disignèd John disuests[5] young Britaine's Duke,
But Antichristian's prince, our Sauiour's foe,
Bringes Lewis in, and doth him straight rebuke;

---

[1] Henry the 2nd, the first Plantagenet. H.
[2] = stirred. G.
[3] Richard 2nd. H.
[4] Marcellus, so called by Hanniball. Ч.
[5] Transition-form of ' divests.' G.

Egles of England, yeeld to swans of Poe,
A Monarch falles by monkes, Fates wills it so.
  Titus suruiues, though Flaminius burne,
  Worster is safe, and Lewis doth returne.

At Thrasimenus valiant Titus fell,
In Prusia's court; his sonne reuengde his death :[3]
From happie heauen, though John to haples hell
Headlong did slide, his sonne shall weare the
    wreath ;
The dolphen flyes, and Mars begins to breath :
  Tempestuous whirle-windes, breake the Temple-
      gate
  Of Peace; the peers the king, the prince the
    barons hate.[4]

Ciuill dissention and disloyall armes,
Cleerly declares Clare's hidden enmitie :
A fatall starre foretelleth future harmes ;
The legions meete, each doth the other spye,
Eccho resounds; S. George, S. George, both cry :
  Gracchus is stabd, young Scipio peace maintaines,
  The barrons tam'd, all-conquering Longshanckes
    raynes.

---

[4] Titus Flam : was slaine at the battle of Thrasimenus, whose death was by his sonne reuenged in the poisoning of Hanniball. H.

[4] Henry the 3. H.

Rome's enuious tribunes, that ignoble tribe,
The vitious issue of a vertuous dame :
Did the base mindes of poore plebeians bribe,
To gaine them honour with their countrie's shame.[1]
They dead ; the world did ring with Romanes'
    fame.
    So Clare and Mountford shall, who being slaine,
    Edward shall vanquish Caledonia's plaine.

Acon is tane, and Tunis feares his stroakes;
He louèd peace, yet bare a warrior's shield :
Cambria disdain'd to weare his sister's yoake,
The ensignes spred, both striue to win the field,
The bridge is past, and Leoline must yeeld :[2]
    Marius departs, proscriptious gin to cease,
    The prince of Warre shall end his dayes in peace.

Destruction graz'd on fertill Italy,
Till Scylla's legions vanquisht Marius' might :
So Ciuill Warres shall feed on Britany,
Till Leolinus, that all-daring knight,
Is tane by Edward, in vnequall fight :
    When Marius fell, Concordia gan to smile,
    So Wales will amplify faire England's stile.

---

[1] Caius and Tiberius Gracchus. H.
[2] The saying of Leoline himselfe, as Powell hath laid down in his life. H.

Resplendant Iuno leaues her sacred throne,
Young Gaueston bewitcht great Edward's hart :[1]
The minor gods bewaile Saturnia's mone ;
Bohume and Beaumont takes the Marchers part,
And false Matreuers stabbes Carnaruan's hart :
 For Cæsar's office Scipio striues in vaine,
 And March too soone retells his triple gaine.

When that the Romane eagles graspt of yore,
Scipio with auncient Lentulus[2] did striue :
For Julius' priesthood, whose deserts were more,
But when that Pompey's legions did not thriue,
They tasted gall within the honie's hiue.
 So Wigmore seekes in vaine to get a crowne,
 But by Lord Mountacute[3] is tumbled downe.

Terra's proud issue tam'd, immortall Ioue
Rides in his chariot through the azurde skie,
Adornd with Valure, Mercy, Peace and Loue ;

---

[1] Queene Isabel wife to Edward the 2d. was next heire
to Charles, king of France, whose title our present king
doth enioy. H.

[2] Scipio and Lentulus two worthy Ro. stroue vehemently in the campe of Pompei, for the Bishoprick of
Rome, but the battels ioyning and Cæsar winning, their
strife ended with their liues. H.

[3] Misprinted 'Mountaoute'. G.

So Cæsar rode in Rome with maiesty ;
Scipio would liue, life Cato would deny.
    So Wigmore's honor seekes, but must not part,
    Matreuer's[1] hand, hath stabd Matreuer's hart.

Warre's thunderbolt, with his Egiptian pearle.
Illustrious Venus and her martiall bride,
Phillip's faire sister, with great Mercia's earle,[2]
Submits to Henault's mounting-minded bride :
Vengeance and Fury scourge inhumane pride.
    Egipt is lost, and Anthony must die,
    March is immurde, and twise he may not flie.

When Anthony did Cleopatra loue,
And did Augusta's chamber-bed forgoe :
Bellona, Cæsar's irefull minde did moue
To worke reuenge on chaste Octaiua's foe :
Marcus is slaine, he must his loue forgoe,
    As Anthony and Cleopatra were,
    So is queene Isabel and Mortimer.[3]

Depressed water's element, some thinke,
Is downe supprest by Powers most diuine :

---

[1] As before, = Maltravers.   G.

[2] Ed. the third, married Phillip daughter to the Earle
of Henault.   G.

[3] Lord Roger Mortimer, Earle of March, and Queene
Isabel, compared to Anthony and Cleopatra.   H.

Some iudge that Terra doth the moisture drinke ;
Yet certes shall men see with mortall eyne,
When deadly water shall with ayre combine,
   Great Mortimer whose name from waters sprang,
   Shall waue in waues of ayre, and there shall
      hang.

Vermilion-colloured clowdes of purple Warre,
Are by the radiant beames of Edward's raigne,
From England's territors exilèd farre ;
But stay—me thinkes—Bellona soundes againe,
And calles forth Mars to fight in Aquitaine ;
   Stay Cæsar stay, let valiant Drusus goe :
   Great Arthur's heire, can vanquish Artois foe.[1]

When that Tiberius did the septer sway,
Of Alba's empire, great Saturnia's king,
Germanicus, whose head was deckt with bay,
Fought still abroad, and conquest home did bring :
So Edward did,[2] whose praise the Spanyards sing:
   Let Beaumont witnes fearfull Phillip's flight,
   And Iohn which yeelded to the Gascoigne knight.

The wandring planets of the burnisht skye,

---

[1] Edward the Blacke Prince compared to Germanicus.
H.

[2] Edward the Blacke Prince ayded the Earle of Artois
against King John of France. H.

Are by the vncomprisèd spheare of Ioue,
Thrust here and there, as men condemn'd to
        dye;
Heauen were nought, if Heauen did not moue:
So Nature taught, so Nature's sonne did proue.[1]
    Like vnto these, or like a comet bright,
    Through euery region Casar sent his light.

The Zodiak's lamp in the eclipticke line,
Twice vrged his courser to a swift careere.
The Hitrurian[2] sonne doth in the East decline;
In Europe's West his praise did first appeere;
O climatericall disaster yeere!
    Cæsar thy glory in the West did rise,
    The poison'd East thy ruine did deuise.[3]

So siluer streames and toplesse Apenine,
Which doe confront terrestriall paradise,
Must not great Edward's wandering fame confine:
Mars and Bellona stratagems deuise,
That he with Honor's wings should mount the
        skyes.

---

[1] Aristotle. H.

[2] Etrurian. G.

[3] Germanicus appeased Germany, but ended his dayes
by poison in Assiria. H.

Exilèd Peter doth implore his ayde,
Iberia quakes, to see the crosse displayd.[1]

Reuolting Henault, and relenting John,[2]
Are terrified at Bruse and Balliol's fall:
No Salike law, can barre bold Phillip's sonne,
His matchlesse valure caused a kingdome's thrall:
Whilst slothfull Charles immur'd him in a wall,
    Germania's terror wan a glorious field;
    So Cambria's monarch made a king to yeeld.

Carelesse of death, like to a thunder-bolt,
England's Crasinius[3] with a massie lance,
And not vnlike a fierce vntamèd colt,
Glides like the siluer Rheine through yeelding
    France;

---

[1] Edward, prince of Wales restored Peter, king of
Spaine, into his kingdom by the conquest of Henry, his
bastard brother, at the battle of Nazers. H.

[2] John, Lord Beaumont, tooke part with the English
against the French nation, but afterwards he fauoured
the factiō of John, king of France. H.

[3] The Lord Audley at the battle of Poytiers behaued
himself most valiant, as Crasinius did in Pharsalia, who
bad Cæsar be of comfort, and take courage before he
fought, and that day he should praise him aliue or dead,
which he performed, for he lost his life in the pursuite of
honor, and for the safety of Cæsar. H.

Blinded with age great Boheme falls by chance :
    Caligula is borne, the sinke of shame,
    Richard misled, deserues an endlesse blame.

The wordle's faire mistresse, empresse of the Earth,
Ordaines a triumph for Augustus' heire :
So Gascoigne triumphes at young Gascoigne's birth ;
Wonder of armes set in Victoria's chaire,
To Troynouant with tropheys doth repaire.
    Rome's senators attended Alba's starre,
    So Albion peeres did waite on Albion's carre.

Two glorious sonnes, rules the celestiall globe,
Cheering the world with their transpearcing rayes :
Garnisht with saphires, and a iasper robe,
—Vntimely chaunce—Time's wonder ends his
    dayes:
Æmilius mournes amidst her tropheys praise.
    Troie's hope is dead, and Priam's Hector slaine :
    Edward hath lost his sonne, his sonne a raigne.[1]

Impartiall Death maskt in a sable weede,
Passeth the Romanes' watch and Prætors guard,
And to Tiberius' royall tent doth speede ;

---

[1] Ed. the 3. compared to Paulus Aemi. who in his greatest glory lost his chiefest ioy, namely his two sonnes. H.

196

Phisicke resists, and Death by art is bard,
But art doth yeeld, for Death was too too hard :
  He, laid in graue, his nephewe's sonne doth
    raigne :
  The scourge of Rome, and Europe's empresse
    slaine.

So when that death of Edward made an end,
Essence of value, substance of renowne :
Whome peace for iustice, warres for rule commend,
Exalting vertue, putting vices downe ;
His bones entombd, his worthy sonnes doe crowne
  Their nephew Richard, second of that name :
  The first, though not the last, disgrac't by Fame.

Melpomene thou dismal Muse appeare,
And moralize the anthemes which I bring :
Richard misled by Bushy, Poole and Vere,
Ignoble Scroope in his new empire's spring
Inchaunting charmes vnto his eares did sing :
  Flattry corrupteth kings, but good aduise
  Makes counsellors gratious, and the princes wise.

When Neroe's sonne was borne in Neroe's campe,
Quirinus' father, Rhea's valiant spouse,
In his red spheare enlightnèd had his lampe,
Leauing his yron roabes and brazen house,
Did to Bellona cups of blood carowse.

197

Saturne then ioynd with Mars, which did foretell
That Neroe's sonne for murther should excell.

Whom Brutus freed[1] by death from Tarquine's
stroakes;
Princes of peace, for Warres admirde of all:
The world's arch monarches rent their chainèd
yoakes,
Consulls and tribunes do a Senate call,
Their voice is one, Caligula must fall.
  Nature doth swarue and from her limits passe,
  The imperious lyon, got an abiect asse.

So when chaste Alice, Richard forth shall bring,
In Edward's campe, Victoria's sacred seate:
Prophets like starres, ensuing harmes shall sing,
The peeres—like Alba's knights—were all repleate
With wrath; disdaine was in a mightie sweate
  In working waies, the king for to depose;
  Which being done, the nobles Darby chose.

The Northerne planet great Northumberland,
Whose peerles issue neuer shall decaie,
Till Nature doth confound both sea and land.

---

[1] Romanes. H.

And shapeles Chaos comes his part to play :
Vertue must liue though men be turned to claye.
  This glorious moone, true badge of Honor bright,
  Disdaynes the sunne, and did not borow light.[1]

Foreseeing Gaunt, like to a carefull sire,
Seeing that lost by sloth which labour wonne :
Doth contermaund his soueraigne's hot desire,
And like a blast doth caulme the scorching sunne,
Which by illuding sycophantes is wonne :
  Two combatants[2] on their earth-threatning
      steedes,
Attend the trumpet's sound in yron weedes.

The reuerent consulls Yorke and Lancaster,
Doe conuocate a senate of the peeres,
And equalizing Woodstocke did preferre,
Due banishment to those ambitious peeres ;
The barons ioyned to this, the champions sweares

---

[1] The half-moone is the armes of the Percies, Earles of
Northum. H.

[2] Hen. Bullingbrooke, Duke of Heref. was accused by
Th. Mowbray, Duke of Norfolke, of treason, which he not
being able to proue, was contented to maintaine his alle-
gation by combat, which his aduersary did accept. But
better aduice being taken, they were both banished the
land, Hereford for the terme of ten years, and Mowbray
for the date of life. H.

Mowbray for aye, ten yeares must Harford part,
Griefe galles the one, and kills the other's hart.

The gallant courser in the listed[1] race
Dismounts the ryder, scornes his curbing raine :
Stamping with ioy his freedome doth embrace,
And doth his pristine seruitude disdaine,
Leauing his ryder breathlesse on the plaine.
    So raging Burdeux tumbles downe his kinne,
    And runnes from sin to vice, from vice to
        sinne.

In his imperiall pallace, Pleasure's bowre,
Rome's mightie monster did himselfe repose :
Sacking Cythereis fort, fair Venus towre,
The raging multitude their wrath disclose :
For his Prætorian guard they did inselose ;
    Chœrea did split his hart ; oh happie thing !
    T'was good he dide, twas bad to kill a king.[2]

So Honor's spurre did pricke the Percies blood,
To tumble Richard from his bloudie throne :
Wishing great Herford to transpasse the flood,
To come and sit on Iacob's sacred stone.[3]

---

[1] = Racecourse : so Shakespeare " the very *list*, the very utmost bound ". (King Henry IV. iv. i.). G.

[2] Caligula slaine by his own friends. H.

[3] The stone where the kings of England's chaire is

Where he might raigne as king, and rule alone.
As Claudius rose, so Herford came to raigne ;
As Nero fell, so Edward's sonne was slaine.

Now Gaunt's great issue in his throne is set,
Whose sacred science this my Muse should tell :
For Margaret's sake, that sprang from Sommerset,
For her it should, if Cambria did not tell :
For lawes vnheard, this monarch did excell.
  Who gaue him wings to mount, he threw to
    ground,
  Claudius who ran so faire, is Claudius found.[1]

In Silence' vault my Muse shall hide his fame,
Who dide the grey goose wings with purple red :
Praise he deseru'd, though he deserued blame,
Sertorius-like his warlike troopes he led,
For by alluring hope they both were fed :
  Had men and Fortune equaliz'd his minde,
  His conquests Seuernes neuer had confinde.[2]

---

placed at their coronatiōs, is reported to be that stone
whereon Jacob laid his head whē the angel appeared to
him in his dream : Genes : brought frō Scotland by Edward the first. H.

  [1] Henry 4. The extremitie of his lawes are set down
in Powel's Annales. G.

  [2] Owen Glēdour compared to Sertorius. H.

Victorious Hotspurre and his valiant sire,
The king's great steward, Woster's reuerend lord,
With neuer-daunted Dowglas doe conspire,
Whose endles praise our Annales doe record :
With these doe Glendoure ioyne and Wigmor's
    lord,
    To pull the scepter from the tyrante's hand,
    And giue it him that should by right com-
      mand.[1]

Dowglas and Hotspurre, peerlesse for their might,
Are ouermatcht by Henrie's matchlesse sonne :
Who like a lyon rows'd him in the fight :
Glendowre himselfe is by himselfe vndone,
Northumberland is sicke and cannot come :
    Like to a tyger in his eager chase,[2]
    Great Monmouthe's praise doth run from place
    to place.[3]

Tumults appeas'd and armor set aside,
The stately citty of the highest God,
Diuine Ierusalem, Iehouah's bride,

---

[1] Edmund Mortimer Earle of March was designed heire
apparant in the dayes of Richard 2. if the King dyed
without issue. H.

[2] The battle at Shaftsbury. H.

[3] Henry the 5. borne in Monmouthshire in Wales. H.

Being whipt with warre and famine's pinching
    rod,
Implores the helpe of this all-conquering lord :
  His soule defilde with sinne, by merits sought,
  That to redeeme which Jesus' blood had bought.

His royall Nauy, like a sea of wood,
Attends his princely presence in the bay :
But see how meager Death still enuying good,
With fatall stroake his enterprise doth stay :
The cædar falles in time, so kings decay :
  Why stay your shippes, he treades the sacred
    path,
  Jerusalem his soule and body hath.

Henry the Fift, his Life and Death.

AVAUNT proud Rome and bragge not of
    thy men
    Nor thy ætheriall Cæsars' warres declare :
Cease peerlesse Plutarch, with thy sacred pen,
The world's archmonarches aptly to compare
Reason doth vrge, and this alledge I dare,
  That England's Homer portraid hath his warre,
  Which doth excell the worthiest Cæsar's starre[1]

---

[1] Henr. 5. H.

What telst thou me of famous Hasdruball,
Of Canna's chance, and Varro's ouerthrow :
Æmilius' death, and conquering Hanniball,
Of Sylla's legions, and a Parthian bowe,
Of Titus valure, Cato's wrinckled browe,
 Of Syracuse, and strong Numantia's wall,
 Or Phillip, Persia, Iugurth, Iuba's fall.

Of noble Drusus and proud Saturnine,
Of Scipio's death, and Gracchus' infamy :
Of Marius' trophies, and sterne Cataline,
How Cæsar vanquisht France and Germany,
And twise returnd as foild from Britany :
 The world admir'd their victories to see,
 Yet none of these must be comparde with thee.

Let Athens praise the lawes which Solon gaue,
And Marathon extoll Miltiades,
Write Caria of Mausolus' stately graue,
And let Cycilia wish Demosthenes,
Let[1] Salamina praise Themistocles :
 Greece did admire their tryumphes for to see,
 Yet all these cannot [be] compare[d] with thee.

Let Sparta now conceale Lycurgus' fame,
And Lacedæmon hide Lysander's praise :

----

[1] Misprinted ' But '.   G.

Cease Argos now, to shew th' Olimpicke game,
Let silence cloud or maske those golden dayes,
When Epires' monarch acted tragicke playes :[1]
  But what of him? or what are these to thee ?
  For thou alone doest farre exceed those three.

Though Alexander wan Darius[2] crowne,
And forc't the Easterne emperour leaue his tent,
Burning Persopolis, that regall towne :
Seeing thy valure freely giues consent
That two bright sonnes should rule the element :
  With thee great prince we aptly may compare,
  Rich Europe's paragon, and phœnix rare.

Thou didst not want Parmenio's aiding hand,
Nor valiant Perdica's aspiring minde :
Which might Alanson's quarels fierce withstand,
As long as Langlie's gallant-issued minde
Had faithfull Suffolke's loue to him combinde.[2]
  They wan, they lost, they liue though they are
    dead,
  They liue in heauen, and dide in Conquest's
    bed.

---

[1] Pyrrhus. H.

[2] The Duke of Yorke and Earle of Suffolke were the
onely men of nobilitie that ended their lines in the battell
of Agincourt. H.

France did ten yeares withstand the Romanes'
        might,
Both parties oft with equall courage plaide :
Yet thou[1] before the sun shewd twice his light,
Mads't great Mompensier flye as all dismaide,
To see thy kingly banner forth displaide.
    Like to Crassinius, Yorke the va[n]ward led :
    True valure is by hope of honor bred.[2]

Henry two diadames doth now combine,
Europe's faire daughters, eldest sisters twaine,
By marriage of a maide, a nimph[3] diuine:
Whilst Lewis liues, as emperour he must raigne,
Henry as heire apparant doth remayne :
    When Katherin is betrothd his beauteous wife,
    Peace conquers Warre, and Concord endeth strife.

Immortalizèd virgin, sacred queene,
Britaine's Aurora, harbinger of day :
Fairer then thought could thinke or eye hath seene,
Rich Vertue's port, and Honor's cleerest bay ;
Thrice blessèd wombe fram'd of ætheriall clay,

---

    [1] Misprinted 'that'. G.
    [2] Crasinius was the first captain that charged the enemy
in the Field, which office of valure, Edward the Duke of
Yorke enioyed at Agincourt. H.
    [3] Misprinted 'mimph'. G.

Which didst enclose that glorious Theodore,
Whose sonne did Britaine's regalty restore.

Her amber-tresses like to wyers of gold,
That shadowèd her white vermilion face,
Like Vulcan's chayne did Venus' champion hold ;
Who triumphed erewhile, now sucs for grace,
Vndecent action for a captaine's place :
 Thy eyes are now bewitcht with eyes diuine,
 Thy heart consents to honor Katherine.

If I had Zeuxes ait to paint thy lookes,
Did I enioy Mæonian Homer's quill :
To pourtraiture thy praise in golden bookes,
Thy vertues rare would æqualize my skill ;
Thy sacred paps sweete nectar did distill.
 Had'st not thou beene, our eyes should neuer
  view
 Our present peace and pleasures to ensue.

Stay ranging Muse, thy wandring course restraine !
When Ioue's all-seeing eyes did view this king,
He sent his harauld to that spatious plaine,
Where the three fatall sisters, then did spinne :
To know when Henrie's life did first beginne,
 And if his thred were not already spunne,
 That Lachesis should make it quickly runne.

His wisest onne did place his golden wings,

Holding a siluer rodde,—all-charming wand!
Wherewith he could inchant all mortal things :
With this attire he claue the ætheriall land,
Where Ioue and Iuno doth the gods command :
    When that he came vnto the appointed place,
    He told his message with a comely grace.

Sisters—quoth he[1]—for so they were indeed,
Th' omnipotent and all-commanding Ioue,
Which doth on nactar[2] and ambrosia feed,
Iuno, Apollo, and Cythereis loue,
With all the gods that rules the sphere aboue,
    Entreats, cōmands, of you faire sisters three,
    To end his life, though not his dignitie.[3]

Atlas you know is old Alcides dead?
You know the waight of heauen's massy throne :
The planets houses couered all with lead,
Ioue's pallace varnisht with rich rubies' stone,
The gates of iuory and Indian bone :
    He that doth heauen's heauiest waight sustaine,
    Must patience haue to tollerate his paine.

---

[1] Mercurie's oration. H.
[2] Nectar. G.
[3] He dyed in a chamber at the Deane of Westmi. lodging, named Ierusalem. H.

Therefore—quoth he—this is my father's will,
—For Ioue his father was, or Fame doth lye—
That you which power haue great kings to kill,
Would shorten Henrie's life that he might dye :
A heauenly thought deserues æternitie.
    Atlas is old, and Atlas must haue aide :
    All feare the heft,[1] Henry was nere afraide.

The Sisters[2] stood amazde at his request,
Each looke at other's eyes as in a glasse :
Whereat sterne Clotho eldest of the rest :
Brother quoth she—for Ioue their father was—
Shall Fates be rulde by gods ? ahlas ! ahlas !
    They reuell still, but we poore wretches worke,
    We labour, they in caues of Pleasure lurke.

The world's poore impes may iustly now complaine
Of humane sorrow, man's still growing griefe :
How birds and beasts a longer life do gaine
Then man, poore man ; and man's commanding
    chiefe,
If you deny them helpe, where is reliefe :
    Men say that Fates are certaine, now they see
    Ioue made vs constant in inconstancy.

---

[1] Weight, pressure. It is a living word in the United
States (New England). G.

[2] The Fates answere. H.

The angry god invellopèd in ire,
Wrath in his face and fury in his lookes,
His eye more redde then was the reddest fire :
Shewes ancient monuments of sacred bookes,
Which earst he wrote by the Idalian brookes.
    There might you see what acts the gods did
       frame :
    Amongst the rest Ioue might the Sisters blame.

Out of this place he drawes his argument,
And doth confute this sugred sophistry :
Then reades another act of Parliament,
Which did confirme Ioue's royall empery,[1]
His great perogatiue and dignity :
    Then doth he powre forth sacred eloquence,
    Selected flowers of Learning's quintessence.

What if proud Terra's issue, Briareus,[2]
Would combat with your great ætherial sire ?
Entring Castalia, where the sacred Muse
Liues still inspirde with yong Apollo's fire ?
What if the giants could so high aspire,

---

    1 = empire   It occurs repeatedly in Shakespeare : *e. g.*
" in large and ample *empery* " (Henry v. i. 2.). " ambitious-
ly for rule and *empery* " (Titus Andron. 1. 1.) "the Romans
empery " (*ibid* : i. i.) et *alibi*.   G.
    2 Mercinys reply.   H.

Would not they touch the christalizèd sky,
Vntuning heauen's sweetest harmony?

What god should then the heauen's waight sus-
    taine,
Whilst Bacchus in his Indian tyger's carre
Would shake the orbes and that celestiall plaine,
When faire Victoria, conquering queene of Warre,
Brighter than Venus, or the brightest starre,
    Doth giue to Ioue a crowne bedeckt with gold;
    Could Atlas then heauen's heauiest waight
        vphold?

His age is great, and yeares will strength remoue,
Therefore faire Sisters well aduisèd bee,
To answere Ioue and all the gods aboue :
Though loth they were, yet all did well agree
To cut his thred for meere necessitie.
    Then Atlantiades did soone depart,
    And Atropos did stabbe great Henrie's hart.

Thus dide the phænix of the vastie round,
Whose worth my Muse should euer memorize :
And eccho-like his martiall deeds resound,
But that he did his countrey scandalize
In following Henry which did tyranize.
    She gaue thee breath to liue, and men to fight,
    Yet thou depriu'st her of her cleerest light.

When noble Henry ended hath his daies,
Bedford with conquering swords Vernoi shal fill,
And spend his blood to gaine immortall praise :
Beauford and Beaumont shall good Humfrey kill,
And Warwicke gaine the popular good will.
    Poole is exilde from wofull Margaret,
    And Yorke malignes the Duke of Somerset.

Mars mounts his ensignes on our highest towers,
And decks our helmets with Ambition's plumes :
Reuenge, sad massacres and silent showres
Distills, cities are burnt, whose dankish fumes
Contaminates the ayre ; now Yorke presumes
    With Sarum's earle and Warwicke's willing
      hand,
    To gaine the crowne, and with the crowne the
      Land.

The Ciuill Warres.

LUTONIAN princesse, sacred Proserpine,
Licence Megæra and Ctesiphone,
Which neuer saw the sunne's all-pleasing
    shine :
Enter this vale of humane misery,
And consecrate to endles memory

These Ciuill broyles in characters of brasse,
Let forth these warres, which did all warres
surpasse.

Heere Mars' pauilion, there Bellona's tent,
The lanciers' here, and there the carbines stands :
The bilmen strikes, the archers' bowes are bent :
Here raging Fury flies with burning brands :
Distorted limmes are pilde on purple sands :
   Here gassamores are cract, there helmets crazd.
   Here gorgets cut, there vaines of azure razd.

Now doth the courser neigh, the clarions sound,
And Wrath ymounted[1] on a flaming steed,
Doth both the legions' fortitude confound ;
The moistlesse Earth for very griefe doth bleed,
To see the gardner spoyle the sowen seed.
   Heere might you see what age could neuer tell :
   Whilst lyons fought, the forrests baron's fell.

Here ambuscadoes watch the sallying scout,
There Hanniball entraps Marcellus traine :
Here wings are plac't, and sqadrons round about,
Scipiades must leaue disloyall Spaine,
And like Anchises, clippe the Elizian plaine.

---

[1] I have ventured to supply 'y' for the missing syllable
in this vivid line. G.

Nature hath dig'd for men more kind of granes,
Then Indian Ganges hath translucent[1] waues.

No valiant Martius, stout Corioloene,
Did now the raging multitude withstand :
Tumultuous windes haue left the rocky lane,
Where sterne Hypodates with mace in hand,
Their lawlesse force, by force doth countermaund.
    Eurus will blow and shake the islands' king,
    Rebells will rise, and belles of discord ring.

Vnworthy I, to mount that sacred hill,
And Clodius-like see female sacrifice :
Virgill sang this, and none but Virgill will
Aduenture Valure's worth to memorice ;
Thrice glorious obiect, fit for princely eyes.
    Pardon great Homer, my all-daring Muse,
    Let cherill's[2] folly, cherill's fault excuse.

The lesser starres makes Phœbe shine more bright,
So may my infant Muse, comparde to thine,
Make thy heroicke poems' splendant light,
Seeme fairer farre in men's iuditious eyne :

------

[1] A Miltonian word, *e.g.* " Under the glassie, cool,
translucent wave " (Comus 861) : " the Eastern ray, *translucent*, pure " (Samson Agonistes, 548)   So in Pope
later : = semi-transparent. **G.**
    [1] Transition-form of churl : sometimes cherel. **G.**

Comparison makes vertue seeme diuine.
　Yet giue me leaue with my vnworthy pen,
　To blazon forth the acts of worthy men.

Cease mournfull Rome thy sad enlangoring,[1]
Those fatall fields neere to Campania fought :
Wherein the very prime of Marius' spring,
The spring of griefe which Carbo deerly bought,
Ambitious Conquest, rulde great Scylla's thought. [2]
　Speake not of these proud Rome, nor make thy
　　mone,
　Or if thou speak'st, make not comparison.

What of stout Varro, and Affranius lost,
Massilia's ruine Scæua's piercèd sheeld :[3]
Home by Brundusium, Cæsar's shippes were tost ;
Euer renown'd Pharsalia's bloody field, ;
How Iuba fell, and Diator did yeeld. :
　Pompey in Egipt by Pothinius slaine,
　And endles shame which Ptolomy did gaine.

Cæsar is stabd,[4] and Alba's doth lament,

---

[1] Lamentation (?) : but I do not remember the word elsewhere. G.

[2] The ciuil wars of Marius and Sylla. H.

[3] The battell in Spaine, where Cæsar was victor. H.

[4] Cæsar slaine in the court of Pompey. The battell of Phillippia. The fielde at Actium. H.

Antonius doth the tyrant's plea refute :
Irefull Octauius to reuenge is bent,
Cascas and Cassius, Cicero and Brute,
For countrey's freedome frame a faithlesse suite.
   Lawes silent are when armies rule the towne,
   Who conquered kings, by kings are tumbled
    downe.[1]

Enuious desire of honor, loue to raigne,
Seuers their mindes whome Nature did combine :
Two Romaine nauyes cut the ocean maine,
One brother's losse, doth cause another's gaine,
Nothing is worse then potentates' disdaine.
   Rome smild with ioy, when Ciuill Warres did
    cease,
   England admirèd more at perfect peace.

In thirteen battells England's strength was tryde,
Gaunte's issue striues with Clarence' progenie :
Through euery place Destruction's steel did ryde,
Making debate and endles enmitie,
Twixt subiects loue, and princely soueraigntie.
   The lords conspire, and at Saint Albon's meete,
   Here's Warwicke's tent, there Yorke doth man
    the streete.

---

[2] The first of Saint Albon's battells. H.

Vnder the castell, Somerset is slaine,
Here Clifford falls, and there Northumberland ;
Great Buckingham renewes the fight againe :
In vaine the lion doth the beare withstand,
Where Warwicke leades his all-subduing band :
   The rose doth wither, and the daysie[1] spring,
   The queene escapt, but Warwicke hath the king.

O whither shall she fly ? whose ayde expect,
Who is encombred with a thousand woes ?
What peasant boore will prince's griefes respect ?
By flight she scapes the furie of her foes :
Thus to the North this Amazonian goes.
   Griefe flies to those, who are opprest with griefe,
   Societie in woe is some reliefe.

When Rome's two Scipios fell—two glorious
    starres—
In Andeluzia or illuding Spaine.—
None durst, but Scipio, vndertake those Warres ;
Euen so when Clifford was for England slaine,
And Percie's pride lay breathlesse on the plaine,
   None durst the ragged Staffe and Beare with-
    stand,
   But Clifford's sonne and great Northumberland.

---

[1] Daysie, in French, signifieth Margaret. H.

The trumpets wake the champions to the field,
Who rode in tryumph through Epæon's towne
To Westmoreland ; and Margaret must yeeld :
Whose vertues did deserue a golden crowne :
His browes are circulizde with paper browne.
    Themistocles doth yeeld to Xerxes' might,
      Yorke ouermatcht, giues place to Henrie's right.[1]

Penthisilea bends her course to Troy,
Showing the spoiles of Larrissea's king,
And Henry, like to Priam, smiles with ioy,
Seeing his queene such tropheys home to bring,
And all the Phrigian virgins Io sing.
    Like vnto this, or like a brauer wight,
      Courageous Margret doth returne from fight.

Neuer discouragde Warwick's royall peere,
Vnconstant Clarence, constant Montacute,
Seeing the southerne coast of Albion cleere,
Did Essex, Suffolke, Surrey, resalute ;[2]
Norfolke doth Mowbray captaine constitute.
    Both armies ioyne, and to Saint Albon's came,
      They flye their foes, where first they ouercame.

---

[1] At Wakefield, Rich. Duke of Yorke being taken by
the Lord Clifford, in reuenge of his father's death, slaine
at S. Albon's, crowned the Duke's head with paper. H.

[2] = re-salute, as before re-tells. G.

[3] The second Battell of S. Albons. H.

Mowbray to Suffolke, Warwicke with the rest,
In haste, poste haste, to Cambria's borders flye :
New rising March doth rowse his spangled crest,
And vnderstanding by a sallying spye
His father's friends and fauorites were nigh,
    With decent gesture, doth them entertaine,
    Imploring aide his right to reobtaine.

Warwicke, who was the speaker for them all,
In modest sort, as well became his age :
Not Duke of Yorke, but doth him soueraigne call :
A name so great doth vertue equipage :
Now each to other doth his honour gage.
    Like Cæsar now he ioynes with Anthony,
    And like to him doth foster enmitie.

When Brutus' hand had stabt great Cæsar's hart,
Octauius' honour every where did finde :
Antonius takes the stout Cæsarean's part,
But when reuenge had satisfide her minde,
Whome mariage chaste, with friendship had
      combinde,
    Ambition makes them striue for endlesse raigne,
    And with their blood to dye the crimson mayne.

So Edward and renownèd Sarum's sonne
Ioyne to reuenge dead Richard's iniury.[1]

---

[1] Richard Earle of Warwicke. H.

But when that Gaunt's great issue was vndone,
Warwicke doth enuy Yorke's prosperitie,
And much disdaines his peerlesse soueraigntie.
Witnesse when Edward durst not here abide,
And Barnet field where noble Warwicke dide.

Henrie's faire queene,[2] great Neapolitane,
Blinded with maskèd Fate, vnconstant Chance,
Did neuer feare her future fatall bane :
Like a fierce coult this iennet proud did prance,
Smiling with ioy to see her smiling chance.
Harke how the drumme doth summon to the
field,
See how she takes her ill beseeming shield.

Stay Naples' pride, Sicilian empresse stay,
Will France for euer showres of vengeance raigne ?[2]
Thy first approch presage[d] this fatall day :
Fire flew from heauen and made our turrets plaine,
When thy Armados cut the ocean maine.
Had Cæsar read that which the poore man gaue,
Egypt had neuer beene Antonius' graue.[3]

---

[1] Margret daughter to Reino, Earle of Aniow, who entituled himself King of Naples, Sycil, and Ierusalem, but enioyed none. H.

[2] = rain. G.

[3] That day in which Cæsar lost his life in the court of Pompey, a poor man tendred him a petition, which he

Had but great Henry, great in maiestie
Joynd with that match which Bedford first did make,
He had not tasted base seruilitie;
But when his minion Suffolke did forsake,
That nimph of ioy, great heire to Arminake,
   Then Yorke's depressèd issue gan to rise:
   An abiect prince each subiect will despise.

Clifford and Percy, proppes of Henrie's state,
—Seeing the southerne lords entend to fight—
Doth the fierce tyger's anger instigate,
Proposing arguments of Henrie's right,
How her decaye augmented Edward's might.
   In Hampton first she did our woe begin:
   Two Hamptons cannot end her endlesse sin.[1]

Fury awakes the murthred lion's whelpe,
And like poore Hector, his deceasèd sire,
Craues of his kinsmen their supporting helpe,
Their smotherd hate hath kindled Murther's fire,
Which none can quench till they haue quencht
     desire;

---

lightly regarded, the contents whereof had he perused, his
life might haue been preserued. H.
  [1] At her first comming, landing at Southampton, some
part of Paule's steeple, and many other churches in England were set on fire. H.

Where Nemesis of late did murther end,
There she begins heroicke bloud to spend.

Like the world's monarch, Yorke's apparant heire
Ioynes with his father's friend, great Neiul's race:
They to Northampton with their troupes repaire,
Where Aniowe's Tamiris with martiall grace
Clifford's triumphant armes[1] did embrace :
   Clifford, whose name as Talbot did in France,
   Made Warwicke feare his colours to aduance.

Octauius now and chaste Octauius' bride,[2]
Conspire the death of tyranizing Brute.
Clifford must fall in top of all his pride :
Who did by armes, great Munster's plea refute,
Doth pleade his cause, but Warwicke gaines the
     suite :
   A headlesse arrow piercst his armèd throate,
   Who in his youth did saile in Conquest's boate.

If Homer liu'd and dwelt in Castalie,
And daily tasted of Parnassus' well,
Inspirde with furious sacred poesie,
Yet would he not our Virgil's worth excell,

---

[1] Query—read as a dis-syllable or is it a misprint for
'armies'? G.

[2] A comparison of Edward and Warwicke with Octav-
ius and Anthony. H.

Whose pæans did these fierce massacres tell.
Delia is praisd with thy all-praysing hand :
No wonder, for thou dweltst in Delos' land.[1]

Eight seuerall battels shall escape my Muse,
Least Pride it selfe should me esteeme as proud :
Let Maro's quill that sacred path peruse,
Couer our temples with a sable cloud,
Cimerian wreathes my head of sorrow shrowd :
    Giue me a brazen pensill not a pen,
    Some drops of blood, to portraiture these men.

The Field of Banbery.

NOW Warre is mounted on Rebellion's steede
        And Discontent perswadeth willing Pride,
His crest to raise, and weare an iron weede :
Long smothred Enuy doth the army guide,
Which made firme loue from true obedience slide :
    'Twas that great Neuill made proud George rebell,
    Whose haughty spirits Warwicke knew too well.

---

[1] This is in allusion to SAMUEL DANIEL, whose
" Civil Wars" appeared in his " Works" in 1601. His
" Delia" or " Sonnets" were famous so early as 1592. G.

Warwicke, that raisde the race of Mortimer,
Whose eyes did see too soone—thy death saies so—
The downfall of immortall Lancaster;
'Twas he that did,—what could 'not Warwick
        doo ?—
Make kings and queenes to loue and feare him too.
    'Twas that great peere, who with one warlike
        hand,
    Crown'd and vncrown'd two kings who rulde
        the Land.

Thus while these royall but disloyall peeres,
Maugre reuenge to him that knew not feare,
Vnnumbred bands of men and swarmes appeares
In north and south, east, west, yea euery where :
They throw away their coats, and corslets weare :
    Wiues, maides, and orphans' eyes are stuft
        with teares,
    And cannot see the spades transform'd to speares.

The shepheard's hooke is made a souldier's pike,
Whom weather-beaten hands must learne aright
His speare to traile, and with his sword to strike
Vpon the plumèd beauer of a knight ;
None must be sparde by Warre's impartiall might
    If euery souldier were a king, what then ?
    Princes should die as fast as other men.

The senator must leaue his skarlet gowne,
And keepe him in some turret of defence :
When Warres once flourish, Iustice must goe
    downe,
Lawes to correct, is law-lesse Warre's pretence,
Valure doth greeue to see ill gotten pence.
    To see a man without deserts to rise,
      Makes Warre, such men not Iustice, to despise.

You that in peace by vse of golden hoords,
Your dunghill race to barons did erect :
You that by English phrase and chosen woords
Make heauens' enuy your toplesse architeck,
Your angels cannot you from Warres protect :
    The Campe and Court in manners different are,
      Words may in Peace, but deeds preuaile in
        Warre.

For robes of honor furr'd with miniuere[1]
You must haue brest-plates of well tempred
    steele,
And on your agèd heads strong helmets weare ;
All states must turne when Fortune turnes her
    wheele :
That man which pleasure tastes must sorrow feele.

---

[1] Miniver = a kind of fur usually employed in royal
robes. Since more common. G.

Who sees the wracke of mightie empery,
He loues his life too well that will not dye.

When kings must fight, shall subiects liue in
     peace ?
What coward is of such a crauant race,
That loues not honor more than idle ease ?
Great Romane, I applaud thy worthy phrase,
To liue with shame, is worse then dye with praise.
     All which haue being, alwaies cannot bee,
     For things corrupt must die, and so must wee.

Could Cressus[1] mightie mines from Cyrus' hand,
His captiue carkasse or his state defend ?
Wealth cannot Warre, nor siluer, speares withstand:
By strife we see the greatest States haue end,
And most they marre by Warre, who most would
     mend.
     When old Warres cease, then straight their[1]
     springs anew,
     For harmes still harmes, and euils do ills ensue.

No sooner had the gladsome eyes of Peace
Beheld this warlike, sea-inuiron'd Ile,
But Disobedience, heire to sluggish ease,
Did weake beleefe subdue with subtile stile;

---

[1] = there.   **G.**

Grace winnes the heart, but words the eares
beguile,
'Twas Warwick's tongue, whose speech did all
men please,
Whose words were such, or very like to these.

The Earle of Warwick's Speech,

YOU know great lords, your very eyes did
see
The spotlesse honor which my house
and I
Did euer beare this kingdome; who but wee
Did checke the pride of wilfull tyranny ?
And with our grandsires, we esteemde it good,
For England's weale to spill our dearest blood.

Witnesse the dismall fall of Salisbury,
And Richard, Duke of Yorke, in Wakefield slaine,
The wracke of my decaièd familie;
Why did we this, what profit did we gaine ?
'Twas but to shew our country our good will,
Which now we also do, and euer will.

How many times haue I in complete steele,

---

[1] Crœsus. **G.**

Yea mounted on my steed, pursude the chase?
Witnesse these weary limbes ; for age must feele,
If youth hath runn'd astray or tedious race.
  Witnesse these siluer haires which now appeares;
  Cares makes vs old, though we be yong in yeares.

When as these eyes, impartiall eyes of mine,
Beheld my king illuded and misled
By baser men, true honor did repine
To see great maiestie with basenesse wed :
  For which I waged warre, and warring wan,
  And winning, chose a tyger for a lambe.

Both you and I great lords, yea all the State
With vniuersall voice adiudg'd him wise :
Who now hath prou'd a tyrant and vngrate :
Humilitie makes Time's obseruers rise.
  For you I chose him king, and spent my blood,
  But tryall saies, good seeming is no good.

Now therefore friends let Warwick's tongue in-
    treate,
Since that our hopes of Edward's loue despaire.
That Lancaster may repossesse his seate,
Whom we vnkindly thrust from Honor's chaire ;
  The reason is, which gouernes our pretents.
  Tyrants are worser farre then innocents.

Thus this enragèd lord doth instigate

With spurlike words swift coursers to the race :
Enuy ambition breeds, ambition hate,
Hate discontent breeds, discontent disgrace ;
These be Warre's angry sounds,peruitious race.
　Those vices by Iniustice nourisht are :
　Affection[1] in a iudge is worse then Warre.

Blessed that state, thrice happie is the Land
Where sacred Iustice is esteemede diuine :
And when the iudge on one eare holds his hand :
My pen applaudes that sentence iust of thine,
Rome's holy prince, peace-louing Antonine :
　As I am Marcus, I am not thy foe,
　But being iudge, I must be iust also.

That lawe-deryding peere, disdaining lord,
Warwick, doth his rebellious ensignes reare,
And vowes reuenge on Edward, with his sword ;
Hastings and Stanley do withstand the Beare,
True honor neuer yeelds to seruile feare.
　He is a friend that loues when Fate doth frowne,
　He shall haue thousands that doth weare a
　　crowne.

Thus while these threatnings like some blazing
　starre,

---

[1] = Partiality or favouritism.　G.

The wracke of some great emperour do portend :
Their friends on either side addresse for Warre :
Great William Earle of Pembrooke doth entend,
Ere Warre begin to make of Warre an end :
    And for that purpose for his friends he sent,
    To whom as thus he shewed his right intent.

The Earle of Pembrooke's Oration.

YOU that did euer with your swords main-
      taine,
      The vndoubted title of the whiter Rose :
By whose great ayde great Edward did obtaine,
The royall crowne, and homage held of those,
    Which now rebell; deere friends correct this
      sinne,
    'Tis as much praise to keepe, as praise to winne.

If speech might spur you to this glorious race,
Where endlesse honor is the purchast fee,
Selected words my ruder speech should grace :
We pricke in vain his sides, whose feete are free.
    You euer did the house of Yorke adore,
    True loue encreaseth daily more and more.

Giue not occasion to the enuious pen,
To brand you with the badge of infamie :

Be firme in resolution, worthy men,
And thinke vpon your auncient libertie.
  Behold why Warwick doth these Warres entend:
  A bad beginning hath a worser end.

Looke with indifferent, not respecting eyes,
Vpon these two coriualls in the Warre :
Edward, a king, couragious, honest, wise,
Warwicke, whose name is like a blazing starre,
  That some ensuing harmes doth foretell :
  Enuy doth still worke ill, but neuer well.

For whom doth he this bloody battell wage ?
For aged Henry, and the prince his sonne :
Who but for him had led a quiet age,
But they poore princes, were by him vndone :
  I finde it true which hath bene often sed,
  Beares must sometime with humane flesh be fed.

It is not loue to either of these twaine,
That doth enforce this proud, ignoble peere
These wandring troupes of rebells to maintaine ;
But tis Ambition whom he holds most deere,
  That doth compell his willing hands to fight :
  Vnsettled braines bloud still respect, not right.

Nay, what if Henry should enioy the wreath,
Thinke you by yeelding fauour to enioy?

Friends, when Warres rise, say kings should neuer
    breath,
Princes in neede men of regard imploy.
  To this iust action loyall friends be mou'd,
  The firmest faith in danger great is prou'd.

Thus hath this lord as with a touch-stone tride,
The courage of his country-men, and loue :
The voyce of all is on Warres ; Warres they cride ;
The prince's vertues do the subiects moue,
Dangers and perils eminent to proue.
  The noble earle with speede pursues his fate,
  Delay brings danger to the surest State.

When Fame reported this to Edward's eare,
Hope vanquisht feare and gaue encouragement :
To see them firme who euer faithfull were.
Then to Lord Stafford, Southwike earle, he sent,
To muster all his friends incontinent :
  Then gaue he ioynt commission to these twaine,
  As equalles when they came in campe to raigne.

Thus these two captaines as those two of yore,
When Rome's selected youth in Canna's bled,
Equal in power, but not in iudgement's store :
As Varro, Stafford from the battell fled,
As Paulus, so renownèd Pembrooke sped.

Thus lord-like stout, Æmilius forth doth goe,
To chase the pride of his rebellious foe.

Stafford and hee,—weake staffe to leane vpon,—
No Stafford he, nor sprung from Buckingham,
Nor let that name so base a man bemoane :
His cowardize escandalizde his fame,
Lassiuious lust did explaiten[1] his shame.
   These two to Banbary with armies bend,
    Thence Stafford fled, there Herbert's life did
    end.

There might you see a troope of warlike men,
Conducted by the glories of their clyme :
Vnworthy I, with my vnworthy pen,
To æternize in layes vndecent rime,
Their memories, which liue in spight of Time.
   These two as Fabius and Marcellus weare,
    Rome's guarding target and offending speare.

Richard was valorous, but his brother wise,
Youth made him forward, age the other stayde :
Richard for action, Pembrooke for aduise :
If both their worths were in a ballance wayde,
Neither should Fate's partiallitie vprayde,

---

[1] = expleite *i. e.* complete. There is also explate, transition-form of explaine, unfold. G.

The differences betweene these brothers are,
Cne Peace affected most, the other Warre.

There might you see the champions of the Beare,
Mounted on lustie coursers, scoure the plaine :
There might you see the sonne of Latimer,
With rashnesse charge, with feare returne, and
    slaine :
They neuer feare, who neuer feelèd paine.
   There might you see, O I am greeu'd to say
   What years confirm'd, consumèd in a day.

There might you see that worthy man of men,
Richard, with his victorious sword in hand :
Like a fierce lyon passing from his den,
Or some sterne boare, whose anger plowes the land :
Securely passe through euery conquer'd band.
   As a round bullet from a canon sent,
   This knight alone through fortie thousand went.

And backe return'd to his amazèd traine,
But more enraged with anger then before,
Begins to kill, where he before had slaine :
Like a close myzer he augments his store,
The more he slaies, he loues to slaie the more.
   All this thou didst ; what latter age can tell,
   Of one that better did, or halfe so well ?

Thus like Alcides, all composde of ire,

Whose fiery lights shut[1] sparkes of fortitude :
This champion doth to greater deeds aspire,
Still pressing on the Hydra multitude,
Till like to sheep they fled in order rude,
 Then to his tent with tryumph he doth goe :
 Valure doth loue to spoile, not chase the foe.

But see vnconstant Chance, and seeing weepe,
For euery word requires a siluer teare :
Whiles carelesse Victory did sweetly sleepe,
And Conquest by desert did honour weare,
—When most we liue secure, we most should feare—
 Sixe hundred men conducted by a squire,
 Made those that chaste with praise, with shame
  retire.

But ere that these confused warriours fled'
Whom vnexpected horror did amaze :
They sold their liues for liues ere they were dead,
Their conquering blood their honors did emblaze ;
But all were not deriuèd from one race :
 Some stallions in a field, some asses bee,
 And so of men there be, of each degree.

Richard,thou can'st not mount thy steed and flye,
Nor thou great lord : experience makes thee stay ;

---

   [1] = shoot. G.
    235

To feare the name of death is worse then dye :
Tut men borne base, a baser word will say,
' I care not how I scape so liue I may.'
    Ye slaues to feare whom I abhorre to see,
    That loue life more then praise or honestie.

Still do they striue till that vnnumbred presse
Like bees of Hybla swarmèd euery where:
Courage in danger doth it selfe expresse.
Submission to a lyon breeds but feare,
But rauenous beasts their prostrate subjects teare :
    By such, great Richard falls, and Pembrooke
        dies,
    Conquering twise twentie thousand enemies.

Mount sacred spirits with cleare Conscience' wings
To the ninth heauen, whereas your glorious eye
May gaze on the immortall king of kings :
Liue you in peace, but we in misery :
Man cannot happie be before he dye.
    Vnto your glorious tombes I sacrifice,
    These dismall anthems and sad elegies.

Cease mournfull Muse, to chaunt these Ciuil broiles,
Vnciuill Warres, and sence-amizing[1] times :
Brothers by brothers spoild,—vnnaturall spoiles,

---

[1] Transition-form of ' amazing '. G.

The guilt whereof to Ioue's tribunall climes ;
Oh subiects fit for Thæban Statius' rimes.
All Warres are bad, but finall end doth tell,
Intestine Warres all other Warres excell.

Witnesse the same, the Macedinian downe,
When Pompey did the Senate's cause defend,
And Cæsar sought the world's imperiall crowne :
Witnesse Phillipe's and Antonius' end,
Milde Otho's death which authors so commend.
  Richard now riseth at his nephewe's fall:
  A conscience cleare is like a brazen wall.[1]

Now England's Traiane sprung from Troiane race,
Doth Oxford helpe and Darbie's aide implore,
Froth-facèd Neptune with his trident mace
Doth guide his argosies to Milford's shoare,
At Bosworth field he slaies the tuskèd boare.
  Leicestrian dales their crimson goare did fill,
  A scarlet streame from Richard did distill.[2]

Cheiney, thy armes and sinewes are not strong
Enough to match with Albion's maitiall king :
Brandon, thou dost thy youthfull vigor wrong.

---

[1] Richard 3. H.
[2] The battle of Bosworth. H. [See Sir John Beaumont's " Bosworth Field " in our edition of his complete Poems. G.]

To combat him who to the field did bring
Those cruell parts which Colingbourne did sing :
  Now Consolation's wings doth reare my minde,
  To shew his praise, who sprang from Priam's
    kinde.

Great impe of kings,[1] heroicke Theodore,
England's Augustus, famous prince of peace,
Great treasurer of sacred Vertue's store,
Eden of pleasure which didst all men please,
Comfort of Albion, and thy countrie's ease :
  From the foure golden fountaines did arise,
  Like vnto those that sprang from Paradise.[2]

Oh that I had all Witte's excelling witte,
To eternallize thy deeds, immortall king :
My pen thy trophies should, and triumphes writte,
The triple lauor[3] of this round should ring
With thy great name, which my great Muse should
    sing.
  But since that Nature did the same denie,
  Accept my will, ætheriall dietie.

---

[1] Henry 7. H.
[2] Arthur, Henry, Margaret, Mary. H.
[3] Transition-form of ' laver' : = the dome of the sky.
G.

Elizabeth![1] O princely, perfect name,
Combinde with thee, O cheerfull, cordiall knot:
No priuate quarrell could white Albion fame :
With blood and rapine fierce dissention blot,
Fury itselfe, within it selfe did rot.
   Two parted Roses which so long did striue,
   Grew on one stalke, and both began to thriue.

From that faire stalke great Arthur first did rise,
Arthur who match't with Castile's Katherine :
Childlesse he dide, and death he did despise,
His body was intombde in gorgeous scrine,[2]
His soule ascended, for it was diuine.
   Henry, then prince and heire apparant was,
   Henry, which did all former Henries passe.[3]

The snow-white cliffes which Albion do confine,
Whose subiecte[4] sands are deckt with margarites
Clearer then is the clearest christaline,
The towring waues which rule the narrow streights,

---

[1] Elizabeth, eldest daughter to Edward the 4th was
married to Henry the 7th, by which marriage both the
houses of Yorke and Lancaster, so long seuered, were
vnited. H.
  [2] Shrine. G.
  [3] Henry 8. H.
  [4] Misprinted ' subiects'. G.

Which do adumbrate sleepy rockes' deceits,
  Could not debarre his thoughts, but he did goe
  To conquer France, and England's greatest foe.

Wolsey then liu'd, high-minded, worthy clarke,
Which did erect those glorious towres of yore,
Learning's receptacle, Religion's parke.[1]
O that some eagle-mounting thought would soare
To finish that which he began before.
  Oh that some prince—for none but princes can—
  Would perfect that excellent worke of man.

The siluer Isis and the gliding Thame,
When billowes resalute the verdant strand,
Should warble pæans to his mightie name;
The leaden age is past which rulde the land,
Saturne is come, and Saturne doth command :
  Whose hopes were dead—rich students, neuer
    feare,
  —Most rich in hope—some will your turrets
    reare.

Nurse of ingenious spirits, Athens' praise
Chiefe benefactor of what ere is mine :
O might I see some mightie monarch raise
Those halfe built walles and parted towres com-
    bine,

---

[1] Christ Church in Oxford. H.

Then Christ might yet be iustly tearmèd thine :
  As Christ is best, so should His houses bee,
  And in perfection haue a sympathie.

Henrie's triumphant carkasse laid in graue,
Couered with gold in Cæsar's ancient towre,
Edward succeeds : a prince though yong,[1] yet
    graue ;
The skye which whilome smilde begins to lowre,
And showres of sorrow on the land to powre.
  He endes his life before it scarce began :
  What is more short then shortest life of man.

When Nature fram'd this prince, oh goodly
    creature,
Compos'd of pure and elementall fire :
Turnd in a heauenly mowld, diuinest feature :
She saw herselfe deceiu'd, and wroth with ire,
When life began, his end she did desire.
  What enuie so could thee proud Nature sting ?
  Nothing should make and marre, the selfe same
    thing.

The gods did enuie man's felicitie,
And therfore did to Nature condescend :
That this yong king, great king of Maiestie,

---

[1] Edward 6. H.

In sixteene yeares his vitall course should spend :
His life hath end, and all our ioyes haue end.
    Nature doth hasten to the house of Death,
    And shee consents to steale away his breath.

Now Spayne and England ioynes[1] : that peace I
        loue,
That concord doth augment the common State ;
Pray God it doth both firme and faithfull proue,
But for to match with Spayne, oh cruell fate,
Could Mary so her countrey ruinate ?
    Guiltlesse shee was, but those that made the
        match,
    Vnder their wings did egges of serpents hatch.

Oh now me thinkes I could in dismall blacke
Shadow my lookes, and neuer wish the light :
Writing red lines of blood, more blacke then
        blacke,
The massacres of man's amazing sight.
After these duskie cloudes, comes clearest light,
    Mary is dead, Elizabeth doth raigne,
    Her conscience cleare, no corasiue could staine.

---

[1] Queene Mary, married with Phillip, Prince of
Spayne. H.

The losse of Elizabeth.

AIRE virgin, empresse, royall princely
maide,
Sprung from the damaske Rose, the
Rose's bud :
'Tis true as truth it selfe which men haue saide,
The end is best, though all the meanes be good :
She was the last and best of Henrie's blood.
  Henry did well in all, excell in this,
  In getting of this maide, our greatest blisse.

He vaquisht Bolleine and strong Turnus' towne,
And rode in tryumph through the English pale :
Placing the diademe of France, that regall crowne,
Vpon his sister's temples ; and withall
Made the twelue peeres to feare their finall fall.
  But what of these ? if Bullain had not bin,
  We all had liu'd for aye in endles sin.

Astronomers did dreame and fondly saide,
That twelue designèd signes did rule a spheare :
Virgo did guide the earth ; oh heauenly maide !
But now sky-teachers, wise men neuer feare,
To say she is in heauen, for sure shee's there.
  Oh shee is gone ! with her our pleasure's fled,
  They liu'd in her, they dide when she was
  dead.

Bright gem of honor, Albion's glorious starre,
The cynosure of England's hemispheare :
Princesse of peace, Cytherian queene of Warre,
Rides through the cloudes on her cælestiall beare,[1]
Conquering Deathe's ebon dart and sharpest speare.
 Fathers of peace put on triumphant weedes,
 A gratious king, a gratious queene succeedes.

Reason's first founder, Nature's eldest sonne,
The Stoikes' prince, did also erre in this :[2]
Repugnant natures neuer raigne in one :
Perfect my griefe, more perfect is my blis,
I smile with ioy, yet teares my cheekes do kisse.
 A present salue hath cured a pensiue sore,
 Britaine is now, what Britaine was of yore.

The wandring Brute, who sprang from Priam's
  kinde,
Though artlesse men with their malignant muse,
Still bearing burning enuie in their minde,
Britaine's first monarch, warlike Brute abuse,
Of all the northern world, this Isle did chuse.
 With fire and sword he did obtaine his sute,
 With peace and ioy we chuse a second Brute.

---

[1] = bier. G.
[2] Aristotle, Plato. H.

Peace, valure, learning, science hee did bring:
Thou feare of God, Whom thou doest onely feare,
Imperiall monarche, Truth and Concorde's king,
No champion then did weild his fruitlesse speare,
No chaine did tye the milde vntaméd Beare,
   Saturne then liued, no Sinon did amisse,
   All men were free—no slaue by Nature is—

Oh sacred age, and blessed times of yore,
When iust Astræa rul'd this circled plaine :
Then each man liu'd alike, and liu'd withstore,
No Persian blood did Salamina stayne,
No Vandals Rome, nor Romane gouernd Spayne,
   No Canna's chaunce did cause Saturnia mourne,
   No sencelesse Nero wisht new Troy to burne.

No Manlius sought a diademe to gaine,
No iust Papirius sude for Fabius' bloud :
Claudius as then did not Virginia stayne,
No consulls fell at Alia's flaming flood,
Red Chærea was not dewde with Fabys' blood,
   Albans and Romanes knew no single fight,
   Saffetius did not yeeld to Martius might.

The vnspotted spowse of martiall Collatine,
Did not consent to Sextus' lawlesse lust :
Each virgin was ybound with Vesta's line,
Camillus needed not the Ardeans trust,
245

Nor Sceuola his hand in flames to thrust.
  But see, oh see how age doth follow age,
  Worse after worse, as actors on a stage,

Thrice happy Britaine, strong vnited Ile,
Disioynted was by her first monarche's fall :
Then Albanact was slaine by Humber's guile,
Cæsar then conquer'd it, who conquered all,
Hunes, Pictes and Danes tryumph't in Britaine's
    fal.
  Vaile Sorrowe's roabes, Ioue's father comes
    againe,
  The golden age begins with Iacob's raigne.

The lords great Stuart, Albion's mightie king,
Our second Brute, like to the morning starre,
To England's Court doth light of comfort bring,
Now Concord's boult doth Ianus' temple barre,
Binding in chaines the sternest god of Warre.
  Vertue and valour triumph euermore,
  Augustus liues adornd with Crassus[1] store.

---

[1] = Crœsus.   G.

To the Maiestie of King James, Monarch of all Britayne.

LL haile great monarch[1] of the greatest
        Ile,
        The northerne world's vnited lawfull
        king,
Pardon my rudest reede['s] vndecent stile :
Though I want skill in thy new empire's spring,
Yet doe I loue, and will thy prayses sing.
   Me thinkes I do on Claros kingdome stand :
   No maruaile, for Apollo rules the land.

On true obedience' knee I pardon aske
Of thy diuine heroicke maiestie ;
It was thy merites great, impos'd this taske
On my weake pen,—badge of infirmitie!
Too weake indeede to prayse thy excellency.
   Each cherril's[2] muse doth now salute thy grace :
   Shall I alone be mute and hide my face ?

Maro extold Augustus' peacefull daies,
The liricke poet sung Mecena's fame :
Ennius did Scipio Affricanus praise ;

---

[1] James the 1. of England and 6 of Scotland.   H.
[2] Transition-form of churl, as before.   G.

If all they liu'd and saw thy sacred name,
Each verse they made should sure containe the
    same.
    But if they reade thy gift,[1]—oh princely worke!
    For shame they would in vntrode desarts lurke.

If England's lcade-starre, pride of Poesie,[2]
Could the firme center's regiment transpearse,
And formalize his peerlesse ingeny,[3]
Thy all surpassing vertues to rehearse;
A princely matter fitts a princely verse :
    Yet were his wit too weake thy deeds to praise,
    Which brought vs ioyes in our most mournfull
    daies.

Could Lidgat passe the tower of Proserpine,
And like to Virbius[4] liue a double age,
Penning thy trophies in a golden skrine :
Yet could he not thy merits equipage,
Admiring, most would vse a tapinage ;[5]
    Bocchas and Gowre, the Virgils of their time,
    Could not vnfold thy praise in antique rime.

---

[1] Pasilicon Doron. H.
[2] Chaucer, so called by M. Camden. H.
[3] = genius. G.
[4] Cf. Ovid, Metam. xv. 544. G.
[5] = seek a hiding place. G.

If these foure poets liu'd, like lions foure,
They should thy famous coach of glory drawe
From Vertue's temple to true Honour's towre :
Each should a kingdome haue ; thy foes should
    know
Thy might, and feare their finall ouerthrow.
    But what should muses sing ? the world doth see,
    And seeing, feares Vnited Britany.

Still liuing Sidney, Cæsar of our Land,
Whose neuer daunted valure, princely minde,
Imbellishèd with art and Conquest's hand,
Did expleiten his high aspiring kinde :
—An eagle's hart in crowes we cannot finde—
    If thou couldst liue, and purchase Orpheus' quill,
    Our monarch's merits would exceed thy skill.

Albion's Mæonian Homer, Nature's pride,
Spenser, the Muses sonne and sole delight:
If thou couldst through Diana's kingdome glide,
Passing the palace of infernall night :
—The sentinels that keepes thee from the light—
    Yet couldst thou not his retchlesse[1] worth com-
        prise,
    Whose minde containes a thousand purities.

---

[1] = reach-less, unequalled. G.

What fatall chance is this, and lucklesse fate,
That none can aptly sing thy glorious prayse,
And tell the happinesse of England's state?
O barren time and temporizing dayes,
Fowle Ignorance on sacred Learning prayes.
  But now I doe a diapazon see,
    None but thy selfe—great king—can sing of
    thee.

That Macedonian starre, first prince of Greece,
Sent for that wandring learnèd Stagirite,[1]
To teach his sonne knowledge of knowledges:
His sword was keene, his sense could ill indite:
Thy sword is sharpe, and who can better write?
  He had another to instruct his sonne,
  What he by others did, thy selfe hath done.

Some, Cæsar deemde, the happiest mortall wight,
That breath'd the ayre, or did ascend the skye,
For conquering Scipio's force and Pompei's might;
Some did Augustus iudge more happy, why?
Because he vanquisht Ægypt's Anthony;[2]
  Rome's holy prince, said Nerua did surpasse,
  For learning such a sonne as Traian was.

---

[1] Philip, Aristotle.   H.

[2] Such is the text, except 'he' misprinted 'the'. Is
Augusta or Cleopatra intended?   G.

If those olde wisards which of yore did sing,
Read with impartiall eyes thy peerlesse deeds,
—Great prince of Warre, of Peace thrice happie
        king—
Concord should reconcile their striuing reeds,
And sensures ioyne, which censures enuy breeds.
    Cæsar's acts, Augustus' peace, good Nerua's
        kinde,
    In thee alone, in none but thee, we finde.

The siluer moone plac'd in her circle round,
At her encrease, her equall distant hornes
Vpwards ascends, as scorning abiect ground :
So when the world's great honour first was borne,
That fayre arising sunne, cleere facèd morne,
    Her mounting thoughts did to the heauens toure,
    Scorning the earth, or any terrene bowre.

But when that virgin's goddesse doth decrease,
Her pickèd forkes their course to Terra bend :
So when our England's Luna's light did cease,
The Artike clime an Vnicorne did send,
Whose radiant lusture, night shall neuer end :
    Phœbe's cleere light seemes darke, whilst he
        doth shine,
    He borrowes perfect light of God diuine.

Those that do reade the secrets of the skie,

Whose iudgement is in heauen conuersant :
Which portraiture the signes in heauenly die
Might asseuere that Virgo was on high :
I sawe a starre of late from heauen flie :
   Why cannot this starre then faire Virgo bee ?
   A starre more chaste I thinke we cannot see.

O now my thoughts can diue into the deepe,
Our all ship's guiding starre was fixèd there :
And when Eliza did with honor sleepe,
Mounted vpon her praise-deseruing beare,[1]
She did obtaine of him she lou'd so deare,
   That she might haue his seate, he rule the Land
   Which she of late as empresse did commaund.

The anatomizers of our learnèd daies,
Affirme that Virgo do the belly guide :
No wonder then that Albion's wondrous praise,
That virgin queene which here on earth did bide
So nourisht each poore hunger-bitten side.
   Now she is dead, oh who will them reliue ?
   The present starre doth present comfort giue.

I heard an aged woman often say,
That shee did see a starre from heauen descend :
Which was as true me thought as trees did bray :

---

[1] Bier. G.

For she alledg'd the same, and did commend
A certaine crowe, whose wit she did defend.
 Pardon me Age, for now mine eyes do see
 A starre on earth, more bright than starre can
  bee.

To whom shall I this northerne starre compare ?
To Cæsar, which first did subdue the State ?
To Horsus who no limbe of Christ did spare,
Damming his soule this Land to ruinate ?
Great William's conquest and the Normane's hate ?
 Thus doth my muse all wanting art begin,
 To sing thy vertues, and to shewe their sin.

Cæsar was twice repulst ere he could see,
This litle world, from all the world remote :
Before we sawe thy face we sent to thee,
As to a pilot for to guide our boate :
Which did in seas of suddaine sorrow floate.
 He lost his sword before he conquest wan,
 Wee yeeld thee all our hearts, and all we can.

Horsus by cruell tyrant trechery,
Subdude Ambrosius, that wise prince of peace :
Witnesse the hidden kniues at Salisbury ;
He trauaile brought, but thou doest bring vs ease,
Thy true descent makes greedy warres to cease.

A wolfe possest his heart, a lyon thine,
He worse then man, thou better, more diuine.

William was fierce in warre, and so art thou ;
In counsell sage, thou doest them æqualize,
His sword forc't foes their trembling knees to
    bowe ;
Thou conquer'st hearts, by thy heart's winning
    eyes ;
By force he wan, by merits thou doest rise ;
    He brought subiection, thou doest freedome
        bring ;
    He louèd warre, but thou of peace art king.

Rufus was rude, thou ciuill, gentle kinde ;
He was austere, thy browes hath Mercie's frowne ;
He had a Nero's hart, thou Cæsar's minde,
He hunting lou'd, for pleasure tumbled downe
Many a castle fayre, and stately towne :
    Thou lou'st the chase, yet cities doest adorne ;
    Thou wert for all the world's great profit borne.

Henry was grac't with artes, thou doest excell :
Children did blesse his age but soone did dye :
Children thou hast in health and perfect well,
—God prosper them with pure prosperitie—
Adorne their harts with louing pietie :

He was a worthy king, thou worthier farre,
Thou are our Northerne-Pole, hart's-guiding
   starre.

Soare humble thoughts, and let my abiect pen
Touch the high-mounted Artike Northerne starre,
And there compare this man excelling men :
We should compare the things that equall are,
And who is like this light, this lampe, this starre ?
   Mine eyes distill sweete teares, the teares of ioy,
   To see Troye's issue raigne in new found Troy.[1]

Let Barland cease to write of wisest kings,
And Mellificius with his tuned voyce,
From whose sweet song sprang Learning's sweetest
   springs :
Sing not of Persians' prayse or Caldeans' ioyes
The Grecian's Emperour, Europ's worthiest choyce.
   These three combinde, each sought the other's
     fall,
   Britaine is ioynd, and Concord guides it all.

When Alexander sawe that precious stone,
Vnder whose isye[2] wings Achilles lay :

---

[1] The Troy-Novant of the mythic-legends, = London.
G.

[2] = icy.   G.

Shedding ambitious teares, he said with mone,
Vnhappy I, and ten times happy they,
Whose ensignes praise, sweet Homer did display :
   Then happy art thou king whose raigne we see,
   Homer doth sing thy praise, for thou art hee.

The maiestie of Marius' feareful face
Did terrifie the Cymbrians' crauen minde
Though he were armde with Clothos fatall mace,
And solemne oath to murther did him binde,
A wandring Bucke did feare the Eagle's kinde :
   So did thy princely lookes and grace of God
   Protect thy issue from a traytor's rod.

Now doth my ship in Plentie's ocean sayle,
Pusht with a pleasant gale of Pleasure's winde :
But stay I hear[1] an enuious Momist rayle :
Thy toothlesse threate doth not amaze my minde ;
Barke, for thou canst not bite, I scorne thy kinde.
   That which I write I reade, and both are true,
   I doe not, nor I will not tell what will ensue.

My hope is good that we shall happy bee,
Hopelesse our foes ; they feare, we still secure :
We peace, they Warre : ye[a][2] endlesse peace shall
   see :

---

[1] Misprinted 'here' G.   [2] Qy. 'we. G.

We plenty haue, they pouerty endure,
Religion we sincere, but they impure.
   They liuing seeme to dye, we dying gaine,
   To liue with saints in Paradisus' plaine.

What said the learnèd, those that learning loue,
If causes perish, then effects decay :
Pray for the cause, yea, pray to God aboue
That He may long the Albion scepter sway,
Who shinde like Sol in our Cimmerian day.
   Liue, and liue long, great king, liue manye
      dayes,
Vse that fayre theame, Be as thou art alwayes.

Note—It is scarcely possible to identify our young
Poet's allusions (page 99) to ' Barland ' and ' Mellificius '.
His fine tributes to Chaucer, Gower, Lidgate and Spenser,
are noticeable (pp 92-3). G.

Finis.

Poeme to the Yong Prince.

TO THE WORTHY AND HONOURABLE GENTLEMAN, SIR PHILIP HARBERT, KNIGHT OF THE MOST NOBLE ORDER OF THE BATHE.

HE second time doth my vnworthy Muse
Salute thy milde aspect, thrise noble knight.
Let gracious censure his defects peruse
Whose genius waites on thy heroicke spright,
   Whose loue and life are bent to honour thee :
   And whilest breath lasteth vse both them and mee.

These Poems which my infant labours send
A s messengers of dutie to thine eares,
Are of small value, but if Nature lend
Some perfect dayes to my vnripened yeares,
   My pen shall vse a more iudicious vaine,
   And sing thy glory in a higher straine.
           Your Honour's at commaund.
               William Harbert.

TO THE IVDICIOVS READER.

WHICH in bloudy Warres haue steep'd
     my pen,
   Whose Muse the passing bell of Peace
     did wring,
And how the world did loose a world of men,
Now chuse to touch a more concordant string,
My Prince, his prayse, whose prayse Ile euer sing.
   'Tis no mechanicke hope of hirèd gaine
   That mou'd my minde these labours to sustaine.

No, that ignoble basenesse I abiure,
It was the loue I euer bare the place
Where first I breathèd life, did me allure,
In pleasant paines for to consume a space,
And her to prayse, though with mine owne
     disgrace :
   With my disgrace, why? though my verse be ill
   I do not doubt to please the good with will.

To thee iudicious Reader, do I send
These fruites of youth : 'tis thee I hope to please :
If that my Muse the ignorant offend,
No lines of mine their fury shall appease :
I set iust Warre before an vniust peace,
   I rayle, not I, though I with Plato say,
   To please the wise, must bee the wisest way.

A POEME TO THE YONG PRINCE.

HE lotted seruant to thy infant age
    Thrice glorious issue of a gracious king,
    Least that her twelue-monthes fearefull
      tapynage,[1]
Ingratitude suspect to thee should bring,
Me, though vnworthy, chose thy prayse to sing.
   Her mourning garments she hath cast aside,
   And hopes ere long to entertaine her bride.

The Cleargie with the Barons' borrowed light,
Is now obscured by thy transplendant shine :
The rochet nor the border hath no right
To rule, but that which doth from thee decline :
She ioyes and glories to be onely thine :
   Shee deemes it honour, count it no dispraise,
   For thee with her to spend thy yonger dayes.

No matchles Machauil, nor Arietine,
Doth her plaine-meaning breast with enuy breede.
Her wits doe moderne seeme, and not diuine,
Loyall her loue, though lowly is her weede,
A sympathie there is of word and deede :
   Such as these are, in Wales thine eyes shall see,
   Thousands that will both liue and dye with thee.

---

[1] As before, = hiding or retirement. G.

O was she euer false, vntrue, vnkinde,
Since her obedience did augment thy stile ?
Or since the parted Roses were combinde,
Did euer rebels' blood her brest defile ?
Or did she euer England's hopes beguile ?
   Witnesse the world, and those that liue therein,
   Her spotlesse soule did neuer taste that sin.

Search Truthe's records, not Time's illuding lines,
Then shall thy princely thoughts and eyes be fed
With the strange wonders of those warlike times,
When thy great grandsyres made our channels red
With blood of those that on our shoares laie dead :
   Teaching great Cæsar how to runne away,
   That neuer knew to flye before that day.

Ten yeares did Rome and all the world admire,
For all the world and Rome ten yeares did feare
The lusture of thy bekons set on fire,
Great Odonisis king, Charactaker,
Whose endlesse worth my worthlesse Muse shall
    reare
   To that bright spheare where honor doth re-
    maine ;
   She loues thee dead, thy life her loue did gaine.

What honor or what glory didst thou win
With the Earthes' strength to conquer but an ile,

Maister of the world's mistres, mightie king?
Onely this grac'd the greatnes of thy stile,
Claudius with blood did not his hands defile.
   This triumph Rome did thee as highly grace,
   As when by Scipio Affriqe conquerèd was.

How many legions Cæsar, didst thou send?
How many consuls did returne of thine,
Which sought what others marr'd, by Warres to
    mend?
How many emperours Britaine, did repine,
To see thy honor rise, their praise decline:
   Let Tacitus vnto the world declare,
   No land saue Rome might with this land com-
    pare.

I know yong prince, and am agreeu'd to see
The leeuy'd lookes of squint-eyde Theonym,
Who saies this fault is proper vnto mee,
To iudge all others base, our selues diuine:
No, enuious Momist, 'tis no fault of mine:
   That some are so, I must confesse 'tis true,
   All are not bad of vs, nor good of you.

The mellow fields haue tares as well as corne,
And thistles grow amidst the greenest grasse:
An Anacharse in Tartary was borne.
Vertue, and vice do meete in euery place,

Clodius in Rome as well as Milo was.
　Both good and bad in euery land we see,
　And so are you, if of a land ye bee.

Curbe the malignant pride of Enuie's rage,
And checke the stubborne stomackes of Disdaine,
These penny poets of our brazen stage
Which alwayes wish—O let them wish in vaine—
With Rossius gate[1] thy gouernment to staine :
　Make them more milde, or be thou more austere,
　'Tis vertue vnto vice to be seuere.

I speake not this vnto the learnèd wise,
For them I loue, because the truth they loue :

---

[1] By 'Rossius gate' I understand 'Rossius gait'
Roscian, or the Latin *Roscianus*: and the meaning to be
'theatrical, and so glory-loving'. This perhaps meets
Mr. Collier's difficulty. I may remark that the three
errata pointed out by him in ' Cadwallader' will scarcely
be accepted I must respectfully submit, as such. For 'shut'
our Poet's spelling of ' shoot ', not as Mr. Collier supposes
a misprint or meaning ' closed ', he would read ' shot '
(page 79th, line 1st,) for 'milde ' he would read 'wilde'
but the change would reverse the intended character
(page 81st, line 9th,) and for ' parke ' he would substitute
' sparke'. The reference is to the ' grounds ' of the College
and 'sparke' should make nonsense (page 84th, line 6th).
See my Note at end of our Memorial-Introduction. G.

'Tis the bleard iudgement of Sedition's eyes,
That doth my Muse and my affection moue,
A most vnwilling Satirist to proue :
 Nature hath made me milde, but these hard men
 Turn'd my soft quill into a brazen pen.

Play not the satyr, peace-affecting Muse,
I doubt not but their conscience will prouoke
These Lucilists their follies to refuse,
And make them soft, though they were hard as
  oke :
Conscience makes bad men good, so wise men
  spoke :
 I leaue them to their spurres : my Muse shall
  flye
 Vnto that sphere where Enuy dares not prye.

Vnto that sphere whose circuit doth containe
The neuer spotted essence of his soule,
Whose sacred intellect no worldly staine
Could with Desire's rebelling aide controule :
This guilded sphere is like a golden boulè,
 Which many lesser mazers doth containe,
 So many vertues in this one do raigne.

Why partiall Nature, stepdame to my birth,
Ye mixèd elements, Affection's slaues,
Why did ye frame this vessell but of earth ?

An equall matter to the dead men's graues :
And ioynd thereto a spirit like the waues :
    Low as the Earth although my genius be,
    Yet doth it touch skye-threatning maiestie.

O were my wit but equall to my will,
Were I as wise as I am ignorant,
Here were a place that would deserue my skill :
Had I as great experience as I want,
Then would I in a booke of adamant,
    And inke compos'd by water made of golde,
    With pens of diamond thy prayse vnfolde.

Let Iustice rule the organ of thy speech,
And Clemency adorne thy princely browe :
Vnto thine eares long absent Patience teach,
By those which good men wish, let all men knowe,
None but thy selfe, thy selfe can ouerthrowe.
    Let Pittie check the rod when we offend,
    That makes the good more good, the bad to
        mend.

I witnesse call the seuen hillèd Queene,
How we obey'd, when Lawes obey'd were :
And shall not we be now as we haue bene ?
Feare made vs then vnnaturall bondage beare,
We now securely liue and cannot feare.

Doubt not thereof, but come, experience haue,
We loue to serue, but loathe the name of slaue.[1]

Our gazing expectation longs to see
The true admirèd image of thy syre :
Which Nature hath so rightly grau'd in thee :
As phisicke causes seem'd, they did conspire
To shape thee like to him whom all admire.
   So Sion's sacred finger, Dauid saies,
    Good trees bring forth good fruit, good fruit
    alwaies.

Do not sweete sallets spring from soundest seed ?
And is not man like God, which man did make ?
Can bad effects from causes good proceed ?
Do we see fruite on any withered stake ?
Or do we see in sea a bush or brake ?
   How canst thou then not good and perfect bee,
   That were engraft on such a goodly tree ?

---

[1] Cornelius Tacitus in the life of Agrippa. H.

𝔉𝔦𝔫𝔦𝔰,

MISCELLANIES

OF

The Fuller Worthies' Library.

THE

POEMS

OF

HUMFREY GIFFORD,

GENTLEMAN:

(1580)

Edited, with Memorial-Introduction and Notes,

BY THE

REV. ALEXANDER B. GROSART,

ST. GEORGE'S, BLACKBURN, LANCASHIRE.

PRINTED FOR PRIVATE CIRCULATION.
1870.
156 COPIES ONLY.

Contents.

CONTENTS.

Memorial-Introduction.

ITSON in his 'Bibliographia Poetica' (1802: p 219) and the bibliographical books earlier and later, simply give the title-page, with varying correctness (or incorrectness) of the "Posie of Gilloflowers", having literally nothing to tell of its author, 'Humphrey Gifford, Gent.' For the three quarters of a century nearly, since RITSON recorded the volume, strange to say, the single exemplar in the Royal Library of the British Museum, remains unique.[1] Ellis and Farr—the former in his well-known "Specimens", the latter in the 'Selections' of the Parker Society—have given quotations from the 'Posie'; but neither added a syllable to our knowledge of the Poet.

Our researches have been wide and persistent and warmly seconded by many fellow book-lovers. The result is sadly disproportionate to the expenditure in every form. Nevertheless we are able to give a little, and perchance have opened veins

---

[1] Press-mark 239, G. 33.

of inquiry that may hereafter yield something
more substantive. The Devonians are to a pro-
verb proud of their county : and rich as is her
roll of illustrious names, the memory of the
"sweet Singer" of the 'Posie', is worthy of
pains to recall and preserve, for Devonshire and
all England.

JOHN GUILLIM in his "Display of Heraldry"—
accepting the original name as the Author—thus
wrote under the name and shield of Gifford:
"He beareth SABLE, 3 Fusils[1] in Fess *Ermine*, by
the name of Gifford, a Family of long continuance
in HALSWORTH in Devonshire from whence des-

---

[1] My friend Mr. Shelly of Plymouth, informs me that
in a MS. catalogue of Arms of Devonshire Gentry, A.D.
1689 in the Public Library there, is the following entry :
"Gifford of Brightley, Halsbury and Tiverton, Sable 3
lozenges (= Guillim's ' fusils ', which is only a different
name for the same charge) in fess Ermin. The crest is a
morecock's head erased Proper, having in his bill an ear
of corne Or," Edmondson in his " Compleat Body of
Heraldry " repeats Guillim's misprint of Halsworth. Mr.
Coffin, (as onward) confirms Guillim *supra* from a Heraldry MS. by Richard Coffin, of Portledge, who was Sheriff
of Devon in 1685, as follows: " Gifford of Halesbury
hath long continued there, of whom is descended Hum.
Gifford of the Poultry, London, an industrious gentleman
and of judgement as a collector of rarities and antiquities."

cended that great Collector of choice Rarities, Humfrey Gifford, of the Poultrey Compter, London, Gent ".[1] There is no such place as 'Halsworth' in Devonshire. It is a misprint or inadvertence for Halsbury, or as it is sometimes spelled Halesbury. Turning thither, I find from the present accomplished Rector of Parkham, near Bideford (Edward Hensley, M. A.) within which Halsbury is situate, that the Parish Registers— in admirable preservation from 1547 onward—and the Church itself, abound with notices of the Giffords, Giffards, Gyffords, (all the same): but neither here nor elsewhere, have I come upon much that is definite on our Humphrey Gifford:[2] It were well-nigh endless to reproduce the many Register and monumental 'entries' with which

---

[1] I quote from the 6th edition 1724 folio p 369 : but may state that the little notice of Gifford did not appear until 1660 edition (§ iv. c. 19. page 355), not being in either the 1st. edn. (1610) or 2d. or 3d. edition. I owe thanks to G. E. Adams Esq of the College of Arms for collation of the different editions. Here and elsewhere I have also to acknowledge unfailing help rend ered byMr. W. Winters of Waltham Abbey.

[2] The neighbouring Church of Buckland Brewer's Register, dates only from 1603 (too late) and Alvington's does'nt go back beyond 1700. In the former are several

I have been kindly favoured by Mr. Hensley and
by the Rev. F. O. Giffard M.A. of Hartley Wint-
ney, Hartford Bridge, the latter descending from
the Halsbury Giffords—one of not a few living
representatives high in the service of the State, on
sea and shore, two also viz : Sir H. A. Giffard and
his sister the late Lady Follet, known to a private
circle as ' wooers of the Nine '.

I would mention one small fact from Parkham,
namely, that a Katherine Gyfford of Halsbury,
born October 12th, 1541, was in all probability
the ' Katherine' Gifford married to Thomas
Moncke, of Pudderydge, grandfather of General
Moncke. The Rector recently discovered a slab
in the Church, which was first laid down to the
memory of ' Katherine Moncke, Wydowe ', date
' Nov. 2, 1595 ', and subsequently reversed and
engraved in memory of the wife of Roger Giffard
of Halsbury, 1685, and Bridgett, his daughter,
and Dorothy, his 2d· wife, 1712.[1]

---

entries relative to Halsbury Giffords, so that it is just
possible the missing portion of the Register contained
our Humphrey Gifford's baptism. So too the Parish
Registers of Milton Damerill, whence the paternal Gifford came, date only from 1685. I have to acknowledge
the willinghood to oblige of the several Incumbents.

[1] Mr. Coffin writes me ' The armes of the Monkes shew

Failing to trace our Worthy in Devonshire : and equally failing to connect him with the many pedigree-stems and twigs found in PRINCE's 'Worthies of Devon ' and RISDON's ' Surrey of Devon ' and FULLER's ' Worthies ' (*s. n.* Devon ' Sheriffs ') and POLE's 'Pedigree of the Giffards,' and numerous other authorities, I plunged into the *mare magnum* (not to say chaos) of the British Museum MSS. Various Gifford ' Pedigrees' were fortunately come on : one specially valuable—Harleian MSS. 1041, fol. 58. Starting with a John Gifford of Halesbury (= Halsbury) who came of Joan, wife unto Bartholomew Giffard, of Halesbury, daughter of Peter de Halesbury in Edward Ist's time, grandson of Walter de Halesbery in Henry IId's time, whose ancient 'inheritance' Halesbury was :[1] and passing very many descents and intermarriages, I find an Anthony (latinized 'Antonius' Gifford ' second sonne' of (apparently) a Thomas Gifford, and this Anthony married to a Dorothy Weekes or Wykes (latinized Dorothea), with the following family : —

---

90 quarterings, and those of the Giffords appear twice : but I cannot see that a Thomas Monke of Pudderydge ever married a K. Gifford. G.

[1] Risdon, as before, edn. 1811,p. 242.

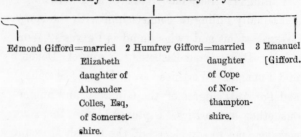

Anthony Gifford = Dorothy Wykes

Edmond Gifford = married   2 Humfrey Gifford = married   3 Emanuel
        Elizabeth   daughter   [Gifford.
        daughter of   of Cope
        Alexander   of Nor-
        Colles, Esq,   thampton-
        of Somerset-   shire.
        shire.

By another 'very ancient' Manuscript, in the
possession of a recognized Antiquary and Geneal-
ogist, (J. B. Pine Coffin, Esq., of Portledge,
Bideford) our Anthony Gifford had for first-born
an Emanuel Gifford " de Tapeley in com. Devon,"
and Edmond 2nd, Humfrey, [latinized *Humphredus*]
3rd, and a William 4th.   Emanuel's descendants
are traced herein : but not Humfrey's.   G. E.
Adams, Esq., of the College of Arms (London)
has also favoured me with a pedigree taken from
the Visitation of Devon, 1620.   It agrees with
that of Mr. Coffin's.   We can hardly be mistaken
in accepting this second (or third) son of Anthony
Gifford—in Mr. Coffin's MS. described as " de
Milton Damerell in com. Devon "—as our Humfrey Gifford, all the more so that the designation
of him as married to a Cope is confirmed by the
pleasantly respectful, respectful yet affectionate
terms, of one of the Epistles-dedicatory of the

" Posie " to Cope of Edon, Northamptonshire. It
will be seen that our Poet was fully warranted by
his lineage, to add and have added *'gent'* to his
name. The marriage to a Cope probably carried
no little romance in it: for various of his Verses,
especially those to 'gentlewomen'—one or more
—have a fire of passion in them, significative of
deeper then mere lovers quarrels : if I err not
pointing to family influences interfering to delay
at least. More of this anon. Meanwhile I note
that the Harleian MS, gives our Humphrey two
sons, Anthony and Dolorus, and three daughters
viz Katherine, Agnes and Elizabeth : while another (Harleian MS. 1080 fol 30) describes Katherine, daughter of Humphrey Gifford, as wife of
Dr. William Kinson, concerning which Doctor (of
theology or medicine I know not) nothing appears
to have survived.[1] With relation to the name of
'Dorothy', of Humfrey Gifford's mother, it is to
be noted that in the acrostics of the opening
verse-prayer, the commencement of the lines (1st
column) makes 'Dorothy', with 'Samuel and
Daniel thereafter, and then the name 'Danvers'.
'Danvers' again comes up in the intermarriages

---

[1] I tried "Notes and Queries" and various private
sources in vain.

of our Poet's other friend-patron, Stafford of
Blatherwick, Sir Humphry Stafford having married Elizabeth, daughter of Sir Thomas Cave of
Stanford, Knt, by his wife Elizabeth, daughter
and co-heir of John *Danvers* of Chamberhouse,
Berks, the covenants of marriage, being dated
October 4th 1547 : and again in the records of the
the intermarriages of the Copes and Staffords, viz
in the Will of Anthony Coope of Bedhampton Esq
1586, one legacy is to "Anne Gyfforde £10
which I owe her by obligation ".[1]

Our quotation from GUILLIM, describes our HUM-
FREY GIFFORD as "that great collector of choice
rarities ". Perhaps the phraseology points to
the title-page of the "Posie": or it may mean
that he was of antiquarian tastes and cul-
ture. Further, he is designated "of the Poultrey Compter, London ". The "Poultry Compter" was one of the "Prisons for Debt" of
the Metropolis—so vehemently assailed in contemporary pamphlets and later, in verse and prose.
Good old STOW thus writes of the Prison, "On
this North side [of the Poultry] some four houses

---

[1] See a very interesting Paper in response to my QUERY
in N. and Q , for September 24th, 1870 (4th S. vi., pp.
250-251) by Mr. B. W. Greenfield of Southampton.

west from this Parish Church of St. Mildred, is a prison-house, pertaining to one of the Sheriffs of London, and is called Compter in the Poultry, and hath been kept and continued time out of mind : for I have not read of the original there of ":[1] and again " The Poultry Counter, being the Prison belonging to one of the Sheriffs of London, for all such as are arrested within the city and liberties thereof. And besides this Prison, there is another of the same nature, in Wood-street, for the other Sheriff......Under the Sheriffs there are divers other officers belonging to both Counters......(1) The first and principal officer next to the Sheriff is the Secondary. Whose office is to return writs, mark warrants, impanel for the Courts, both above and below, and also for the Sessions. (2) The Clerk of the Papers, whose office is to impanel juries for the Sheriffs Court : he enters up judgement, and makes out all processes of the Sheriffs' Courts. (3) Four Clerk sitters......(4) Eighteen serjeants as Mace : and every sergeant hath his yeoman ".[2]

The present venerable holder of the office of Secondary (G. W. Killett Potter Esq)—for it

---

[1] Survey of London, edn. 1720, book iii. p 33.
[2] *Ibid* pp 50, 51.

still exists—has put himself to no small trouble within and without his office, including the Sherriff's, to get at any memorials of our Worthy in connection with the Compter: but fruitlessly, save that with pen and pencil he has given me quaint glimpses into far back days and ways.[1] The conclusion is, that he was a deputy or Clerk, no account of any of whom has been kept. He was not Secondary—or at least no record of his name occurs either in the Secondary office or the Corporation Books of the Town Clerk's office. *En passant* I recall that Christopher Hod-

---

[1] Mr. Potter, as *supra*, furnishes certain details that deserve preservation : " To each of the Compters there was a Secondary or London Under-sheriff. These in early times were great men, who purchased the situation of the Corporation and acted by their first and second clerks : and probably Humfrey Gifford was one of these, who were paid by a portion of their fees. No register was kept of either the Secondaries or of these clerks. Latterly the two Secondaries acted together. I became one by purchase upwards of half-a-century ago. On the death of my colleague I became under an arrangement with the Corporation, sole Secondary : the first and second clerks are done away, and I now act personally, with clerks appointed by myself." It is one of the pleasures of my literary work on the Worthies to have brought me into correspondence with one so well-informed, so courteous, and in a green old age so sprightly as Mr. Potter.

deson Esq., to whom John Hoddeson dedicates
"Sion and Parnassus" (1650)—whereto are pre-
fixed 'commendatory verses' by "glorious John"
(Dryden)—was "secundary of the Upper Bench."

Such is our little all of biographic fact—beyond the 'Posie'—concerning HUMPHREY GIFFORD.
I had hoped through Thomas Milbourne, Esq, the
Historian of St. Mildred's Church—within which
parish the 'Poultry Compter' stood—to have
found family-names and dates and burial : but
after every effort nothing came. We know at
present neither birth nor death-date. His one
pathetic memorial is the 'Posie of Gilloflower s'.

Looking within the Posie for more light, the Epistle-dedicatory to 'Edward Cope' of Eydon, already
noticed, indicates that in some way or other he
'served him'. Whatever his post was, it afforded
literary leisure : for he gratefully acknowledges
that by his worship's 'favourable permittance' he
had 'convenient opportunity' in his service 'to
bestow certain houres' amongst his 'bookes', adding finely, 'with which exercise, of all earthly
recreations I am most delighted'. He also places
his 'Maister' beyond 'all the worlde', his
'parentes excepted '—the except ion a pleasing
one, and illuminative of the memory of Mr.
Anthony and Mrs. Dorothy Gifford. He addressed

JOHN STAFFORD, Esq., of 'Bletherwicke' in similar kindly words, for 'professed curtesies and good
opinions.' The Copes and Staffords intermarried,
as we have had occasion to note. Both were of
ancient and eminent Houses. In its place I anno-
tate briefly the name of Stafford. Of 'Edward
Cope' I have been furnished with a good deal of
interesting detail, sent me by·his present collateral
representative, Sir William H. Cope. The main
facts to our purpose are, that he afterwards became
Sir Edward Cope, knight—that he was a 'strong
Puritan'[1] and that he lies buried in Bury St.
Edmunds, Suffolk, having died in 1620, after three
marriages, relating him successively to the Yelver-
tons, Raleighs and Astons. The 'G. C.' of the
answer-Verses to, a 'Dumpe' in the 'Posie' (pp
139—140—) was most probably a Cope, and so
with other occurrent C's.[2] It may finally be

---

[1] Witness Strype, Annals iii., P. 2, p. 452. The Bishop
is reporting on the justices in his diocese, and thus charac-
terises him "Ed. Cope, *armig.* an honest gentleman : but
that he doth over greatly countenance such preachers as
do impugn all orders established, which some others also
in this commission (i.e. of the Peace) do."

[2] 1 went expectantly to a modern Cope's reprint of his
ancestor Sir Anthony Cope's "Godly Meditacion vpon
XX Psalmes" (1547) : but full and interesting as is the

mentioned that the Canons Ashby Copes became
extinct in the male line, and that the estate passed
to the Drydens by Elizabeth Cope, (Edward's aunt)
who was thus grand-mother to 'glorious John'.[1]
Surely some day the 'fair Cope' wooed and won
by our Poet will be traced. For the present, the
Reader might do worse than turn to these among
other things of the 'Posie', reflecting the lights
and shadows of his love : 'A complaynt of a louer'
(pp 66—68) 'For his Friend' (pp 68—9) 'For
a gentlewoman' (pp 84—87 and 87—89) 'A New
Yeere's gift to a gentlewoman' (pp 97—99) 'Of
the uncontented state of louers" (pp 117—118),
'A renouncing of love' (pp 64—65).

The "Posie of Gilloflowers"—such fanciful title
re-calling Tregso's earlier "Daintie Nosegaie of
diuerse smelles" (1578) and later Chappell's
"Garden of Prudence" (1595)—as explained by
the Author in his Epistle-dedicatory, consists of
prose as well as verse : but in the solitary remain-
ing copy, the former is somewhat imperfect, and I

---

biographic Introduction, the Editor has nothing on either
Edward Cope or our Gifford. The Edward Cope, son of
Sir Anthony named, is not to be confounded with the
friend of our Worthy. The two were second cousins, or
as some call it, first cousins, once removed. (Sir W. H.
Cope, Bart., to me.) [1] Once more I owe thanks to Sir W.

rather think the Verse is deficient of a title-page
for it self. The translator praises highly, as in
duty bound, the Italian and French 'prose' that
he has rendered. There are good *bits* : but on
the whole one has a feeling of emptiness. I have
reprinted a favourable specimen, (pp. 36—40)
which is not without salt of humour.

The Verse of the "Posie" it is necessary to
state, from the somewhat ambiguous language
of RITSON, who describes it as "put together"
and as "collected", is GIFFORD's own. His words
to Stafford of Bletherwicke make this indisputable.
I quote a few of them : "the thing I here present
you with, is a posie of Gillowflowers collected out
of the garden *of mine own invention*". On one
apparent exception see in its own place (pp 113-
114).[1]

H. Cope,and also to Sir Henry Dryden, Bart., for painstaking information.

[1] It may be remarked that as there is not the slightest
reference anywhere in the "Posie" to any prior publication by the Author—original or translated—Mr. Hazlitt's
(conjectural) filling up of H. G. as = Humphrey Gifford,
in a translation of Boccacio (Handbook, p. 42 6a) is probably a mistake. This H. G. was more likely H. Grantham,
translator of Lentulo's Italian Grammar (1575). See Hand-
book. p. 333 *s.n.* Lentulo.

Our Singer tells us too, that his " Posie" consited
of Verses made at leisure-hours, that is, such as
later came to be known as ' occasional verses '.
Many of them bear out this, being self-revealingly
complimentary poems, written *currente calamo*, to
personal friends. Those to ' Gentlewomen ' are
tremulous with emotion : and as I have intimated
would guide us to autobiographic touches if only we
could get nearer the facts, His " Praise of the
contented minde " and " of Friendship " and
" Farewell Court " seem to me penetrated with
a fine and noble scorn of Mammon-worship.
These lines from the first, have the true ring :

" What doth auaile huge heapes of shining golde,
Or gay attyre, or stately buildinges brave : .
If worldly pelfe thy heart in bondage hold ?
Not thou thy goodes, thy goodes make thee their slaue,
For greedie men like Tantalus doe fare :
In midst of wealth they needie are and bare." (p. 55.)

But by far the most noticeable poem of the
" Posie "—and it *is* noticeable, —is the passion-
ate address " For a Gentlewoman ". The sentiment is manly and worthy in itself, the utterance
purged in its disdain of the player with a ' true
heart. ' There is this extrinsic about it also, that
if without the finish and power of our living
Laureate's immortal " Lady Clara Vere de Vere " its

burden and the movement of its measure, recall the later Singer in the quaintest way possible ; not a trick of memory merely but really. Let the Reader judge. Here is Tennyson—

" Lady Clara Vere de Vere,
    Of me you shall not win renown :
You thought to break a country heart
    For pastime, ere you went to town.
At me you smiled, but unbeguiled
    I saw the snare, and I retired ;
The daughter of a hundred Earls,
    You are not one to be desired.

Lady Clara Vere de Vere,
    I know you proud to bear your name ;
Your pride is yet no mate for mine,
    Too proud to care from whence I came.
Nor would I break for your sweet sake
    A heart that dotes on truer charms.
A simple maiden in her flower
    Is worth a hundred coats-of-arms.

Lady Clara Vere de Vere,
    Some meeker pupil you must find,
For were you queen of all that is
    I could not stoop to such a mind.
You songht to prove how I could love,
    And my disdain is my reply.
The lion on your old stone gates
    Is not more cold to you than I.''

Now for our HUMPHREY GIFFORD—let the Reader turn to " For a Gentlewoman ", occupying pp 84 —87, and 87—89.

Without italics, or other emphasis, if the Thinker read attentively and listeningly, he will be sure to catch the prelude here of the more splendid after-lyric.

Other of the flowers of the " Posie " seem to me to have been transplanted to the garden of FULKE, LORD BROOKE, or to speak not in allegory, I recognize the first putting into words of that meditative melancholy, not without flashes of wrath, running through and through the great 84th Sonnet of ' Cælica ' and its associate, Sir Edward Dyer's " Fancy ". I am not aware that this has ever been pointed out : I had not myself observed it when I was annotating Lord Brooke in the places. One little piece in Gifford and Brooke respectively, will confirm our judgment *e. g.* "A dolefull dumpe" (pp. 53—4). The Reader will please turn to and dwell on it.

Now LORD BROOKE :

"Who grace for zenith had, from which no shadowes
  grow :
Who hath seene ioy of all his hopes, and end of all his
  woe ;
Whose loue belou'd, hath beene the crowne of his desire ;

Who hath seene Sorrowe's glories, burnt in sweet Affec-
tions fire :
If from this heauenly state, which soules with soules
vnites,
He being falne downe into the darke despairèd warre of
sp'rits,
Let him lament with me ; for none doth glorie know,
That hath not beene aboue himselfe, and thence falne
downe to woe :
But if there be one hope left in his languish'd heart ;
If feare of worse, if wish of ease, if honour may depart,
He plays with his complaints ; he is no mate for me,
Whose loue is lost, whose hopes are fled, whose feares for
euer be"
                         (Works, Vol. III. pp 104-112) :

Even more striking are the resemblances in Sir
Edward Dyer's " Fancy", as will be seen on turning
to it (Works of Lord Brooke, Vol. III. pp 145-150)
and also in Southwell's " Complaint " (*ibid* pp 150-
154). The " Complaynt of a Louer " (pp 66-68).
and "For his Friende " (pp 68-69) and " a
Dumpe " (pp 138-139) also suggest that Lord
Brooke must have read the " Posie ". Even in
his conceits there are anticipations therein, as of
the ' heart ' of his lady-love being his hiding
place. (Posie, pp 99. Brooke, Vol. III. pp 11, 20
et alibi).
Very fine likewise in its stir and march, is the
summons " For Souldiers ", written be it remem-

bered while the air was full of ominous voices of
the invasion of the Spaniard, that a few years onward, culminated in the Armada. The measure is
peculiar but resonant, and the appeal is thrilling as
a trumpet. One marvels that in the dearth of
effective war-songs this has not long since found
its place. With every abatement, it is worthy to
be ranked with Campbell's, while the earlier has
even a higher tone. I cannot deny myself the
pleasure of quoting a few of the central lines of
this really great lyric.

"The time of Warre is come, prepare your corslet, speare
and shield,
Methinks I heare the drumme, strike doleful marches to
the field:
Tantara tātara, ye trūpets sound, wʰ makes our hearts wh
ioy aboūd.
The roring guns are heard afar, and every thing denounceth Warre;
Serve God, stand stoute, bold courage brings this geare
about.
Feare not ; forth run ; faint heart, faire lady never woone.
Yee curious carpet knights, that speude the time in sport
and play,
Abrode, and see new sights, your coūtrie's cause cals you
away :
Doe not to make your ladies game, bring blemish to your .
worthy name.

387

Away to field and win renoune, wt courage beat your
       enimies down :
Stout hearts gain praise, when dastards sayle in Slaunder's
       seas ;
Hap what hap°shal, we sure shal die°but°once for all.
Alarms me thinkes they cry, be packing mates, be gone
       with speed,
Our foes are very nigh, shame haue that man that shrinks
       at need ;
Unto it boldly let vs stand, God wil geue right the vpper
       hand ;
Our cause is good, we need not doubte ; in signe of cour-
       age geue a showte :
March forth, be strōg, good hap wil come ere it be long.
Shrinke not, fight well, for lusty lads must beare the bell."

                            (pp 59-62.)

Will the Reader next look at " A Merry Iest "
(pp 126—131) : and after studying it say whether
he does not agree with me in recognizing the dim
precursor of Cowper's " John Gilpin " in this
humorously told story ? Substance and structure
and turns of wording, inevitably remind of the
' famous ride'. There is the same näivete, the
same under-play of quiet fun, and the same
simple words. The " Pleasaunt Iest " (pp. 94—
97) and others, have the same vein. How truly
Cowperian the sense-nonsense of the " delectable
Dreame's " " his lippes were placde aboue his

chinne" (page 102) and "foure fingers and a thombe" (page 102) as if these were abnormal. I would similarly invite attention to "A New Yeere's Gift" (pp. 97—99) in a measure adopted by BURNS in some of his raciest songs.

Passing from the Poems in full, there are met with in the ' Posie' now familiar words and phrases that seem to have been primarily used by Gifford, or at least some of them—the limitation being demanded by the antiquarian notes of "Notes and Queries ".[1] Thus in the Epistle to the Reader (page 35) the Shakesperean student is arrested with this sentence. " Such *as take men's purses* from them undesired, passe often by the sentence of a cord, and shall such *as robbe men of their good names*, be suffered to escape scot free ". What if Shakespeare himself read the ' Posie" and consciously or unconsciously kept the words in his capacious memory? Be this as it may one is at once reminded of Othello (iii. 3)

---

[1] These references to Notes and Queries I deem it well to give here : On " call a spade a spade " see 1st Series IV. 274, 456 : 2nd Series, II. 26, 120 : III. 474 : X. 58 : on ' *bottle* of hay' 2nd Series, IV. 87, 176, specially the latter : on ' cock a-hoop' 1st Series, X. 56 : 2nd Series V. 426.

" *Who steals my purse* steals trash ————
But he that *filches from me my good name*,
Robs me of that which not enriches him
And makes me poor indeed."

Othello was first printed in 1622 : the " Posie "
in 1580.   Then, in the " Praise of Musick "
(page 93) occurs a verdict afterwards glorified by
Lorenzo :

" If Musike with her notes divine
    So great remorce can move,
I deeme that man bereft of wits,
    Which Musicke will not love,
She with her silver &c.

Every one remembers the Merchant of Venice
(v. 1)

.... " nought so stockish, hard and full of rage,
But music for the time doth change his nature.
The man that hath no music in himself,
Nor is not moved with concord of sweet sounds,
Is fit for treasons, stratagems and spoils :
The motions of his spirit are dull as night
And his affections dark as Erebus : "

There may be mere accidental use of the same
words in these two instances : but I like to do
honour to my ancient Worthy by thinking of the
possibility of SHAKESPEARE having valued the

" Posie ". Again, in the Epistle to the Reader, we
have the (now) trite "comparisons are odious"
thus, "if comparisons were not odious" (p. 32).
This is by many years anterior to Dr. Donne,
and equally so before Shakespeare's " comparisons
are odorous ". (Much ado about Nothing, iii. 5.)
So too phrases such as these, ' learned backwards '
(p. 36) ' necessary evils ' (p. 43) ' call a spade a
spade ' (p. 101). Our foot-notes mark a number
of interesting words also, with Shakesperean and
other illustrations in them. Altogether I must
be allowed to count on our reprint of the " Posie "
proving a right acceptable addition to our limited
treasury of early English Verse. Throughout, let
the date ' 1580 ' and perhaps 1560 of composition,
be kept in mind. Shakespeare says of " Gilloflowers "

> ...." the year growing ancient
> Nor yet on Summer's death, nor on the birth
> Of trembling Winter, the fairest flowers o' the season
> Are our carnations, and streak'd *gillyvors*
> Which some call, Nature's bastards: of that kind
> Our rustic garden's barren; and I care not
> To get slips of them."

Polixenes remonstrates with saucy Perdita
fruitlessly. I venture to echo him in relation to

our Singer's "Gilloflowers" without fear of a denial :

.........." make your garden rich in gillyvors,
And do not call them bastards."
                        (The Winter's Tale, IV. 4.)

May I hope that our revival of the "Posie" will stir up some Devonshire son to find out more than I have concerning this fine old ' Makkar' Devon ?

ALEXANDER B. GROSART.

St. George's, Blackburn, Lancashire.

Posie of Gillowflowers.

1580.

Note.

The original title-page of the Posie is as follows :

A

POSIE

of Gilloflowers, eche

differing from other in

colour and odour,

yet all sweete.

By Humfrey Gifford, Gent

¶ Imprinted at London

for John Perin, and are to be

solde at his shop in Paules

Churchyard, at the signe

of the Angell.

1580.

4to. 82 leaves, closing on V 2 *verso*, but no Sig U. For
further details see our little Memorial-Introduction. G.

II.

Epistle-Dedicatory of the Prose in the "Posie."

To the Worshipfull, his very good Maister, Edward Cope of Edon,[1] Esquier, Humfrey Gifforde wisheth many yeeres of prosperities.

AUING by your Worship's fauourable permittance, conuenient oportunity in your seruice, to bestow certain houres amongst my bookes,—with which exercise of all earthly recreations I am most delighted—both reasō bids me, and duety bindes me, to make you partaker of some of the fruits of my studies. And farther, your Worship being the onely maister that euer I served, vnto whom — my parentes excepted—I acknowledge my selfe more bounde then to al the worlde besides, I might be sayde to carie a verie bad minde with me, if I shoulde not endeuour by some one meanes or other, to

---

[1] See Memorial-Introduction of notice of this Cope, and the Family. G.

shewe my selfe thankefull for your benefites. And
not knowing better how to doe the same, I haue
—amongst other toies[1] by me taken in hand—
made speciall choice of these translations ensewing,
to present you with, as a pledge of my loyaltie
and testimonie of the duetiful zeale that I beare
you.

The first thing that shall heerein be offered
to your view, is a moste excellent Epistle, written
first in Italian by Maister Clodius Ptholemœus,
which according vnto my simple skill, I haue con-
uerted into English, although not with suche
eloquence as some other might—peraduenture—
haue done it; yet I trust with such diligence
that yee shall finde the intent of the Authour
sufficiently explained. Hee made it for the com-
forting of an acquaintaunce of his, who beyng
fallen into pouerty, did beare it very impaciently :
wherein he hath discharged the duety of a friend
so faithfully, that no man can say so much in the
commendation of it, but that it will deserue a
greate deale more. And what indifferent iudgement it shall seeme too want of the prayse that
I geue it, shall appeare to come to passe through
the imperfection of the Translator, and not any

---

[1] Trifles. G.

default of the Authour, whose[1] abilitie, if it shall
not in all poyntes answeare to the willingnesse
of his mynde, meriteth the rather too be pardoned,
in that he hath done his goodwil.

Next vnto this Epistle, followeth another of the
same mans composition, which for the occasion
wherevpon it was made, is not inferiour to the first.
For the golden examples and diuine sentences that
are cowched in them, I christened this discourse by
the name of a Comfortable Recreation, nothing
doubting but that whosoeuer shall peruse it with
aduised consideration, will acknowledge that
what the title doth professe in shewe, the
treatise will performe in substance. As the
ylnesse of my manner of handeling of it was as it
were a bridle to holde me backe from geuing my
consent that it should come foorth, so the goodnesse of the matter contayned in it, serued me
as a spurre to pricke me forwardes to yeelde to
theyr entreaties that craued to haue it published.

Such other French and Italian toyes as I haue
translated and added heerevnto—If I flatter not
my selfe ouer-much with myne owne follies—are
suche as will bring more delight then disliking to
the perusers of them. I am to craue pardon for

---

[1] Misprinted 'wohse'. G.

my presumption in dedicating them to your
Woorshippe; which I haue done, in that passing
vnder the shadowe of your protection, they shall
of a number that know you, be receaued with the
greater fauour.

Thus hoping that my welmeaning and willing
endeuour shalbe constred in the best parte,
remayning most thankefull to your Worship, for
your benefits bestowed on mee, I put an ende to
my rud preface, wishing unto you and my mistres, with your little ones, and all other your
welwillers many yeeres of prosperities. With
humble and heartie intercession vnto God, that
as yee haue already planted a good and lawdable
begining amongst your neighbours, and liue in
credit in your countrey, with the loue and good
liking of as many as know you, that so yee may
grow and goe forwardes with dayly encrease of
worshippe, vntill it shalbe his good pleasure, that
yee shall exchaunge this earthly mansion, for a
heauenly habitation.

Your seruaunt,

HUMFREY GIFFORD.[1]

---

[1] It may be noted here, once for all, that the orthography of the " Posie " is somewhat arbitary and singular : *e.g.* in above Epistle ' ylnesse ' for ' illness ', ' woor-

Epistle to the Reader of the Prose in the "Posie".

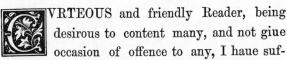VRTEOUS and friendly Reader, being desirous to content many, and not giue occasion of offence to any, I haue sufferedthe importunacie of som my welwillers to preuayle so far with me, that I haue yeelded them my consent for the publishing of this Treatise, not being ignorant vnto what hazard of reproch they oppose themselues, that permit their doings to be layde open to the view of a multitude. For as the better sort will pronounce their oppinions of it, answearable to the veritie of the substaunce that shalbe in the workes contained : so the greater sorte doe commonly giue their verdi[c]t according to the vanitie of the surmises that

---

shippe ' for ' worship ', ' constred ' for ' construed ', ' rud ' for ' rude '. Throughout we adhere to the original text, save in cases of a lacking letter as in ' verdit ' above. G.

shall by them be conceaued : often kindling a
kinde of mislike with the matter, for some secrete
malice that they beare to the man : and more
oftener for a resolute and setled determination that
they haue grounded in them, neuer to like well
of any thing, vnless it meete iumpewith[1] their
own doting and peeuish imaginations, or be some
pigge of their proper farrowing : being in this
poynt not vnlike the crow, who alwaies thinkes
her owne byrdes fayrest. But dayly examples
teach vs, that they which vomitte forth the poysoned rancour of their malicious stomackes, against
the lawdable attemptes of others : most, are such
as of themselues can do least : who neither cary
a minde to undertake any commendable exercise
themselues, nor haue a meaning to permit others
that would, to performe it without their
venemous backbyting. If comparisons were not
odious,[2] I woulde heere liken all such whelpes of
Zoilus, to that crabbed and canckerly naturde

---

[1] Printed as one word, as 'shalbe' is : = *agree exactly
with*. It is found in Shakespeare, *e.g.* " *jumpeth* with the
heart" (Richard III. , iii., 1.) " bring him *jump* when he
may Cassio find " (Othello ii. 3), *et alibi.* G.

[2] See our Memorial-Introduction for remarks on this
phrase. G.

curre, which being layde vpon a bottle[1] of hey,
would neither feede of it himself—being meat
contrary to his complection[2]—nor suffer the poore
hungerstarued beastes to approch neere it quietly :
but would lye still snapping and snarling at them.
But to omitte these preambulations, and come to
the purpose, I tell thee—gentle Reader—if thou
wilt vouchsafe the ouerlooking of this comfortable recreation, with a mind to profit, thou maist
reape benefit, and be greatly bettered by the reading of it.   For the brydling and keeping under of
our disordinate affections : for the restrayning and
contayning of our desires within the compasse of
a contented meane : for the vse and abuse of
riches, and for the gayning and obtayning of the
true and perfect tranquilitie of minde, one may
reade much, and yet not finde it more pithily and
substantially sette downe, then in these Epistles
following ; and especially in the first, where thou
shalt meete with such plentie of sweete and comfortable consolations, collected out of the bowelles
of the Scripture, and applyed so aptly, as will
mooue them, if thou haue neuer so little tast or
feeling in them of God, or godlynesse, to minde

---

[1] = bundle or sheaf : still used in Scotland.   G.
[2] Temperament.   G.

thy Creator, and be thankefull vnto him for His
benefits. And my hope is, that the goodnesse and
excellencie of the matter shall so rauish thy senses
that my imperfections in the translating of them,
shall be passed ouer by thee unespied. Neverthe-
les if either in the edition of this or other my
trifles, anything shal chaunce to escape mee, which
in thy vnpartial opinion shal seeme vnfitting, I
will most willingly submit my selfe to the censure
of thy iudgement, and vppon admonition amende
the fault by repentance, yeelding thee thankes for
thy friendlinesse, answerable to the minde and
good meaning that I shal see thee to advertise me
of it. Bnt if I shal perceaue thee to speake it,
more of malice to reprehend mee then of meaning to amende me, it wil so discomfort and dis-
corage me, and take downe my edge in such sort,
that I doubt I shal very hardly be brought heere-
after to repose confidence again in thy courtesie.
Yet if thou bee learned, and wilt tel me of my
faults louingly, spare not, I will take it most thāk-
fully : also if thou be one of Momus mates and
dost raile at my doings spytefullie I care not: I
will brooke it most patiently, accounting it no
lesse commendation to bee ill spoken of, by one
that is ignoraunt and foolish, then to be well
spoken of by one that is skilfull and wise.

Thus we should doe, and thus—would to God —we could doe : but as it is most easie to professe patience in words when our estate is in quiet: so it is very difficulte to expresse it in deedes, when our affections are distempered. Such as take men's purses from them vndesired, passe often by the sentence of a cord, and shall such as robbe men of their good names vndeserued, be suffere l to escape scotfree ? This may be set downe for a rule that neuer fayles : that as many men would be glad to be better thought of then his dealings shall deserue : so any man would be loth to be worse thought of, then his doinges shall demerit. For to be defrauded of deserued prayse, and pursued with vndeserued reproch, may well bee accounted a double iniurie. To conclude—gentle Reader—I haue bin so charie in the choyce of the things contained in this pamphlet, that thou mayst finde many thinges heerein to delight thee, and not any thing to despight thee. If thou shalt take pleasure, or gaine profit by the reading of them : be thankfull to the authors, and vouchsafe to thinke well of the translator, who when he would thee worst, wisheth thee well.

Thine in all curtesie,
Humfrey Gifford.

IV. Specimen of the Prose of the "Posie."

Maister Gasparinus a Phisition, by his cunning, healeth fooles.

HERE dwelt in times past in Englande, a very rich man who had one only sonne, called Gasparinus, whom he sent ouer too the uniuersity of Padua, that he might there follow his studie : but hee making no account of learning, spēt his time in gaming and rioting, haunting brothel houses, and other suspected places, leading yᵉ most dissolute life that might be : his father thinking that he spent his time in the study of phisicke. He practized in steed of bookes, bowles ; for disputing, dicing ; and whereas he should haue attayned learning, he altogether frequēted loytring. Hauing remayned there yᵉ space of fiue yeeres, he returned into his countrey and shewed by experience yᵗ he had learned backwards, for going about to seem a Romaine, he manifested himselfe to be a Barbarian ; and men noted him and poynted at him, as a common laughing stocke, in the towne where

he dwelt. What griefe it was vnto the poore
father, to see his cost lost, and his onely childe,
as it were cast away, I referre the consideration
thereof to your discretions. Wherfore for the
mitigating of his sorowes, hee called his sonne
vnto him, and opening a chest full of money and
iewels, layde forth vnto him the one halfe of his
goodes—which verily he deserued not—and said,
Take here — my sonne — thy portion of thy
father's heraditamentes, and get thee farre frō
me. For I rather choose to remain without a
child, then to liue with thee in infamie. No
sooner were these words spoken, but he most willingly obeying his fathers commandement, fingering
the money, tooke his leaue and departed. And
being farre distant from him, at the entrance of a
wood neere a riuer, hee built a costly and sump-
tuous pallace, the gates being of brasse, and with
this riuer it was moated about. Herein with a
deuice of sluces, he made certayne little pooles,
whose depth hee woulde encrease or diminish at
his pleasure; into some the water entred the
depth of a man; into some other, y^t it would
reach to his eyes; others, vnto the navel; some
to the middle, and some to the knees; and vnto
euery of these pooles, an yron chaine was fastened.

Ouer the gate of this pallace was a title written, which sayd,

"A place wherein to heale fooles."

The fame of this pallace, in short space, was spread abrode in most places of the world, and fooles repayred thither in great abundance, to be cured, but—to speake more neerer the truth—to bee washed. The maister according to the greatnes of their follies, would plundge them in these pits, and some of these he would heale with whippings, some with watching, some with fasting, and other some by little and little he would restore to their former estate, and vnderstanding, by the tēperature and suttlety of yᵉ ayre. On a time, in a large court without the gates of this pallace, as certayne of the meanest sort of these fooles, were sporting themselues in the heate of the sunne, it fortuned that a Falconer came by, which carried a sparhawk on his fist, hauing a great number of spaniels wayting on him. Who presently beyng espied by these fooles, they maruelled greatly what he meant to ride with that birde and spaniels: and one of them demanded of him what bird it was that he carried on his fist? He answered a sparhawke. And to what end—quoth he—doe

ye keep her? Quoth the gentleman, shee is a
birde greedy at her pray, and I keepe her to kill
partridge with, which is a great bird, and delicate
in tast: these are called spaniels, which spring
and retrine[1] the birdes, and this sparhauke killeth
them, and I eate them. Quoth the foole then:
I pray doe tell me what this sparhawke and
spaniels stand thee in? the Falconer made
answeare: I bought the horse that I ride on, for
sixe pound, the sparhawke cost me twenty
shillings, and my spaniels three pound: and the
feeding and nourishing of all these yeerly, I
value at xx pounds. Now I beseech thee tell
mee, said the foole, how many partridges thou
takest yeerely, and what they be woorth. I
catch—quoth he—about two hundred, and they
are at the least worth twenty shillings. The
foole, but not a foole herin, but rather he shewes
himsels very wise, with a loude voyce cried unto
him, fly, fly, foole that thou art, which spendest
twenty pound yeerely, for the gaining of twēty
shillings, and yet reckonest not the time that is
vaynely consumed. Fly with al speede, for the
Passion of God, fly, for if my maister find thee

---

[1] Query = retrieve: an ancient sporting term for the
recovery of the game once sprung. G.

heere, he will throw thee into a pitte, where thou shalt be plunged over head and eares, and be suffered hardly to escape with life. For I which am a foole, may discerne that thou art more foolish then them which are most foolish of all.

V. Epistle-Dedicatory to the Verse of the 'Posie'.

*To the Worshipfull John Stafford of Bletherwicke[1]
Esquier, Humfrey Gifford most humbly sendeth
greeting.*

CKNOWLEDGING my selfe deepely indebted to your Worshippe for your professed curtesies and good opinion conceaued of me, and desiring by some one meanes or
other to make manifest my thankfull minde, I
haue aduentured the dedication of this trifling toy
unto your protection, not doubting of your fauour-

---

[1] This Stafford was second son of Sir Humphrey Stafford
of Blatherwick, co. Northampton, by Margart Tame, one
of the sisters and co-heirs of Sir Edmund Tame, Knt. He
died November 28th, 1595, leaving Bridget (Clopton) his
wife surviving and Humphrey, his son and heir. The
present representatives are of the O'Briens : but they have
taken the name of Stafford. See a singularly interesting
communication in response to a Query of mine in Notes
and Queries for September 24th, 1870. It corrects Dug-
dale and the County-Histories. G.

able acceptance, in that I bestow it as an earnest-
pennie of my wel-meaning, and testimonie of the
vnfaigned goodwil that I beare you. The thing
that I here present you with, is a Posie of Gillowflowers, collected out of the garden of mine owne
inuentions; which if they shal come too short in
shew and colour, or proue inferiour in sent and
odour to that which is to be looked for of so fra-
grant a flower, let the Gardiner—I pray you—be
excused, who hath done his good-will and indeu-
our in the sowing and setting of them, and lay
the fault in the barrennesse of the soyle wherein
they were planted; which had it byn better, their
vertue would haue proued to be greater. Though
al the flowers herein contayned, carie one name,
yet eche of thē differs from other, both in colour
and sauour, the better to satisfie the diuersitie of
eyes that shall vew them, and variety of noses
that shall smell them. Nowe if the spider shall
happen to sucke any poyson out of them, let not
the flowers be the worse thought of, but consider
that it is his propertie to doe the like, out of the
most pure and delectable flowers that euer were,
and God in geuing vnto her and other such like
creatures this nature, doeth no lesse manifest His
omnipotent power herein, then in his other wonderful works. For reason telleth, and experience

teacheth, that in this vale of misery there is nothing so beautifull but that it hath some blemish,
nor so pure, but that it sauours of some imperfection: so that as long as the world is a world,
corruption must continue amongst vs. Which
filthy dregs and poysoned humors, if they were
not in parte drawen and drayned away by the ven-
omous beastes and wormes of the Earth, they
woulde a greate deale more annoy vs then now
they doe. And it is to be doubted whether life
could any long time be conserued amongst vs. I
might here take occasion to liken the crew of
curious carpers—which more of malice then good
meaning accustomed to cauel at other men's
doings, playing the ydle drones themselues—to
the vememous beastes and wormes before spoken
of : whom, for their congruity in condition and
affinity in disposition, I might bring them within
the compas of one cōparison and conclude that
both the one and the other are necessary euils.
But leste that the old prouerb be obiected agaynst
me, *Ne sutor vltra crepitam*,[1] let the Gardiner
meddle no farther thē his spade, I will leaue thē
to theyr predecessor Zoilus—whose apes they are

---

[1] More exactly ' *Ne sutor supra crepidam* ' (Plautus, 35.
10, 36, *no* 12: Val, Max 8, 12 *fin.* **G:**

in imitating his conditions—and returne agayne
to my Gillowflowers, eftsoones beseeching your
Worship to accept those that I present you, with
no lesse thākfulnes then the Gardiner doth offer
them willingly, wherof he doubtes not, calling
to minde your accustomed curtesie. In one
thinge I haue vsed suche circumspection as my
simple skill would permit me, which is, that the
beauty of my flowers be not blemished with the
weedes of wantonnesse that cōmonly grow in
such gardens. I hope therefore ye shal finde them
rooted out in such sort, that if there remayne
any, my trust is they shal not fall out to be
many. The onely thing that I doubt of in this
my dedication, is that your Worshipp shall haue
cause to account mee a deepe dissembler and one
that hath byn more lauish in promise, then he is
able to pay in performance. For whereas by
my former speeches, yee might peraduenture
looke for some delicate Gillowflowers, it will fall
out to be but a coppy of my countenance ; hauing
done nothing els, but—as the fashion of the worlde
is now a dayes—set a good face on a bad matter.
For—to deale plainly with you—I was neuer
Gardiner in all my life, and the thing that I here
present you with is but a collection of such verses
and odde deuises as haue—at such idle howres as

I founde in my maister his seruice—vpon sundry occasions by me byn cōposed. The one I confesse farre vnworthy your view, and yet such as when ye shal returne home weeried from your fielde sportes, may yeelde you some recreation. The chiefe marke that I leuel at is, the continuance of your Woorship's curtesie and good minde towardes me, which as they already haue surmounted the reach of my deserts, so if I might enioy the fruition of them hereafter, in that fulnesse which I hope for, I shall account all the duetifull endenour that I can possibly shew you, insufficient for the satisfaction of the least parte of them. Thus for feare of being tedious, I ende, wishing your Worship with my good mistres your wife, and all yours, many yeeres of prosperitie, with dayly increase of worship ; and heauen for your hauen to rest in, when the daungerous sea of this life shalbe ouer sailed.

Yours in all dutifulnesse,

H. G.

V.

A Posie of Gilloflowers.

A PRAYER.

D Doe guide my pathes, O Lorde my God,
 T That I walke not astray ;
O O who can mount Thy holy hill,
 E Except Thou leade the way ?
R Renew me with such grace, that I
 M May learne Thy lawes aright :
O Order my steppes, so shal I be
 P Preserued day and night ;
T The wicked Serpent euery houre,
 E Endeuours me to spil :
H Haste to my helpe, so shall I, Lorde,
 R Right well eschew the il.
I In Thee I put mine onely trust,
 A Assist me then at neede,
S Stand on my side ; but Thee alone,
 N None else my sute can speede.
A Amidst the sea of sinne and death,
 C Continually we ride,

𝔐   Making still shipwracke of our soules,

𝔈   Except Thou be our guide.

𝔙   Vnto the[e] Lorde with humble sute,

𝔍   I lift my heart and handes :

𝔈   Encline thine eares to my request,

𝔙   Vnlose my sinfull bandes.

𝔏   Let not vil Satan's crafty traynes,

𝔖   So sore our soules assayle :

𝔇   Do thou protect vs with Thy shield,

𝔗   Then shal he not preuayle.

𝔄   As to a rocke of safe refuge,

𝔍   I stil to Thee doe fly.

𝔑   None els there is I know, that can

𝔠   Cause al my sinnes to die.

𝔍   I doe confesse my force is weake,

𝔈   Encrease my fayth—O Lorde—

𝔈   Expel from me al heresies,

𝔓   Protect me with Thy worde.

𝔏   Let not the fiende that seekes my foyle,[1]

𝔅   Reioyce at my decay;

𝔇   Doe make mee strong in liuely fayth,

𝔘   Vnto Thee still I pray.

𝔄   All trueth, al good and godly deedes,

𝔇   Doe still proceéde from Thee :

𝔑   No man can thinke one holy thought.

---

[1] Fall, defeat.   G.

𝕰   Except their guide Thou bee.

𝖁   Unlesse Thou Lord doe giue encrease,

　𝕽   No fruit our deedes bring forth :

𝕰   Esteemd we are as rotten weedes,

　𝕮   Corrupt and nothing worth.

𝕭   Remember not my sinnes forepast,

　𝕰   Eluminate my wayes :

𝕾   So shall I still with heart and voyce,

　𝕲   Giue Thee all laud and prayes.

𝕳   Happy are they that doe Thee serue,

　𝕵   In thought, and eke in deede :

𝖁   Vnturnèd neuer is Thy face,

　𝕵   From them in time of neede ;

𝕸   Make Lord in mee a stedfast fayth,

　𝕵   For euer to abyde :

𝕵   Frame still my lyfe to keepe thy lawes,

　𝕬   And I shall neuer slide.

𝕭   Remoue from me all Error's blockes,

　𝕭   Right so shall I remaine,

𝕵   In perfect footsteppes of Thy paths,

　𝕯   Deuoyde of worldly paine.[1]

---

[1] It is to be noted that the capital letters commencing
the successive lines of the above poem, when read down-
wards, make acrostics, respectively, " Dorothy, Samuel,
Daniel Danvers," (first line), and " Temperance, Justice,
Prudence " (second line) while the two lines together of
the last thirteen lines conceal the author's name, spelled

TO HIS APPROUED FRIEND.[1]

Serue God	Serue God thy Lord, delight to keepe His lawes,
alwaies;	Alwayes haue care to doe His holy hest.
Commit	Commit not that which may His anger cause :
no euil;	No euill, then, deere friend, can thee molest.
Still feare	Still feare and minde the dreadfull iudgement day.
to sinne;	To sinne breedes death, but mercie doe require,
defie	Defie such thinges, as worke thy soule's decay :
the diuell.	The diuell so shall leese his chiefe desire.
If thou	If thou wilt spend thy dayes in great content,
praise God	Praise God ech houre, serue him in feare and dread.

"Hvmfri Giffard" : on which see our Memorial-Introduction. G.

' Note, that as in the preceding poem the letters placed in the margin are those that begin each line, so here the words opposite each line form the commencement successively thereof, and taken by themselves make a small poem. G.

with hearte With heart contrite thy former sinnes
      lament,
and minde, And minde henceforth a better life to
      lead :
Great ioyes Great ioyes the Lord—as His pure
      Word doth say—
in heauen In heauen aboue, for good men hath
      preparde ;
thy soule Thy soule when that this life shall
      passe away,
shal finde. Shall finde such blisse, as cannot bee
      declarde.

THE LIFE OF MAN METAPHORICALLY COMPARED TO A SHIPPE, SAYLING ON THE SEAS IN A TEMPEST.

ASTE homewardes, man ! draw nearer to
    the shore :
    The skies doe scowle, the windes doe
    blow amaine ;
The rag[g]ed rockes, with rumbling noyse doe rore,
The foggie clowdes doe threaten stormes of raine.
Ech thing foreshewes a tempest is at hand,
Hoyst up thy sayles, and haste to happy land.

In worldly seaes thy silly ship is tost :

319

With waues of woe besette on euery side,
Blowne heere and there, in daunger to bee lost :
Darke clowdes of sinne doe cause thee wander wide,
Unlesse thy God pitie some on thee take,
On rockes of rueth thou needes must shipwrack
    make.

Cut downe the mast of rancour and debate,
Unfraight the shippe of all unlawful wares :
Cast ouer boorde the packes of hoorded hate,
Pumpe out fowle vice, the cause of many cares.
If that some leeke, it make thee stand in doubt,
Repentaunce serues to stoppe the water out.

Let God's pure Word thy line and compasse bee,
And stedfast fayth use thou in anckor's steede :
Lament thy sinnes, then shalt thou shortly see,
That power divine, will helpe thee forth at neede.
Fell Sathan is chiefe rular of these seas :
Hee seekes our wracke, he doth these tempestes
    rayse.

In what wee may, let us alwayes represse,
The furious waues of lust and fond desire :
A quiet calme our conscience shall possesse,
    if we doe that which dutie doeth require :
By godly life in fine obtaine wee shall,
    the porte of blisse : to which God send vs all.

A DOLEFULL DUMPE.

HO so doth mone, and lackes a mate,
to bee partaker of his woe,
And will discourse of his estate,
Let him and I together goe :
And I will make him graunt in fine,
his griefe to bee farre lesse then mine.

Perhappes hee wil, to win the best,
paint forth what pangs oppresse his minde :
How that hee feeles no quiet rest,
how Fortune is to him vnkind :
And how hee pines in secreet griefe
And findes no meanes for his reliefe.

These and such like, a number will
alleadge to witnes their distresse ;
Some rolle up stones against the hill,
with Sisiphus ; some eke expresse,
That like to Tantalus they fare,
and some with Yxion doe compare.

But I not onely feele the smart,
of all those euilles rehearsed before :
But taste the torment in my heart,
of thousand times as many more ;
So that the worst of their annoyes,
Is best and chiefest of my ioyes.

321

I never fed on costly meate,
Since that this griefe opprest mee first :
Dole is the dainties that I eate,
And trickling teares doe coole my thirst :
Care is my caruing knife, God wot,
Which dayly seekes to cut my throte.

Muse not that heere I secret keepe
The cause that first procurde my griefe :
What doth it boote a man to weepe,
When that his teares find no reliefe?
Contentes mee only, this repose,
That Death ere long will end my woes.

IN PRAISE OF THE CONTENTED MINDE.

F all the ioyes that worldly wightes
possesse,
Were throughly scand, and pondred in
their kindes,
No man of wit, but iustly must confesse,
That they ioy most, that haue contented mindes ;
And other ioyes, which beare the name of ioyes,
Are not right ioyes, but sunneshines of anoyes.

In outward view we see a number glad,
Which make a shew, as if mirth did abound,
Whē pinching grief within doth make them sad ;

And many a one in these dayes may bee had,
Which faintly smile, to shroud their sorowes so,
When oftentimes they pine in secreet woe.

But euery man that holdes himself content,
And yieldes God thankes, as dutie doth require,
For all His giftes that Hee to vs hath sent,]
And is not vext with ouer great desire :
All[1] such, I say, most quietly doe sleepe,
When fretting cares doth others waking keepe.

What doth auaile huge heapes of shining golde,
Or gay attyre, or stately buildinges braue :
If worldly pelfe thy heart in bondage holde ?
Not thou thy goodes, thy goodes make thee their
     slaue.
For greedie men like Tantalus doe fare :
In midst of wealth, they needie are and bare.

A warie heede that things goe not to losse,
Doth not amisse, so that it keepe the meane :
But still to toyle and moyle for worldly drosse,
And tast no ioy nor pleasure for our paine :
In carke and care both day and night to dwell,
Is nothing els but euen a very hell.

Wherefore I say, as erst I did beginne,

---

[1] Misprinted ' And '.   G.

Contented men enioy the greatest blisse :
Let vs content our selues to flye from sinne,
And still abide what God's good pleasure is.
If ioy, or paine, if wealth or want befall,
Let vs bee pleasde, and giue God thankes for all.

IN THE PRAISE OF FRIENDSHIP.

EUEALE—O tongue—the secretes of my
thought,
Tel forth the gaine that perfect friend-
ship brings :
Expresse what ioyes by her to man are brought,
Unfolde her prayse which glads all earthly things :
If one might say, in earth a heauen to bee,
It is no doubt where faythfull friendes agree.

To all estates true friendship is a stay,
To euery wight a good and welcome guest :
Our life were death, were shee once tane away,
Consuming cares would harbour in our brest,
Fowle malice eke, would banish al delight,
And puffe vs vp with poyson of despight.

If that the seedes of enuie or debate,
Might yeelde no fruite, but wither and decay,
No cankred mindes would hoorde vp heapes of
hate.

No hollow hearts dissembling partes should play,
No clawback then would fawne in hope of meede :
Such life to lead were perfect life in deede.

But nowadayes desires of worldly pelfe,
With all estates makes friendship very colde :
Few for their friendes, ech shifteth for himselfe :
If in thy purse thou hast good store of golde,
Full many a one thy friendship will imbrace :
Thy wealth once spent they turne away their face.

Let vs still pray vnto the Lord aboue,
For to relent our hearts, as hard as stone :
That though the world one knot of loyall loue,
In perfect trueth might linke vs all in one ;
Then should wee passe this life without annoyes,
And after death possesse eternall ioyes.

A COMMENDATION OF PEACE.

HEN boyling wrath perturbs mās troubled
brest,
Outraging will, bids Reason's lore adue :
Turmoyling cares bereaue all quiet rest,
And hastie yre makes harmefull happes ensue :
Great stormes of strife are raisd through dire
debate,
But golden peace preserues the quiet state.

E   325

A gift diuine, than precious pearle more worth,
Is blessèd peace, to discord deadly foe;
Most plenteous fruits this blooming tree brings
    forth,
When warre and strife yeeld crops of care and
    woe ;
Rash Rancour's rage procures fond[1] furious fightes;
Peace makes men swim in seaes of sweet delights.

If that this peace bee such a passing thing,
That it by right may challenge worthy prayse :
What thankes owe wee vnto our heauenly King,
Through Whome we haue enioyde such happy
    dayes ?
Next to our queene, howe deepely are wee bound,
Whose like on earth, before was neuer found ?

If England would perpend[2] the bloody broyles,
And slaughters huge that foraine realmes haue
    tried,
It should me seemes, be[3] warnd by their tur-
    moyles,
In perfect loue and concord to abide.
But—out alas !—my heart doeth rue to tell,
Small feare of God, amongst vs now doth dwell.

---

1 Foolish. G.   = consider attentively. G.
² Misprinted 'by'. G.

And where that wantes, what hope doth els
    remayne,
But dire reuenge for rash committed crimes?
Heapes of mishaps will fall on vs amayne,
If we doe not lament our sinnes betimes.
Unlesse with speed to God for grace we call,
I feare, I feare, great plagues on vs will fall.

England therefore, in time conuert from vice ;
The pleasant Spring abides not all the yeere :
Let foraine ylls forewarne thee to be wise,
Stormes may ensue, though now the coastes be
    cleere.
I say no more, but onely doe request,
That God will turne all things vnto the best.

FOR SOULDIERS.

E buds of Brutus' land,[1] couragious youths,
    now play your parts :
    Unto your tackle stand, abide the brunt
    with valiāt hearts.
For newes is carried to and fro, that we must
    forth to warfare goe :

---

[1] *Sic:* query = Romans, i. e. Roman-like ?   G.

Men muster now in euery place, and souldiers
 are prest forth apace.
Faynt not, spend bloud, to doe your Queen and
 countrey good :
Fayre wordes, good pay, wil make men cast al
 care away.
The time of Warre is come, prepare your corslet,
 speare and shield,
Methinks I heare the drumme, strike doleful
 marches to the field :
Tantara, tātara, y$_e$ trūpets sound, w$_h$ makes our
 hearts w^h ioy aboūd.
The roring guns are heard afar, and every thing
 denounceth[1] Warre ;
Serve God, stand stoute, bold courage brings this
 geare about.
Feare not, forth run ; faint heart, faire lady
 never wonne.
Yee curious carpet knights, that spende the time
 in sport and play,
Abrode, and see new sights, your coūtrie's cause
 cals you away :
Doe not to make your ladies game, bring blemish
 to your worthy name.

---

[1] = announceth. **G.**

Away to field and win renoune, w^t courage beat
    your enimies down :
Stoute hearts gain praise, when dastards sayle in
    Slaunder's seas :
Hap what hap shal, we sure shal die but once for
    all.
Alarme me thinkes they cry, be packing mates,
    be gone with speed,
Our foes are very nigh, shame haue that man that
    shrinks at need ;
Unto it boldly let vs stand, God wil geue right
    the vpper hand.
Our cause is good, we need not doubt ; in signe of
    courage geue a showt :
March forth, be strōg, good hap wil come ere it be
    long.
Shrinke not, fight well, for lusty lads must beare
    the bell :
All you that wil shun euil, must dwell in warfare
    euery day ;
The world, the flesh and diuel, alwayes doe seeke
    our soules decay,
Striue w^t these foes w^t all your might, so shal you
    fight a worthy fight.
That cōquest doth deserue most praise wher vice
    do yeeld to vertue's wayes.

Beat down foule sin, a worthy crown then shal
      ye win;
If ye liue wel, in heauen with Christ our soules
      shal dwell.

TO HIS FRIENDE.

MUSE not too much—O wight of worthy
      fame—
    At view of this my rude and ragged rime ;
I am almost enforst to write the same,
Wherefore forgeue, if I commit a crime :
The cause hereof, and how it came to passe
I shall declare, euen briefly as it was.

Reuoluing in my mind your friendly face,
Your bountie great, your loue to euery man,
I heard my Wit and Will to scan this case,
If I should write or no ; thus Wil began :
Take pen in hand thou fearefull wight, she said,
To write thy mind what should make thee afraid ?

Not so—quoth Wit—acquaintance hath he small,
With him to whō thou bid'st me write his mind ;
What tho'—quoth Will—that skils nothing at all,
He writes to one that is to all a friend.
Him so to be—quoth Wit—none can denie,
Thou art a foole—quoth Will—then to reply.

Great cause—quoth Wit—shoulde make him to
    refrayne
He would—quoth Wil—declare his friendly?
    heart.
What if—quoth Wit—he chance to reape disdayne
Of such foul fruits—quoth Wil—frieds haue no
    part.
Perchance—quoth Wit—it wilbe taken yll.
Wel meanèd things, who wil take yll—quoth Wil.

He hath no skil—quoth Will—how should he
    write?
Al want of skil—quoth Will—good will supplies.
I see—quoth Wit—thou wilt worke him despite,
For counsell good, thou geuest him rash aduice :
Wit said no more, but Will that stately dame,
Still bad me write, not forcing any blame.

Since Will not Wit, makes me commit offence,
Of pardon yours the better hope I haue;
To shew my loue was all the whole pretence,
That made me write : This onely do I craue :
In any thing if pleasure you I can,
Command me so, as if I were your man.

A RENOUNCING OF LOVE

L earthly things by course of kind,
    Are subiect still to reason's lore :
    But sure I can no reasons finde,
That makes these louers loue so sore.
They frye and freese in myldest weather,
They weepe and laugh, euen both together.

Euen now in waues of deepe despaire,
Their barke is tossèd to and fro ;
A gale of hope expels all feare.
And makes the winde to ouerblow,
Twixt feare and hope these louers saile,
And doubtfull are which shall preuayle.

At night in slumber sweetly laide,
They seeme to holde their loue in aimes :
Awaking then, they are afrayde,
And feele the force of thousand harmes.
Then do they tosse in restlesse bed,
With hammers woorking in their head.

A merry looke from ladie's face,
Bringes them a foote, which could not goe :
A frowning brow doth them disgrace,
And brues the broth of all their woe,
Hereby all men may playnely know,
That reason rules not louer's law.

But reason doth me thus persuade,
Where reason wants that nothing frames :
Therefore this reason hath me made,
To set aside all louely gaynes.
Since reason rules not Venus' sport.
No reason bids me scale that forte.

A WILL OR TESTAMENT.

HEN dreadfull death with dint of pearcing
   darte,
  By fatall doome, this corpes of mine
   shal kill,
When lingring life shal from my life depart,
I thus set downe my testament and will.
My faithfull friendes executors shall remayne,
To see performde what here I do ordayne.

To thee—O world—I first of all doe leaue
The vayne delights that I in thee haue found :
The feignèd shewes wherewith thou didst deceaue,
Thy fickle trust, and promises vnsound ;
My wealth, my woe, my ioyes commixt w^t care,
Doe take them, all doe fall vnto thy share.

And Satan thou, for that thou wert the cause,
That I in sin did still mispend my dayes,

I thee defie, and here renounce thy lawes;
My wicked thoughts, my vile and naughty waies,
And eke my vice doe to thy lot befall,
From thee they came, doe take them to thee all.

To thee, O earth, agayne I do restore,
My carrion corpes, which from thee did proceede :
Because it did neglect all godly lore,
Let greedy wormes vpon it alwayes feede ;
Let it in filth consume and rot away,
And so remaine vntil the iudgement day.

But my poore soule, whō Christ deerly bought
Which hated sinne, and loathèd to offend,
Together with ech good and godly thought,
Into thy handes, sweete Jesu, I commend :
O Sauiour Christe, doe guide my steppes so well,
That after death, she stil with Thee may dwell.

A COMPLAYNT OF A LOUER.

F euer wofull wight had cause, to pipe in
bitter smart,
I which am thrall to Cupid's lawes, with
him may beare a part.
Whose ioyful daies alas are gone; whom daily
cares doe tosse :

But wote yee why I thus take on ? my lucke is
    turnde to losse :
Ere cruell loue my heart possest, no cares did vex
    my head,
But since he harboured in my brest, my golden
    dayes are fled.
Time was when Fortune did allow, great gladnesse
    to my share,
But ah, for that time is not, now doth grow my
    cause of care.
Time was when I liude in delight, and reapt of
    ioyes my fill ;
But now time is, workes me despite, would waste[1]
    had tarried still.
No hap so hard, no griefe so great, whereof I feele
    not part,
Now shiuering colde, now flaming heate, anoyes
    my wofull heart,
So that hope is the onely stay, on which my life
    dependes,
Which if it once be tane away, my date of liuing
    ends :
God graunt my hope, such hap may see, that
    good successe ensue,

---

[1] = was, i. e. the past. G.

Which if it long prolongèd be, through griefe I
  die: adiew.

FOR HIS FRIENDE.

 THAT in freedome liued of late,
      And neuer stoupt to Cupid's lure,
      Haue now made change of my
        estate,
And thousand torments doe endure.
As late abrode I cast my lookes,
In Fancie's lune[1] I fast was cought,
And Beauty with her bayted hookes,
Hath me alas in bondage brought ;
I loue, but lacke the thing I craue,
I liue, but want my chiefest good,
I hope, but hap I cannot haue,
I serue, but starue for want of foode : ◄
Then[2] so to loue, what state more yll ?
Such life affoordes small time of ioy,
Such wauering hope doth often kill :

---

[1] *Sic :* and if correct = lunacy : but query 'lume', *i.e.*
loom ? 'Lunes' = lunacies, is used several times by
Shakespeare, *e g.* "these dangerous unsafe *lunes* " (Winter's Tale, ii., 2), " his pettish *lunes* " (Troilus &c., *ii.*
3). G.   [2] = than.

To serue and starue what worse anoy?
Yet wil I loue whiles life doth last,
And liue while any hope remaines,
And hope when dismal dayes are past,
To haue reward for all my paynes.
Loe thus I liue by hope sustaynd,
Yet through despayre, die euery houre,
In sorrow clad, in pleasure painde,
Now fed with sweete, now choakt with sowre.
Deare dame, in humble sort I sew,[1]
Since mine estate to you is known,
Voutsafe my dolefull case to rew,[2]
And saue his life who is your owne.

SOMEWHAT MADE OF NOTHING, AT A GENTLEWOMAN'S REQUEST.

E gladly would haue me, to make you
some toy,
And yet will not tel me whereof I should
write:

---

[1] = sue. **G.**

[2] To rue or rew, in the sense of to pity:
"And at the dore of death, for sorrow drew
Complayning out on me that would not on them rew."
(SPENSER's Fairy Queen VI. viii. 20 : Nares, edn.
Halliwell and Wright). **G.**

The strangeness of this, doth breed me annoy,
And makes me to seeke what things to endite.
If I should write rashly what comes in my braine,
It might be such matter as likes you not best,
And rather I would great sorrow sustayne,
Then not to fulfill your lawfull request;
Two dangers most doubtful oppresse me alike,
Ne am I resoluèd to which I might yeelde;
Wherfore by perforce I am forcèd[1] to seeke
This slender deuice to serue for my shield.
Since nothing yee geue me to busie my brayne,
Nothing but your nothing of me can yee craue,
Wherfore now receue your nothing agayne;
Of nothing, but nothing, what els would ye haue.

OF THE INSTABILITY OF FORTUNE.

HO wisely waies false Fortune's fickle
          change,
     Which in short space turnes loue to
          mortal hate,
Shal find smal cause to deem it wondrous strange,
To fleete from happie life to worse estate:
For whie, her sweete is alwaies mixt with sowre,
If now shee fawne, she frownes within an houre.

---

¹ Misprinted 'foretd'.   G.

Her smiles are wyles, to cause men hope for hap,
Her traynes breed paynes, though pleasant be the
　　show,
Him whom she now doth dandle in her lap,
Straightway sustaines a wretched ouerthrow.
And whom thou seest at foote of wheele downe
　　cast,
Within short space, she hoyseth up as fast.

The raging seas, which dayly ebbes and flowes,
The wauering winds, which blow now here, now
　　there,
More constant art then Fortune's flattering vowes,
Who in one hoode a double face doth beare :
To trust her lookes, when she doth fleere[1] or laugh
Is nothing els but trust a broken staffe.

Pollicrates—as auncient writers tell—
On Fortune's wheele most highly was aduanste,
And many a yeere shee fauoured him so well,
That no ill hap long time vnto him chaunst ;
Yet in the end, to show her double wayes,
With hemping[2] roape, shee causde him end his
　　dayes.

If thou wilt shun all sorow and distresse,
By Fortune's threates doe set but little store,

---

[1] Sneer. G.　　　[2] =hempen. G.

If thine affayres haue euer good successe,
Yeeld hearty thankes to God, thy Lorde therefore.
If great annoyes doe fall upon thee fast,
Thinke them due plagues for some offences past.

By prayer then, make leuell with the Lorde,
Repentant hearts haue mercie when they call:
Loue Him with feare, delight to reade His Worde,
So great good haps vnto thee will befall.
So shalt thou leade thy life without annoyes,
And after death possesse eternal ioyes.

OF THE VANITIE OF THIS LIFE.

 READE in poets' faignèd bookes,
    That wise Vlysses wandring came,
    Where Circes through her fawning
        lookes,
Did worke his men a spightfull shame.
  She causde them quaffe great bowles of wine,
And presently they turnde to swine.

But hee which followed vertue still,
Refusde to taste this proffered charme,
And would not worke her beastly will,
As one that doubted farther harme ;
Her witchcraftes, and enchantmentes straunge,
Were not of force this man to chaunge.

The world with his alluring toyes,
Is Circe's witch, of whom they write :
Which tempts vs with her sugred ioyes,
And makes vs swimme in such delight
That wee so play with Pleasure's ball,
As if there were no God at all.

If man would way,[1] what enemies
Are alwayes prest him to deuoure,
Mee thinkes from sinne hee should arise,
And make defence with all his power.
For why, the world, the flesh, the deuill,
Doe neuer cease to worke vs euill.

These so bewitch our foolish braines,
That nought wee force eternall paine :
And euery one in sinne remaines,
As if hell were a fable vaine.
Alas wee are seducèd so,
That all true hearts do bleede for woe.

The sheepe doth yeerly yeelde his fleese,
The plodding oxe the plow doth draw,
And euery thing in willing wise,
Keepes and obayes dame Nature's law :
But man in witte, which should excell,
Against his Lord doth still rebell.

---

[1] Weigh. G.

Ech doth deferre from day to day,
And thinkes the morow to amend :
But Death arestes vs by the way,
And sodainly some makes their end ;
O wretched case that they bee in,
Which die, and not lament their sinne !

Thou silly man, still feare the Lord,
Thy former sinnes with speede forsake :
The iudgement-day in minde record,
In which ech soule account must make :
Confesse thy faultes to God therefore,
Repent, amend, and sinne no more.

OF THE VANITIE OF THE WORLD.

S I lay musing in my bed,
    A heape of fancies came in head,
    Which greatly did molest mee ;
Such sundry thoughtes of joy and paine,
Did meete within my pondring braine,
That nothing could I rest mee :
Sometimes I felt exceeding ioy,
Sometimes the torment of annoy,
Euen now I laugh, euen now I weepe,
Euen now a slumber made mee sleepe.
  Thus did I with thoughtes of straunge device,

Lye musing alone in pensiue wise :
I knewe not what meanes might health procure,
Nor finish the toyle I did indure.
And still I lay, and found no way,
That best could make my cares decay.

Revoluing these thinges in my minde,
Of wretched world the fancies blinde,
Alone a while I ponder :
Which when I had perusèd well,
And saw no vertue there to dwell,
It made mee greatly wonder.
Is this that goodly thing—thought I—
That all men loue so earnestly ?
Is this the fruit that it doth yeelde,
Whereby wee all are so beguilde?
Ah Jesus ! how then my heart did rue,
Because I had folowed them, as true.
Alas wee haue lost the heauenly ioyes,
And haue beene deceaued with worldly toyes :
Whose fancies vaine, will breed vs paine,
If Christ doe not restore againe.

O wretched man, leaue off therefore,
In worldly thinges put trust no more,
Which yeelds no thing but sorow :
To God thy Lord with speede conuert,
Because thou most vncertain art,

343

If thou shalt liue too morow :
Leaue of to quaffe, to daunce and play,
Remember still the iudgement-day,
Repent, relent, and call for grace,
For pardon aske, whilst thou hast space.
Who doeth from his heart repentaunce craue,
Forgiuenes—saieth Christ—of me shall haue.
Hee will not the death of a sinner giue :
But rather hee should repent and liue.
Still laud the Lord, peruse His Word,
And let thy deedes with it accord.

A LESSON FOR ALL ESTATES.

AST thou desire thy golden dayes to
spend,
In blissful state exempt from all annoyes?
So liue, as if death now thy life should end,
Still treade the pathes that leade to perfect joy[es] ;
Bee slow to sinne, but speedie to aske grace ;
How are they blest that thus runne out their race.

Ech night ere sleepe shut vp thy drowsie eyes,
Thinke thou how much in day thou hast trans-
grest :
And pardon craue of God in any wise,
To doe that's good, and to forsake the rest :

344

Sinne thus shake of, the fiend for enuie weepes,
Sound are our ioyes, most quiet are our sleepes.

Haue not thy head so cloy'd with worldly cares,
As to neglect that thou shouldst chiefly mindé :
But beare an eye to Sathan's wily snares :
Who to beguile, a thousand shiftes will finde ;
Vaine are the ioyes the wretched world allowes,
Who trust them most, doe trust but rotten bowes.

Shunne filthy vice, persist in doing well,
For doing well doth godly life procure :
And godly life makes vs with Christ to dwell,
In endlesse blisse that euer shall endure.
Wee pray thee Lord our follyes to redresse,
That wee thus doe, thus liue, this blisse possesse.

A DREAME.

IN pleasaunt moneth of gladsome May
    I walkt abroad to view
    The fieldes, which Nature had bedeckt
With flowers of sundry hew.
The sight whereof did recreate
    My senses in such sort,
As passeth far beyond my power,
    Thereof to make reporte.

345

Then sat I neere a pleasaunt wood,
  And listened with desire :
Unto the small birdes chirping charme,
  Which set my heart on fire.
Of goldefinch and of nightingale
  I there might hear the voyce :
The wren, the robin and the thrush,
  Did make a heauenly noyse :
Whose sweet melodious harmonie
  My senses so bereft,
That I in this delightfull plot,
  A pray to sleepe was left.
In slumber mine, an auncient dame,
  Before my face appeares :
Whose hollow cheekes and wrinckled face,
  Did argue many yeeres.
Her vesture was as white as snow,
  Her countenance very sad,
It semèd by her watry eine,
  Some inward griefe shee had :
For why, great streames of trickling teares
  Distillèd downe her cheekes,
And thus to mee with trembling voyce,
  This aged beldam speakes ;
My friende—quoth she—bee not dismay'd,
  At this my sodaine sight ;
Ne let the speeches I shall vse,

Thy fearefull minde afright.
I am not of the Furies broode,
  No damnèd sprites of hell:
But Hee through whome my being is,
  Aboue the skies doth dwell.
And Lady Concord I am calde,
  From forraine realmes exilde:
Once Mutuall Loue my husband was,
  And Plentie was our childe:
But ah, quod shee, a hagge of hell
  That long hath sought their spoyle,
Hath slaine them both, unlesse they dwell,
  Within your English soyle.
Heerewith there yssued from her eine,
  Of teares, abundant store:
And sighes so stopt her feeble voyce,
  That shee could speake no more
The sight wherof—mee thought—did rayse,
  Great dolours in my breast:
Yet praying her for to proceede,
  She thus her minde exprest:
Uile Couetousnesse, that Furie fell,
  Hath wrought us all this woe:
To Concord and to Mutuall Loue,
  Shee is a deadly foe:
Time was, when wee were well esteemde,
  And calde ech countrie's stay:

But Couetousnesse now rules the roast,
   And beareth all the sway.
And were it not that in this Land,
   I finde some small reliefe :
I had beene dead long ere this time,
   Through greatnesse of my greefe.
Debate and Rancour night and day,
   On this vile dame attend ;
Whom shee to worke her beastly will,
   About the world doth send.
These two haue raysde such warre and strife,
   In partes beyond the seas,
That now few nations in the Earth,
   Enioy their woonted peace.
Now gold is reuerenced as a god,
   Eche hunts at priuat gayne :
Men care not how their soules shall speede,
   So wealth they may attaine.
Of conscience now few make account ;
   Him men esteeme most wise
Which to beguile his neighbour poore,
   Can craftiest meanes deuise.
This sayd, mee thought the auncient dame,
   Did vanish straight away,
And I awaking heere withall,
   Went home without delay ;
Where taking paper, penne and inke,

With speede I there enrolde
The circumstaunce of all the tale,
That Concord to mee tolde;
Which made me wish that euery one,
Would Mutuall Loue imbrace:
And that no spots of couetousnesse,
With sinne their deeds deface.

A DREAME.

AYD in my quiet bed to rest
    When sleepe my senses all had drownd,
    Such dreames arose within my breast,
As did with feare my minde confound.
  Mee thought I wandred in a wood,
Which was as darke as pitte of hell:
In midst whereof such waters stoode,
That where to passe, I could not tell.
  The lion, tiger, woolfe and beare,
There thundered forth such hideous cries:
As made huge eccoes in the ayre,
And seemed almost to pearce the skies.
  Long vext with care I there aboad,
And to get forth I wanted power:
At euery footsteppe that I troad,
I feard some beast would mee deuoure.
  Abiding thus perplext with paine,

This case within my selfe I scand :
That humaine helpe was all in vaine,
Unlesse the Lord with vs doe stand.

Then falling flatte vpon my face,
In humble sorte to God I prayde :
That in this darke and dreadfull place,
Hee would vouchsafe to bee mine ayde.

Arising then, a wight with winges,
Of auncient yeeres mee thinkes I see :
A burning torch in hand he bringes,
And thus began to speake to mee :

That God, Whose ayde thou didst implore,
Hath sent mee hither for thy sake :
Plucke vp thy sprites, lament no more,
With mee thou must thy iourney take.

Against a huge and loftie hill,
With swifteft pace mee thinkes wee goe :
Where such a sound mine eares did fill,
As moued my heart to bleede for woe ;

Mee thought I heard a woefull wight,
In doleful sorte powre forth great plaintes ;
Whose cries did so my minde afright
That euen with feare ech member faintes :

Fie—quoth my guyd—what meanes this change,
Passe on a pace with courage bolde ;
Hereby doth stand a prison strange,
Where woonderous thinges thou maist beholde.

Then came we to a fort of brasse,
Where peering through greate iron grates,
We saw a woman sit, alas
Which ruthfully bewaylde her fates.

Her face was farre more white then snow,
And on her head a crowne shee ware,
Beset with stones that glistered so,
As hundred torches had bene there.

Her song was woe and weale away,
What torments here doe I sustayne !
A new mishap did her dismay,
Which more and more increast her payne ;

An vggly creature all in blacke,
Ran to her seate and flang her downe :
Who rent her garments from her backe,
And spoyld her of her precious crowne.

This crowne he plaste vpon his hed,
And leauing her in dolefull case,
With swiftest pace away he fled :
And darknesse came in all the place.

But then to heare the wofull mone,
And piteous grones that she foorth sent,
He had no doubt, a heart of stone,
That could geue eare and not lament.

Then—quoth my guide—note well my talke,
And thou shalt heare this dreame declard :
The wood in which thou first didst walke,

Unto the world may be comparde :
  The roaring beasts plainly expresse,
The sundry snares in which we fall ;
  This gaole is naméd Deepe Distresse,
    In which Dame Vertue lies as thrall—
Shee is the wight which here within,
  So dolefully doth houle and crie ;
Her foe is calléd Deadly Sinne
  That proffered her this villany.
My name is Time, whom God hath sent,
  To warne thee of thy soule's decay ;
In time therefore thy sinnes lament
  Least time from thee be tane away.
As soone as he these words had sayd,
  With swiftest pace away he flies :
And I hereat was so afrayde
  That drowsie sleepe forsooke mine eyes.

FOR A GENTLEWOMAN.

IKE as a forte or fencéd towne,
    By foes assault, that lies in field,
  When bulwarkes all are beaten downe,
Is by perforce constraynde to yeelde :
So I that could no while withstand
  The battery of your pleasant loue,

The flagge of truce tooke in my hande,
 And meant your mercy for to proue.
My foolish fancie did enforce
 Me first to like your friendly sute,
Whiles your demaunds bred such remorce,
 That I coulde not the same refute.
I bad you take with free consent,
 All that which true pretence might craue,
And you remaynde as one content,
 The thing obtaynd that you would haue.
Such friendly lookes and countenance fayre,
 You freely then to me profest,
As if all troth that euer were,
 Had harboured beene within your breast.
And I which saw such perfect shewes,
Of fraudlesse fayth in you appeare,
Did yeelde my selfe to Cupid's lawes,
 And shewde likewise a merrie cheere ;
No louing toyes I did withholde,
 And no suspect did make me doubt :
Till your demeanure did vnfolde
 The wilie traines ye went about.
Who sees a ruinous house to fall,
 And will not shift to get him thence,
When limmes be crusht, and broken all,

It's then too late to make defence.
When pleasant bait is swallowed downe,
    The hookèd fish is sure to die :
On these Dame Fortune oft doe frowne,
    As trust too farre before they trie.
Of[t] had I wist , who makes his moane,
    It's ten to one he neuer thrives.
When theeues are from the gibbet throwne,
    No pardon then can saue their liues :
Such good aduice as comes too late,
    May wel be calde, Sir Fore Wit's[1] foole ;
Elswhere goe play the cosoning mate
    I am not now to goe to schoole,
But cleerely doe at length discerne,
    The marke to which my bow is bent,
And these examples shall me warne,
    What harme they haue that late repent.
Your sugred speech was but a baite;
    Wherwith to bleare my simple eyes,
And vnder these did lurke deceipt,
    As poison vnder hony lies.
Wherefore since now your drift is knowne,
    Goe set your staule[2] some other where :
I may not so be ouerthrowne,

---

[1] = foreknowledge : foreweting, (A.S.) G.
[2] Stale or decoy. G.

Your double dealings make me feare.
    When steede by theeues is stolne away,
I will not then the doore locke fast ;
Wherfore depart without delay,
Your woi.ls are winde, your sute is wast ;[1]
    And this shalbe the finall doome,[2]
That I to your request will giue,
Your loue in me shall haue no roome,
Whiles life and breath shal make me liue.

FOR A GENTLEWOMAN.

HAT lucklesse lot had I alas ?
    To plant my loue in such a soyle,
As yeeldes no corne nor fruitfull grasse,
But crops of care, and brakes of toyle ?
    When first I chose the plot of ground,
In which mine anchor foorth was cast,
I thought it stable, firme, and sound,
But found it sand and slime at last.
    Like as the fouler with his ginnes,
Beguiles the birdes that thinke no yll,
By fylèd speech, so diuers winnes

---

[1] = past, *not* ' waste '. Cf. page 67. G.
[2] Sentence, or iudgment. G.

The simple sort to worke theyr will.

But I whom good aduice had taught,
To shun their snares and suttle charmes,
Am not into such daunger brought
But that I can eschew the harmes.

The skilfull faulconer still doth proue,
And prayse that hawke which makes best whing,
So I by some that seemd to loue,
Haue had the proofe of such a thing.

From fist they did pursue their game,
With swiftest whing and egar minde,
But when in midst of flight they came,
They turnde their traynes against the winde :
Yee haggards[1] straunge, thereíore adiew !

Goe seeke some other for thy mate,
Yee false your faith, and proue vntrue ;
I like and loue the sole[2] estate.
Not like Vlisses' wandring men,
In red seas as they past along,

---

[1] An untrained hawk and (metaphorically) a loose
woman. It is a Shakesperean word *e.g.*, " wild as *haggards* of the rock " (Much Ado about Nothing, iii. 1)
" loved this proud, disdainful *haggard* " (Teming of the
Shrew iv. 2.) " if I do proue her *haggard* " (Othello iii. 2.)
G.

[2] Single or bachelor state. G.

Did stoppe their eares with waxe as then,
  Against the suttle mermayds songue.
So shall their crafty filèd talke,
  Hereafter finde no listening eare,
I will byd them goe packe and walke,
  And spend their wordes some other where :
By proofe, experience tels me now,
  What fickle trust in them remaynes,
And tract of time hath learnd me how,
  I should eschew their wylie traines ;
Such as are bound to louer's toyes,
  Make shipwracke of theyr freedome still ;
They neuer tast but brittle ioyes,
  For one good chance a thousand yll.
Cease now your sutes and gloze no more,
  I meane to leade a virgin's life :
In this of pleasure find I store,
  In doubtfull sutes but care and strife. [1]

---

[1] As in the preceding, the listening Reader will catch prelude-notes of " Clara Vere de Vere" in above poem. G.

A GODLY DISCOURSE.

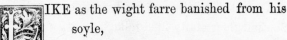

IKE as the wight farre banished from his
    soyle,
    In countrey strange, opprest with grief
    and pain,
Doth nothing way his long and weary toyle,
So that ye[1] may come to his home againe :
And not accounts of perils great at hand,
For to attayne his owne desirèd Land.

Such is the state of vs Thy seruantes all,
—Most gratious God—that here on earth do dwell :
We banisht were through Adam's cursèd fall
From place of blisse, euen to the pit of hell :
Our vice and sinnes, as markes and signes wee
    haue,
Which still we beare, and shal doe to our graue.

When that all hope of remedy was past,
For our redresse when nothing could be found ;
Thine onely Sonne, Thou didst send downe at last,
To salue this sore, and heale our deadly wound ;
Yet did they please to vse Him as a meane,
Us banisht wights for to call home agayne.

And for because Thy Godhead thought it meete,
The sacred booke of Thy most holy wil,

---

[1] Query = he ? G.

Thou didst vs leaue a lanterne to our feete,
To light our steppes in this our voyage still,
Directing vs what to eschew or take :
All this thou doest for us vile sinners' sake.

Graunt vs sound fayth, that we take stedfast
holde,
On Christ, His death, which did our raunsome pay,
So shall we shune the daungers manifold,
Which would vs let[1] and cause vs run astray.
The wicked world, the flesh, the diuel and all,
Are stumbling blockes, ech howre to make vs fall.

This dungeon vile of Sathan is the nest,
A denne of dole,[2] a sinke of deadly sinne.
Heauen is the hauen in which we hope to rest ;
Death is the dore whereby we enter in.
Sweete Sauiour, graunt that so wee liue to die,
That after death we liue eternally.

IN THE PRAISE OF MUSICKE.

HE bookes of Ovid's changed shapes,
A story strange do tell,
How Orpheus to fetch his wife,
Made voyage into hell.
Who hauing past olde Charon's boate,

---

[1] Hinder. G.   [2] = Dule, sadness, woe. G.

Unto a pallace came,
Where dwelt the Prince of damnèd sprites,
  Which Pluto had, to name.
When Orpheus was once arriude,
  Before the regall throne :
He playde on harpe, and sang so sweete,
  As moude them all to mone.
At sound of his melodious tunes,
  The very soules did moorne,
Yxion with his whirling wheele,
  Stood still and would not turne :
And Tantalus would not assay,
  The fleeting floodes to taste :
The Sisters with their hollow siues,
  For water made no haste ;
The greedy vulturs that are faynde,
  On Titius heart to gnawe,
Left off to feede : and stood amasde,
  When Orpheus they sawe ;
And Sysyphus which roules the stone
  Agaynst a mighty hill,
Whyles that his musike did endure,
  Gaue care and sate him stil.
The Furies eke, which at no time,
  Were seene to weepe before,
Were moude to moane his heauy happe,
  And shedde of teares greate store.

If Musicke with her notes diuine,
 So great remorce can moue,
I deeme that man bereft of wits,
 Which Musike will not loue.
She with her siluer sounding tunes,
 Reuiues man's dulled sprites,
Shee feedes the eare ; shee fils the heart,
 With choice of rare delights,
Her sugred descant doth withdraw,
 Thy mind from earthly toyes,
And makes thee feele within thy brest,
 A tast of heauenly ioyes.
The planets and celestiall partes,
 Sweete harmony containe,
Of which if creatures were depriud,
 This world could not remayne :
It is no doubt the very deede
 Of golden melodie,
That neighbours doe together liue,
 In loue and vnitie.
Where man and wife agrees in one,
 Sweete musike doth abound,
But when such stringes begin to iarre,
 Unpleasant is the sound.
Amongst all sortes of harmony,
 None doth so well accord,
As when we liue in perfect feare,

And fauour of the Lord :
Who graunt vnto vs sinfull wightes,
  Sufficient power and might,
According to His mercy great,
  To tune this string aright.

A PLEASAUNT IEST.

SOMETIMES in Fraunce it did so chaunce,
    One that did seruice lacke :
    A country clowne went vp and downe,
  With fardell[1] on his backe :
When that this swad[2] long trauailde had,
  Some seruice to require :
His fortune was, as hee did passe,
  A farmar did him hire.
When Aprill showres, y[t] brings May flowers,
  Made Spring time bud and sprout :
This country swaine, for maister's gaine,
  Did ride his fieldes about :
Now as he road, in ground abroad,
  In prime of pleasaunt Spring :
Hard by their towne, this country clowne,

---

[1] Burden. G.
[2] Country bumpkin, or silly fellow. G.

Did hear two cuckowes sing :
One of them sat fast by a gate,
  In their towne fielde, which stoode
In place neerby ; hee might discry
   The other in a wood.
These cuckoes seemde, as lobcocke[1] deemde,
  With enuie to contend :
Which of them twaine, in playnesong vaine,
  The other could amend.
Thus sange they long, their woonted song :
  Theire towne fielde cuckoes throate
Was nothing cleer, which chaunged the cheere,
  Of farmer's man, God wote.
His horse hee ties, and fast hee hies,
  Upon a tree to stand :
And made a noyse with cuckoe's voyce,
  To get the vpper hand.
Hee thought not good, hee of the wood,
  Should beare away the prayse :
To make him yeeld, to him of fielde,
  Himselfe the cuckoe playes :
' Cuckoe, ' quoth hee, upon the tree,
  And ' cuckoe ' ' cuckoe ' sayde ;
With ' cuckoe ', ' cuckoe ', and ' cuck ' ' cuck '
  ' cuckoe ',

---

[1] Lubber. G.

Long time these cuckoes playde.
As they thus stand, from woodes at hand,
   Two wolues for pray that sought,
By chaunce espyed, the horse fast tyed,
   That lobcocke thither brought;
To him they hye, and presently,
   In peeces did him teare:
Whereat amasde, the lobcocke gazde,
   And pist himselfe for feare.
When wolues were gone, comming downe anone,
   Homewares hee hide with speede:
And there doth tell, all that befell,
   Of this unluckie deede.
His maister swore, being wroth therfore,
   He would none other nay,
But that the slaue and foolish knaue,
   The price of horse should pay.
But to proceede: it was agreed,
   The wiues that there did dwell,
The case should scan, of this poore man,
   If hee did ill or well:
It being seene, he did it in
   Defence of all the towne:
With one intent, they gaue consent,
   For to acquite the clowne.
They eke him gaue a garland braue,
   Adornd with many a rose:

And great and small, him captaine call
  Of cuckoes, where he goes.
Now in my minde, hee were vnkinde,
  That would wish any ill,
Unto a wight, in township's right,
  That shewd so great good will.

A NEW YEERE'S GIFT TO A GENTLE-WOMAN.

F pure good will, not meaning ill, might
      boldly, might boldly,
     Presume to tell his minde :
I wold not vse, in terms diffuse, thus coldly, thus
    coldly
  To shew my selfe a friend.
But now adayes, so sinne preuailes,
That fayth decaies, and friendship fayles,
Most men are so infected with ielous musing
    braines ;
That Trust as one reiected, forsaken cleane remaines.
  And thinges are constred cleane awry,
  When nought was meant but honestie.

Thus much I say, as by the way, reciting, reciting,
  What daunger may ensue :
Because that I suspiciously, in writing, in writing,

Doe send my minde to you.
Some will surmise, that I pretend,
By such deuice some naughtie end :
But let them speak and spare not, I force it not a
    beane,
For al their talke I care not, whilst guiltles I
    remaine.
    Such as haue not transgrest the lawes,
    Doe neuer feare to pleade their cause.

But now sweete hearte, it is my part, to open, to
    open,
    The summe of mine intent :
I send this bil, for pure goodwill, in token, in token,
    That former yeere is spent ;
It is in deede a simple shift,
To serue in steede of new yeere's gift :
Though slenderly I make it, your pardon let mee
    haue,
If in good part you take it, no more of you I craue :
    So shall you binde mee day by day,
    To pleasure you in what I may.

But I offend, such words to spend, in seeking, in
    seeking,
    That you should pardon mee :
If oft I doe, that breeds in you, misliking, mis-
    liking
    Corrected let me bee.

My selfe to you I yeelde and giue,
As prisoner true, whilst that I liue :
So may you be reuenged, for my presumptuous
    heart :
Which hath perhaps offended, to play so leawd a
    part.
    Condemne mee to bee prisoner still,
    So may you boldly worke your will.

Proceede my deere, the case is cleare, now stay
    not, now stay not :
    Give iudgement out of hand :
If you ordaine, perpetuall paine, I way[1] not, I
    way not,
    Your iust decree shall stand.
And if you will award it so,
That I must now to prison go :
Your heart shall be the prison, wherin I will
    abyde,
Vntill by right and reason, my case be throughly
    tride.
    O God, how happy should I bee,
    If such a gaile enclosèd mee.

---

[1] = weigh *i.e.* gainsay.

A DELECTABLE DREAME.

S late abroad asleepe I lay,
  Mee thought I came by wondrous
    chaunce :
Whereas I heard a harper play,
  And saw great store faeries daunce :
I marchèd neere, drawne by delight,
  And prest these gallant dames among :
When as their daunce being ended quite,
  Of him that playde they craue a song ;
My presence nought appalde their minde :
  Hee tundè his harpe, his voyce was cleere,
And as a foe to woman kind,
  He sang this song that foloweth heere.
'A woman's face is full of wiles,
  Her teares are like the crocadill :
With outward cheere on thee she smiles,
  When in her heart shee thinkes thee ill ;
Her tongue still chattes of this and that,
  Then aspine leaf it wagges more fast,[1]
And as she talkes shee knowes not what,
  There yssues many a troathlesse blast.
Thou farre doest take thy marke amisse,

---

[1] Misprinted 'fa' : but the companion rhyme 'blast'
suggests the word meant, *as supra.* G.

If thou thinke fayth in them to finde,
The wethercocke more constant is,
   Which turnes aboute with euery winde.
O how in pittie they abound!
   Their heart is milde, like marble stone!
If in thy selfe no hope bee found,
   Be sure of them thou gettest none.
I know some pepernosèd dame,
   Will tearme me foole and sawcie iack,
That dare their credit so defame,
   And lay such slaunders on their backe.
What though on mee they powre their spite,
   I may not vse the gloser's trade,
I cannot say the crow is white,
   But needes must call a spade a spade '.

Heerewith his songue and musik ceast,
   The faeries all on him did frowne :
A stately dame among the rest,
   Vpon her face falles prostrate downe :
And to the gods request did make,
   That some great plagues might be assind
To him, that all might warning take,
   How they speake ill of womankind.
Heerewith—a wonder to bee tolde—
   His feete stoode fast vpon the ground,
His face was neither young nor olde ;
   His harpe vntoucht would yeeld no sound,

Long hayre did grow about his scull,
   His skinne was white, his blood was read :
His paunch with guts was bombast[1] full,
   No dogge had euer such a head :
His coulour oft did goe and come,
   His eies did stare as he did stand :
Also foure fingers and a thombe,
   Might now be seene in eyther hand ;
His tongue likewise was plaguèd sore,
   For that it played this peeuish parte ;
Because it should offend no more,
   'Twas tyed with stringes vnto his heart :
Yet in his mouth aboad shee still,
   His teeth like walles did keepe her in ;
Which now grinde meate, much like a mill :
   His lippes were placde aboue his chinne.
Thus was hee chaungd, that none him knew,
   But for the same hee was before :
By silent signes hee seemde to sue,
   That gods would now pursue no more,
And hee would there without delayes,
   Recant all that which erst hee spake.
Hee pardoned is ; on harpe hee playes,
   And presently this songue did make :

---

[1] Stuffed. G.

'Amongst all creatures bearing life,
　A woman is the worthyest thing:
Shee is to man a faythfull wife :
　She mother was to Christ our King:
If late by mee they were accusde,
　I haue therefore receiued my hyre :
Unlesse they greatly bee abusde,
　They neuer are repleate[1] with yre :
They neither chide, fight, brawle, nor lye,
　The gentlest creatures vnder sunne :
When men doe square[2] for euery fly,
　To make them friends the women runne,
And where they chaunce to fixe their loue,
　They never swarue, or seeke for chaunge :
No new perswasions can them moue,
　'Tis men that haue desire to raunge :
Like turtles true they loue their spowse,
　And doe their duties euery way :
They see good orders in the house,
　When husbands are abroad at play :
And to conclude they angells are,
　Though heere on earth they doe remaine;

---

[1] = filled. Shakespeare uses it in the very same way :
" eyes *replete* with wrathfull ire ", Henry VI. i. 1.)
et alibi. G.
　[2] Quarrel : another Shakespearean word frequently. G.

Their glittering hew, which shines like star,
   And bewtie braue declares it playne.'

This sayde, the faeries laught,
   And seemde in countenance very glad;
To speake my minde, I then had thought,
   How some were good, and some were bad :
But—marke ill happe—a friend came by,
   Who as hee found mee sleeping so,
Did call mee vp with voyce so hye,
   That slumber sweete I did foregoe.

TO HIS MOST FAYTHFULL FRIEND.

 THING most straunge to tell, of late did
       chance to mee,
   Whiles yᵗ I tooke my pen in hād, to writ
    my minde to thee ;
As I had thought in hast to pach[1] a verse or two,
Without regarde, as common friends, accustomd
    oft to doe :
I could not for my life, mine eies so waking keepe,
But that a sodain slumber came, which made mee
    fal asleep ;

---

[1] Patch. G.

In dreame I seemde to see, appeare beforc mine
   eine,
A comely lady well be seene, attirde in decent wise ;
Most modest were her lookes, most cheerefull eke
   her face,
Methought therin was picturd out, a worthy
   matrō's grace :
O thanklesse wretch, shee said, and canst thou so
   neglect
My worthy lawes ? is there w^t thee of frends no
   more respect ?
Dost know to whome thou writest ? is he a common
   frende ?
Suffiseth it in cōmon sort, that thou shouldst show
   thy mind ?
Hath his desarts deserude of thee no better meede ?
Is this due guerdon for y^t love, which did from
   him proceed ?
In that he had in deedes, byn alwaies friend to
   thee,
Let him peceiue by friendly words, thee thankfull
   stil to be ;
He lookes not for thy deeds, he knowes thy
   power is smal,
And wilt thou then depriue him, wretch, of words,
   of deeds, and al ?

Brute beasts requite good turnes, it cannot be
    denied,
Wilt thou thē be vngrateful, which hast reasō
    for thy guid?
Shal friendship dwell in beasts, and men be found
    vnkinde ?
Shal they for loue, shew loue agayn, and thou
    forget thy friend?
With that shee gaue a becke, and bad me to awake
And said, doe shew thy thankful mind, and so
    requittall make:
Herewith shee did depart, my slumber past away,
I felt my cheeks bedewd wᵗ tears through words
    yᵗ she did say :
Her bitter sharpe rebukes, did make me muse a
    space,
Chiefly in that they did proceede, out from so
    fayre a face,
But then I cald to minde, that Gratitude she was,
That thākfull dame, whose custom is frō friend to
    friend to passe.
I tooke my pen in hand, with purpose to declare
The circumstance of this my dreame, wᶜ cloyd my
    hed with care,
Herein also I thought her precepts to obey,
And al the plot of thy deserts, most largely to
    display ;

But when my dreame was done, I found such litle
    store
Of paper, that I could not haue, wherin to write
    the[e] more.

¶ ONE   THAT   HAD   A   FROWARDE
    HUSBAND,   MAKES   COMPLAYNT
    TO   HER   MOTHER :   WRITTEN   IN
    FRENCH, BY CLEMENT MAROTT.

ND is there any wight aliue,
        That rightly may compare.
        Or goe beyond me, silly wretch,
    In sadnesse and care ?
Some such may be, but this I say,
    One must goe farre to seeke,
To finde a woman in this worlde,
    Whose griefe to mine is like :
Or hath so iust a cause of moane,
    In dumps of deepe despite ;
I linger on my loathsome life,
    Depriud of all delight.
Men say the phœnix is a birde,
    Whoee like cannot bee found ;
I am the phœnix in this worlde,

Of those that care[1] doth wound.
And he that workes me all this woe,
    May be the phœnix well,
Of all enragèd senslesse wightes,
    That in the earth doe dwell.
I moane not here as Dido did,
    Being stryken at the heart,
As woorthy Virgill doeth recorde,
    With dint of Cupid's dart :
Nor in my playnts some louer name,
    As Sappho did of yore :
But husband is the cause heereof,
    Which makes my griefe the more.
For louers if they like vs not,
    We may cast of agayne,
But with our husbandes—good or bad—
    Till death we must remayne.
I doe not speake these wordes, as if
    His death I did desire,
But rather that it might please God,
    His thoughts so to enspire,
That hee might vse me as he ought,
    Or as I doe deserue,
Since that I him—as duety byndes—
    Doe honour, loue, and serue.

---

[1] Misprinted 'that those',   G.

And seemes it not desert thinke you ?
    At his commaund to haue
The beauty greate, and other giftes,
    That Nature to mee gaue ?
Ist not desert, such one with him
    In loyall bed to lie,
As alwayes hath most faythfull byn,
    And will be till shee die :
To looke on him with cheerefull face,
    To call him spouse and friend,
To coll[1] and kisse ; all this he hath,
    With franke and willing mynde,
And all thinges els as God commaunds,
    And duety doth allowe ;
Yet am I dealt with at his handes,
    Alas, I know not howe !
Hee thanklesse man, doth ill for good,
    Agaynst all right and lawe ;
Hee had of mee good fruitfull corne,
    And payes me chaffe and straw ;
For meeke and humble curtesie,
    Fierce cruelty he geues,
For loyalty, disloyalty ;
    And that which most mee grieues,
Is when in sweete and humble sorte,

---

[1] Embrace. G.

I come to make my moane,
 His heart no more is mollified,
  Then is the marble stone.
The cruell lyon ready bent,
 With pawes and teeth to teare,
When that the silly hounde doeth yeelde,
 His malice doeth forbeare.
When Attalus the Romayne host,
 Did erst subdue in field,
His heart to mercy was enclinde,
 As soone as they did yeelde.
Black Pluto eke the Prince of hell,
 Uneasie to bee woone,
When Orpheus had playde on harpe,
 His rankour all was done.
By sweetnesse and by curtesie,
 What is not wrought alas ?
Nerethlesse the sweetenesse feminine,
 Which others all doth passe,
Can nothing doe before the eyes,
 Of my heardhearted feere,[1]
The more that I submit my selfe,
 The straunger is his cheere ;
So that in wrongfull cruelty,
 And spite he doth excel

---

[1] =companion: husband.   F.

The lions wilde, the tyrants stoute,
 And monsters eke of hel.
As ofte as I reuolue in mynde,
 The greatnesse of my harmes,
I thinke how foorth the fowler goes,
 With sweete and pleasant charmes ·
To take the birds; which once betrayd,
 He eyther killes straight way,
Or keepes them pende in pensiue cage,
 That flie no more they may :
And so at first, I taken was,
 By his sweete fleering face,
And now depriude of ioy alas :
 Am handled in like case.
Now if the birdes—as some auouch—
 Doe curse his keeper still,
In language his, why curse I not,
 The anthor of my yll ?
That griefe doeth euer greater harme,
 Which hidden lies in brest,
Then that which to some faithfull friend,
 By speaking is exprest ;
My sorrowes then shall bee reuealde,
 Some stedfast friend vnto ;
My tongue thereby vnto my heart,
 A pleasure greate may doe.
But unto whom shoulde I disclose.

My bondage and my thrall ?
Unto my spouse ? No, surely no,
   My gaynes should bee but small ;
Alas to whom then shoulde I moane ?
   Should I some[louer choose,
Who in my sorowes and my griefes,
   As partner I might vse ?
Occasions great do counsell me
   To put this same in ure :[1]
Mine honour and mine honestie,
   Forbid such rashnes sure ;
Wherefore ye louers al, adew,
   Unto some other goe :
I will obserue my vowèd fayth,
   Though to my greatest foe.
To whome shal I powre forth my plaints ?
   To you most louing mother :
For they by dutie do belong,
   To you, and to none other ;
To you I come to seeke reliefe,
   With moyst and weeping eies :
Even as the hart[2] with thirst opprest,
   Unto the fountaine hies.
If any salue in all the world,

---

[1] Misprinted 'use' = ure : but 'sure' needs 'ure' for
rhyme. G.   [2] Misprinted 'heart', G.

May serue to cure my wound :
Dame Nature says undoubtedly,
  In you it must be found.
Now if some succour may be had,
  Assisted let me be,
But if it lie not in your power,
  Yet spend some teares with me.
That your'r with mine, and mine with your's
  Might so keepe moyst the flowre,
That erst proceeded from your wombe,
  And wasteth euery houre.

HIS FRIEND W. C.[1] TO MISTRES F. K. WHOM HE CALLS HIS CAPTAINE.

S soulders good, obey their captaines will,
    And readie are to goe, to ride, or runne :
    And neuer shrinke their duety to fulfill,
But what they byd, it by and by is done.
  So rest I your's—good captayne—to dispose,
  When as you please, to combate with your foes.

---

[1] Ritson suggests that this poem may have been the pro-
duction of the great *CAMDEN* : and it is not impossible,
seeing that in 1576 he preflxed Verses to Rogers'
"Anatomy of the Mind " : (Bibliographia Poetica p 151)
But it is more likely this W. C. was one of the Copes.
See more in our Memorial-Introduction. G.

Your foes, sayd I? alas what may they be,
That haue the heart to harm so sweete a wight?
Who dare attempt to try his force with thee,
Shall conquerd be, ere he begin to fight.
　　Let thousand foes agaynst thee come in field,
　　Thy beauty great will make them all to yeeld.

To yeeld, sayd I? nay rather would they choose,
By thee subdude, to liue in bondage still,
Then lead such life as conquerors doe vse,
In thy disgrace, and wanting thy good will.
　　But strike the drumme, and let the trumpet sound,
　　To take thy part, whole legions wil be found.

So many eares as euer heard thee speake:
So many eyes as haue thy feature vewde,
So many handes thy puysance hath made weake,
So many heartes thy beauty hath subdued;
　　Ech of these eares, ech eye, ech hand, ech heart,
　　—Sweet captain—stil are prest to take thy part.

Ech eare, to heare when Enuy seekes thy foyle :
Ech eye to spy who worketh thine anoy,
Ech hand, with blade to conquere them in broyle :
Ech gladsome heart, for victory to ioy.
　　Thus euery part the trusty friend will play,
　　For thy behoofe, whom God preserue alway.

382

THE COMPLAYNT OF A SINNER.

IKE as the thefe in prison cast,
 With wofull wayling mones,
 When hope of pardon cleane is past,
  And sighes with dolefull grones :
So I a slaue to sinne,
 With sobs and many a teare,
As one without Thine ayde forlorne,
 Before Thy throne appeare.

O Lorde, in rage of wanton youth
 My follies did abounde,
And eke, since that I knewe Thy trueth,
 My life has been vnsound.
Alas I doe confesse
 I see the perfect way :
Yet frayltie of my feeble fleshe,
 Doth make me run astray.

Aye me, when that some good desire,
 Woulde moue me to doe wel,
Affections fond make mee retire,
 And cause me to rebell.
I wake, yet am asleepe,
 I see, yet still am blinde ;
In ill I runne with hedlong race,
 In good I come behinde.

Loe thus in life I daily die,
    And dying shall not liue,
Unlesse Thy mercy speedily
    Some succour to me geue.
I die, O Lorde, I die,
    If Thou doe mee forsake,
I shall be likened vnto those
    That fall into the Lake.

When that one prop, or onely stay,
    Holdes vp some house or wall :
If that the prop be tane away,
    Needes must the building fall.
O Lorde, Thou art the prop,
    To which I cleaue and leane :
If Thou forsake, or cast mee of,
    I still shall liue in paine.

Although my hard and stony hart
    Be apt to runne astray :
Yet let Thy goodnesse me conuert,
    So shall I not decay :
Sweete God, doe rue[1] my plaints,
    And sheelde me from annoy :
Thē my poore soule this life once past
    Shall rest with Thee in ioy.

---

[1] See foot-note in page 69, No. 3. G.

¶ OF THE VNCONTENTED ESTATE OF
LOUERS.

HO so attempts to publish aud display,
　　Of Cupid's thrals the strange and awk-
　　　　ward fits,
Doth seeke to count the sand amidst the sea,
And wades beyond the compasse of his wits :
　Whose griping greefes and passions to disclose,
　Is to describe a world of care and woes.

More easie its to weild the weightie charge,
That Atlas hath in bearing up the skies :
Then to vnfolde, and picture out at large,
The vncouth cares in louers brests that lies :
　Whose rest is toyle, whose ioy is endlesse
　　greife ;
　They often sue, but seeldome findereleefe.

Yf Plutoe's denne, that vgly pit of hell,
Great griesly plague and tormentes hath in store,
I dare auouch that those in loue which dwell,
Do tast them all, and twice as many more.
　Which makes mee say, and not without goods
　　cause,
　Thrice happlesse wights, that yeelde to Cupid'
　　lawes.

As Aetna hill doth belke[1] forth flakes of fire,
And hydeous sounds are harde within the same:
So louers burne through inwarde hot desire,
And hollow sighes burst out amidst the flame:
   Where scorchèd harts dispaire and anguish gnaw,
   Lyke greedy gripes, that peck Prometheus' maw.

In mirth they moane, yet smile amidst their woe:
In fire they freese, in frost they fry straightway :
Swift legges to runne, yet are not able goe :
Such is the state, in which poore louers stay.
   As houering Hope dooth hoyst them vp on hye,
   Feare clips their wings, so that they cannot flye.

They fayne in hell, one onely plague to fall,
For iust reuendge to those that doe amisse :
But they that loue, are subiect to them all,
And neuer feele one lightning howre of blisse :
   That — to conclude — thrice happyy is their
     chaunce,
   That neuer knew to treade the louer's daunce.

---

[1] Belch. G.

A NEWYERE'S GIFT TO MISTRESSE C. P.

SWEET wight be glad, pluck vp your
  sprites,
 Old friendship is renewd :
Milde Concorde hath thrown down the broth,
 That Discord lately brewd .
Fowle Enuie, Malice, and Debate,
 In teares their time doe spend :
In that the platforme which they layde,
 Came not to wishèd end.
The mightie Ioue, which ruleth all,
 Their prayers heard, no doubt :
Else could not their hot kindled wrath,
 So soone bee quenchèd out :
Thus farre their furie did preuaile,
 A time and place was set,
Whereas[1] at their appoynted houre,
 To try it out, they met,
And dealt : for vowes had rashly past,
 So long foes to abide :
Untill the one, the other's force,
 In open field had tried :
I shrinke, to thinke what horror great,
 Now gripes your heart through feare.

---

[1] Here as elsewhere = whereat or simply where. **G.**

I seeme to see ech member quake,
    As if yee had been there :
To heare my Muse vnto my eares,
    This dolefull tale to tell :
Put feare to flight, cast care aside,
    All things are ended well :
But Rancour vile, couldst thou powre forth,
    Thy spite vpon none other :
But that to combat thou must bring,
    My father and my brother ?
And I my selfe with eies must see,
    And view this dolefull sight ?
Goe packe, thou hast sustaind the foyle,[1]
    For all thy poysoned might :
For by the blowes that they did giue,
    Theyr friendship doth encrease,
And in their heartes establisht is,
    An everduring peace.
The seedes that thou in them didst plant,
    Are pluckt vp by the roote :
Thy sister Discord neuer shall,
    Againe set in her foote.
For if in dealing of their blowes,
    Their handes had not bene blest :
A late repent had made them rew,

---

[1] = fall, defeat. G.

For harbouring such a gest,
But of vngrate discurtesies,
    Wee iustly might complaine :
In that entreaties would not serue,
    To make them friendes againe :
If in their mad and brainesicke heads,
    Dame Reason had borne sway :
But Malice, Rancour, and Debate,
    Had banisht wit away.
So that occasion of this broyle,
    Was not our faythfull friendes :
But these forenamèd furies fell,
    And other hellish fiendes,
Whose daily driftes are to deface,
    Of friendes the pure estate :
And makes them harbour[1] in their hearts,
    Great heapes of deadly hate :
In that things past betwixt them are
    Forgiuen and forgot :
Let vs imbrace and loue them so,
    As if this happened not.
If straunge it seeme that straunger I,
    in verse to you doe write :
Assure your selfe, it doeth proceede,
    Through greatnesse of delite,

---

[1] Misprinted ' barbour '. **G.**
389   I

That I conceaue in that I see,
  them reconcilde so well,
Whome no perswasions latelie serude,
  their furies to expell.
These simple verses to your viewe,
  I haue thought good to sende,
In token of a good Neweyeere,
  And so farewel, I ende.

A STRAUNGE HISTORIE.

YEE that would heare a story straunge,
    To this example rare,
      Attentiuely take heede :
Which pictures heere, before your face,
    A worthy wight indeede :
A phenix, well she may be calde,
    Whose lyke cannot be founde,
      Chast Camna was her name :
Endued with such comely giftes,
    As none can tell the same.
All wiues that in those dayes did lyue,
    This woman did excell
In constant loue towardes her spouse,
    As doth my story tell.
Sinatus was her husband cald,
    a gentleman by blood :

Whose graue aduice in time of neede,
did neighbours his, much good.
In such chast loue this man and wife,
togither did remaine,
That no man could their spotlesse life,
With any blot distaine.

In selfe same citie where they dwelt,
A tyrant vile bare rule;
Sinoris was his name :
Who being taken with her loue,
Did wooe this worthy dame.
When after many onsets giuen,
Hee had sustaind repulse,
His trauayle spent in vayne ;
Her worthy spowse Sinatus then,
Hee causèd to be slaine.
For he surmisde the feruent loue,
That shee to husbande bare,
Did hinder him from his desires,
And eke procurd his care.
This done, afresh this tyraunt vile,
Pursues in cursèd suite
Of her ; then[1] that hee did before,
Hee reapes none other fruite.
The secret flames of Cupid's fire,

---

[1] = Than, and so onward. G.

Now broyled so in his breast :
That nought but Camna could restore,
Sinoris' wonted rest.

Resolued fully was he then,
    To take this dame to wife,
        Though baser in degree :
When no meanes els could serue his turne,
    To cracke her honestie.
Then suite was made vnto her friendes,
    Who waying well his wealth,
        Would haue her needes consent.
She after great denialles made,
    At length did seeme content.
Sinoris, when he heard this newes,
    Was passing measure glad :
And order gaue in al post hast,
    For marriage to be had.
To temple of Diana then,
    With speede these couple goe :
And with them sundry worthy wightes,
    The marriage rites to doe.
In outwarde shew shee did expresse,
    Great sounds of mirth and ioy :
But in her heart shee did contriue,
    This tyrant to destroy.

Ere that they fully were assurde,
    Chast Camna bad one bring,

To her a drinking glasse :
Of which shee must to husband drinke,
As there the custome was.
She tempred had a pleasaunt drinke,
With balefull poyson strong :
Of which shee dranke one part,
And to Sinoris gaue the rest :
Which so did pricke his heart,
That phisicke's skill could not preuaile,
To save his vading[1] life ;
Which well did please the minde of her,
That then should be his wife.
When Camna saw that her deuice,
Did frame euen as shee would :
Shee greetes Diana's image there,
With thankes a thousand folde :
And meekely kneeling on her knees,
Ah Goddesse, then she sayde,
Thou knowest from murdring of my selfe
How hardly I haue stayde.
Thou knowest quoth shee, what bitter pangues,

---

[1] So in Euphues (sign. x i. *b.*) " And how in the *vading* of our daies, when we most should, we have least desire to remember our end." Samuel Rowlands, in his " Good Newes and Bad Newes " (1622) has ' v ' for ' f '—" When Hodge comes home, heel'e tell his *vather* newes." (Epigram). Perhaps Shakespeare's " leaves all *vaded* " (Richard II. 1. 2.) is another example. G.

Hath gripte my heart with griefe :
Since my deare husband's death :
And onely hope of iust reuenge,
  Prolongèd hath my breath ;
Which since I see now come to passe,
  With gladnesse will I die,
    And seeke that soule to finde
In life and death, which then my selfe,
  To me was deerer friend.
And thou, thou caitife vile—quoth shee—
  Which did my mariage craue :
In steede now of a mariage bed,
  Prepare thy selfe a graue.
But seeing then Sinoris dead,
  To husbande's sprite shee cryed :
Oh, let not thy sweete company,
  To me now be denied :
Come meete me now my louing mate,
  Who still I tender most :
And saying so, her armes abroad,
  Shee yeelded vp the ghost.

A MERRY IEST.

SOMETIMES in France, a woman dwelt,
  Whose husband being dead :
Within a yeere, or somewhat more,
An other did her wed.

This good wife had of wealth great store,
    Yet was her wit but thin :
To shew what happe to her befell,
    My Muse doth now begin.
It chauncèd that a scholler poore,
    Attirde in course aray,
To see his friends that dwelt farre thence,
    From Paris tooke his way :
The garments were all rent and torne
    Wherwith the wight was clad :
And in his purse to serue his neede,
    Not one deneere[1] he had :
He was constrained to craue the almes,
    Of those which oft wowld giue,
His needy and his poore estate
    With something to relieue.
This scholler on a frostie morne,
    By chaunce came to the doore
Of this old silly woman's house,
    Of whom wee spake before.
The husband then was not at home,
    Hee craueth of the dame :
Who had him in, and gaue him meate,
    And askt from whence hee came.
I come—quoth hee—from Paris towne :

---

[1] = a penny (French). G.

From Paradise?—quoth she—
Men call that Paradise, the place,
    Where all good soules shalbe.
Cham[1] zure my vurst goodman is dere,
    Which died this other yeere:
Chould geue my friend a good gray groate,
    Some newes of him to heare.
Hee saw shee did mistake his wordes,
    And thought to make some glee:
And saide, your husbande is in health,
    I lately did him see:
Now by my troth,—quoth shee—cham[1] glad,
    Good scholler doe declare:
Was not he wroth, because I sent
    Him from this world so bare?
Indeede—quoth hee—he was displeasd,
    And thought it farre vnmeete,
You hauing all, to send him hence,
    With nothing but a sheete.
—Quoth shee—good scholer let me know,
    When thou returnst agayne?
Hee answerd, Dame I will be there,
    Within this weeke or twayne.
Shee sayde, my friend if that iche[2] durst,
    Presume to be so bolde,

----

[1] = I am. G.   [2] = I might dare. G.

Chould pray thee carrie him some clothes,
　　To keepe him from the colde.
Hee said he woulde with all poste haste :
　　Into the towne shee hies,
Hat, doublet, shert, coate, hose, and shoes
　　Shee there for husband buyes.
Shee praying him in earnest sorte,
　　It safely to conuey,
Did geue him money in his purse,
　　And so he went his way.
Not halfe of halfe an howre was past,
　　Ere husband her's, was come;
What newes shee heard from Paradise,
　　Shee tolde him all and some.[1]
And farther did to him declare,
　　What token shee had sent;
Whereat her husband waxed wroth,
　　And woondrous ill content.
He calde her sotte, and doating foole,
　　And after him doth ride;
The scholler was within an hedge,
　　And him a farre espide.
He was afrayde, and downe doeth fling,
　　His fardell[2] in a dike;

---

[1] = whole and in details. G.　　[2] Burden, as before. G.

The man came neere, and askt him newes,
     Of one whom hee did seeke,
That bare a fardell at his backe :
     The scholler musde awhile,
Then answearing said, such one I saw,
     Passe ouer yonder style.
With hasty speede he downe alightes,
     And doth the scholler pray,
Till he the man had ouertane,
     So long the horse to stay.
Untill he passèd out of sight,
     Full still the scholer bides;
Who taking then his fardell on
     His horse, away he rides.
When he returned and saw himselfe,
     By scholer flouted so,
Your selues may iudge what cheere he made,
     If he were wroth or no,
He sware I thinke a hundred oathes,
     At length *per mundum toots,*
For that he had no shoes to weare,
     Martch homewardes in his bootes.
His wife did meete him at the doore,
     Hayee cought man ?—quoth shee—
No dame—he sayde—he caught my horse :
     The diuel take him and thee.
With that shee laught, and clapt her hands,

398

And sayde cham glad ich sweare,
 For nowe he hath a horse to ride,
  He wilbe quickly there.
When that her husband well had wayde,
 That remedy there was none,
  He takes his fortune in good parte,
   And makes no farther mone.
Now whether that this honest wife,
 Did loue her first good man,
  To such as shall peruse this tale,
   The case I leaue to scan.

TO HIS FRIEND.

F thou wilt shun the pricking briers,
 And thornie cares that folly breedes,
 Put bridle to thy fond desires,
Make reason mistress of thy deedes.
 Attempt no thing by rash advice,
 If thou thus doe, then art thou wise.

Where Wit to Will is slaue and thrall,
Where fond affection beareth sway,
Ten thousand mischiefes doe befall :
And vertue cleane is cast away,
 For hauing rashness for theyr guide,
 Such cannot choose but wander wyde.

Their credite quickly lies in dust,
Which yeelde as bondslaues to their Will,
And follow euery foolish lust;
Such leaue the good, and chuse the yll,
 The wayes of vertue those foregoe,
 And tread the pathes of care and woe.

Wilt thou possesse eternall ioyes,
And porte of blisse at length attayn?
Still prayse the Lorde with heart and voyce,
From doyng yll thy steps refrayne.
 These things obserude, be sure at last,
 In heauen with Christ, thou shalt be plast.

A NEWEYEERES GIFT TO MAISTER G. R.

HE curtesies yee haue to mee profest,
 The bounty great that doth from you
  proceed,
Woulde make me deeme that day to be most blest,
In which I might stand you in any steede,
 When if I flinch, cry on me open shame,
 And where you come, doe bafful[1] my good name.

---

[1] To treat with indignity. Qy.—the transition-form of
'baffle'. It is found in Spenser (Fairy Queen, B. vi. vii.
27) and in Shakespeare (Richard II. i. 1.) G.

If yee doe muse that I but now begin,
For to expresse that heart hath long concealde,
Assure your selfe, my secrete thought within,
So pricke me foorth it needes but be reuealde.
  And eke desire, doth bid me let you know,
  The loyall zeale and duety that I owe.

As I confesse there is not in me ought,
To answeare that my *Velle*[1] would fulfill,
So—make account—right farre hee must be sought,
That doth surmount or passe me in good will.
  Which as in wordes I haue geuen out to some,
  My deedes shal try, if once occasion come.

A crew there are, whose nature is to gloze,
And vaunt in words, when heart thinks nothing˘
      lesse ;
Assure your selfe, that I am none of those,
But will performe what here I doe professe,
  If that I shrink, when you haue cause to rid
      me,
  Doe cast me off, and vtterly denie me.

Of fortune's giftes since slender is my part,
Take here in signe of happy yeere at hand,
These ragged lines, true herauldes of my heart,

---

[1] Query = the old French ' value' *i. e.* valour ? It is
printed in Roman as if to indicate an exotic word. G.

By which yee may my meaning vnderstand ;
   Their maister hath geuen them in charge to tel,
   When he would worst, y^t hee doth wish you
     wel.

A TRANSLATION OUT OF THE FRENCH.

 HEAUENLY God, all beastes that doe
       remayne,
       And nourisht are with fruite that thou
       doest send,
Within the wooddes, the mountaynes, and the
     playne,
Thy holy hest and lawes doe not offende,
The scudding fish that swimmes amidst the sea,
The pretie birdes that play them in the ayre :
Sunne, moone aud stars, ech thing doth Thee
     obey,
And at Thy voyce doe tremble all for feare,
But man alas, yea man, whom Thou doest make,
More perfect farre then all things els that liue ;
Man whom Thou wouldst Thy proper shape to
     take,
To whom for guyde, Thou reason eke didst geue,
And wit, and sense for to discerne aright,

What thing to take, what likewise to refuse,
He, he, vile wretch, and most vnthankefull wight,
Thy maiesty, and honour doth abuse.

A COMPLAINT OF A SINNER.

 LORD most deare, w^t many a teare,
    lamenting, lamenting,
     I fall before Thy face,
And for this crime, done ere this time, repenting,
    repenting,
   Most humbly call for grace.
Through wanton will I must confesse,
Thy precepts still I doe trangresse;
The world with his vayne pleasure,
Bewitcht my senses so,
That I could finde no leasure,
   My vices to foregoe.
I graunte I haue through my deserte,
Deserud great plagues and bitter smart.

But yet sweet God, doe stay Thy rod, forgeue me,
    forgeue me,
   Which doe Thine ayde implore,
O cease Thine ire, I Thee desire, beleeue me,
    beleue me,
   I will so sinne no more.

403

But still shall pray Thy holy name,
    In the right way my steppes to frame,
So shall I not displease Thee,
    Which art my Lord of might.
My heart and tongue shall prayse Thee,
    Most humbly day and night ;
I will delight continually,
    Thy name to lawde and magnify.

With sighes and sobs, my heart it throbs, remem-
      bring, remembring,
    The fraylty of my youth ;
I ran a race, deuoyd of grace, not rendring, not
      rendring,
    Due reuerence to Thy truth.
Such care I cast on earthly toyes,
    That nought I past for heauenly ioyes ;
But now it me repenteth :
    My heart doeth bleede for woe,
Which inwardly lamenteth,
    That euer it sinnèd so.
With many a sigh, and many a grone,
    O Lord to Thee I make my mone.

Though furious fires of fond desires, allure me,
      allure me,
    From Thee to wander wyde :

Let pitifull eyes, and moystened eyes, procure
    Thee, procure Thee
    To be my Lorde and guyde.
As Scripture sayth, Thou doest not craue,
    A sinner's death, but wouldest him saue :
That sinfull wretch am I O Lorde,
    Which would repent and liue ;
With ceaslesse plaints I cry, Lorde,
    Thy parodn to me geue.
O Lorde for Thy sweete Jesu sake,
    Doe not shut vp Thy mercie-gate.

Mercy, mercy, mercy, graunt me, I pray Thee, I
    pray Thee,
    Graunt mercy, louing Lorde!
Let not the diuel which meanes me euill, betray
    me, betray mee,
    Protect me with Thy Worde.
So shall my heart find sweete reliefe,
    Which now feeles smart and bitter griefe ;
O Lorde, I doe request Thee,
    To guyde my steppes so well,
That when death shall arest me,
    My soule with Thee may dwell
In heauen aboue, where angels sing,
    Continuall prayse, to Thee theyr king.

A DUMPE.

THE pangues, the priuie mones,
    The inward secret smarte,
    The griefes, the heauie grones,
  That vexe my dolefull heart,
So plundge my life in paines,
  And reaue me of all ioy,
That death is onely meanes,
  To ridde me from annoy

I graunt that vitall breath, preserueth life in me,
Yet liue I so, that death more welcome farre
    should be:
No wight was euer so perplexèd with despite,
I liue to taste ech woe, and die to all delight.

Although by outward looks, some deeme me void
    of thought,
Lookes are no certayne bookes, but bear false titles
    oft.
For sundry times I iest, when ioy—alas—is small,
And laugh amongst the rest. yet have no lust[1] at
    all.

Loe thus in secrete strife, my lingring dayes are
    led,

---

[1] Cf. our Lord Brooke in index of words, I. 158.   G.

I die yet am aliue, I liue, as being dead.

The more I beare it out, as if I felt no yll,
The greater griefes, no doubt, doe grow within
me still.

The thing which doth amate[1], and most anoy my
mind,
Is that my hard estate, no remedy can finde.
As one that loathes to liue, and daily calles for
death,
These lines to thee I giue, in witnesse of my fayth.

A DUMPE BY HIS FRIEND G. C.[2]

Y heauy heart in dolours drownde,
Consumes and pines away :
And for me wreth[3] nought can be
found,
To cause my cares decay.

---

[1] = perplex. **G.**

[2] Probably one of the Cope Family, in answer to the
preceding. **G.**

[3] This looks like a misprint for 'wretch,' which un-
questionably is the meaning here: but as in 'wrethcock'
'wrethocke', and 'wretchcock', used indiscriminately to
indicate a miserable, stunted or half-starved domestic fowl,
Gifford may have intended to spell 'wreth' as either=
wretch as a noun, or 'wretched' adjectively. Hence I
leave it so. **G.**

Yee eyes of mine, helpe to bewayle,
    Powre foorth your brinish teares,
To rue, alas, his wretched state,
    In whom no ioy appeares.
How should I wretch take any rest,
    How can my heart feele ioy,
When as the wight, that loues mee best,
    Lyes plundgèd in annoy ?
Whereto serue teares, but to bewayle,
    The losse of such a friend ?
Weepe eies, alas, weepe on your fill,
    And neuer make an end.
His troubled state, if to redresse,
    The spending of my blood,
Or that small pelfe that I possesse,
    Could doe him any good :
Then should your eies somtimes permit,
    Mee silly wretch to sleepe,
But out alas, it may not bee,
    Wherfore cease not to weepe.

Such inward griefe doth mee assayle,
    Through thought of his estate :
That if I long of succour fayle,
    All helpe will come too late :
O Sacred Loue, to cure these woes,
    Use thou some speedie meanes :

Or els, alas, with some short death,
Despatch mee of these paines.

FOR HIS FRIEND.

ATE being new fangled, so fancie did
moue,
I was fast entangled in nets of blinde
loue,
—Good friends, doe beleeue me—I chose out a
trull,[1]
Which daily doth giue me a shrewd crow to pull.
Fauour with her fellowes raisde coales of desire,
Bewtie was the bellowes, that first blew the fire.
Thus was I enflamèd, no reason was left me,
My senses were lamèd, my wits were bereft me.
In hope of some fauour, I then fell a wooing :
Such was her behauiour, she sought my vndoing.
Small is my promotion, most foolish, what ment I,
To yeelde my deuotion, to such a dame daintie ?
Since loue first soiournèd, such ease doe I feele,

---

[1] Another Shakesperean word, *e.g.* "The Dauphin and
his *trull* " (1 Henry VI., ii. 2) : like an Amazonian *trull* "
(3 Henry VI., i. 4) : "his potent regiment to a *trull* "
(Anthony and Cleopatra, iii. 6) *et alibi* : = a mistress. **G.**

As Yxion turned about on the wheele.
Although by deseruing, she ought to be mine,
With Tantalus staruing, in griefe still I pine.
And through her controlling, my rest is as ill,
As Sisiphus rolling the stone vp the hill.
Thus is my state chaungèd, deepe dolours do fill
    mee,
My mirth is estraungèd ; good Death come and
    kil me :
Whiles I heere in moning, the time out doe linger,
My griefe and my groning is falne in my finger.
My finger, my finger, my finger, beleeue me :
Alas little finger, ful sore thou dost grieue me !
Was euer a finger perplext in such taking,
I thinke my poore finger will neuer leaue aking.
The cause of my sadnes at length I coniecture,
Is loue with [t]his madnes, that breedes this
    infecture.
I force out[1] a pinne, it forth now is gotten :
Yet whole is the skinne, the flesh is not rotten.
I heard when it fel, now feel I no euil :
Dame daintie farewell, adew to the deuill.

---

[1] Misprinted 'not'.   G.

A STRAUNGE HISTORIE.

 YOUNG man once by chaunce that lost
  his way,
  Through deserts wilde, as on a time
  hee past;
Foure lyons fierce, that sought to gaine some
  pray,
With gasping throte hee saw make at him fast.
Who running swift, to shunne this daunger great,
Espied a well; small trees about it greewe,
By which hee honge, and in the same did leape,
Their ramping[1] pawes and malice to eschew.
Thus as hee thought the peril to escape,
Hee did discry a mightie Dragon fell,
With open mouth most hidiously to gape,
Him to deuour, in bottome of the well.
Then lifting up his head, hee lookèd out,
And might perceiue the lions still remaine,

---

[1] Large, strong. So Shakespeare : '*ramping* fool ' (King
John iii. 1.) 'the *ramping* lion ' (3 Henry **VI.** v. 2).
Also Milton later, has the same word : cf. Samson Agonistes
1, 139 : Paradise Lost IV. 343, and vii. 466. The word is
evidently from the heraldic 'rampant '. An heraldic
' rampant lion ' stands on one hind leg, with the fore-paws
elevated, in the attitude of striking. Hence 'rampant
paws ' or 'ramping pawes '. G.

Which in such sort beset the well about,
That of escape all hoping was in vaine.
Thus as with Death himself besiegde hee saw,
A chaunce befell, which made him more dismayde :
Two beastes, one white, the other blacke did knaw,
The litlle twigges that him from falling stayde.
With daunger thus beset on euery side,
Hee in a hole behind his backe did finde,
A honny pot, which some man there did hide :
Now casting all his care out of his minde,
Hee with one hand the honny sweete did tast :
The other did from falling him sustaine :
Untill the beastes had gnawne the twigs at last,
That downe hee fell and ruthfully was slaine.
This well, the world doth truly represent,
In which we liue in daunger euery houre :
By lions foure, the elements are meant,
Which dayly seeke all mankinde to deuoure.
The Dragon fell, doth signifie our graue,
The twigges self-loue, the beasts, the night and
  day,
The honny pot, the great desire we haue
To worldly ioyes, euen to our soule's decay.
Ech one therfore, I earnestly aduise,
Heere in this world to vse themselues so well :
And spend their dayes in such a godly wise,
That after death, their soules in heauen may dwell.

FAREWELL COURT.

The Preface to a Treatise ensuing, compyled by the Authour, vpon a theme giuen by his approued friend and kinsman, Maister A. D.

 HAUE, according to my promise, though slenderly, compiled this simple discourse on the theme that yee gaue me, which was your Farwel to the Court: which although it be nothing so well handled, as by some experienced courtier, it might haue beene done: neuerthelesse it being considered, that my education hath beene so far distant from the Court, that I neuer sawe the fashions of the Court, I hope that the priuiledge of a pardon may bee purchased for my excuse in this behalfe. I haue herein introduced Witte and Wil as two domestical counsellers, alwayes attendant on a man marching in this vale of miserie: The one giuing him trustie and wholsome admonitions, how hee should here direct his life to the glory of God, and his soule's health: the other with the flattering alluremets of the sinfull flesh, enticeth him to the pursutes of the pleasures of this worlde, in the end drouning him in the puddle of al abhomination, to the vtter confusion both of body and soule. Vnder the person of Wit is prefigured a man, hauing a certaine care-

---

[1] Query—Danvers? See page 49. G.

full regarde of his calling, which is once in a man's
life instilled into the harts of those whome God
hath sealed vp vnto saluation, and causeth them
cleane to cast away the vile and vaine vanities
that the wicked world accounteth as precious, and
addict all their doings towards the attainement of
lyfe euerlasting. Vnder the person of Will is pic-
turde out how a man letting slippe the bridle of his
affections, is caryed from the precious paths of
perfect felicitie, to the ineuitable daungers of
drowning Caribdis : and so passing the sea of the
world, not stopping his eares with the waxe of
vnderstanding, the voluptuous pleasures thereof,
as subtill Sirens, entice him to the folowing of
them, whome they presently drown in such
delights, that he hath neuer further regarde to the
preseruing of his soule, but imitating the nature
of bruite beastes, addicteth himselfe onely vnto
that, which his owne sensuall appetite shal allowe
to be good. Although this may, peraduenture
seeme vnto you a too far fetched circumstance,
little or nothing pertinent to the purpose : yet my
hope is, that when yee haue thoroughly perused it,
yee shall not finde the theme that yee gaue me,
left altogether vntouched. The best is, I know
your thankfull disposition to be such, that how-
soeuer it be, being willingly offered, I, shal not

of you be vngratefully accepted. Thus referr-
ing the view heereof to your discret consideration,
I wish you and yours abundance of such prosperitie, as your heart desireth.　H. G.

FAREWELL COURT.

 ' YOUTH, when fancie bare the sway,
　　Within my peeuish braine :
　And Reason's lore by no meanes could
　My wanton Will restraine :
My gadding minde did pricke me forth,
　A courtier's life to proue :
Whose golden shewes, and vaine delights,
　My senses then did moue.
Not halfe so fast the bowdged[1] shippe,
　The water in doth drinke :
When foes by force of roring gunnes,
　Endeuour her to sinke.
As when the floodes of fond desires,
　Came rumbling in my head :
Which clean extinguisht Vertue's sparks,
　That Nature there had bred.
No power I had the sinfull snares
　Of filthy vice to shunne:

---

[1] Transition-form of ' bulged '=broken or leaking. G.

My good desires did melt away,
   As snow against the sunne :
If Wit sometimes would goe about,
   Mee wisely to perswade,
How that I spent my time amisse,
   And vsde a naughtie trade :
Then wilfull Will would bee at hand,
   And plucke me by the sleeue :
And tell me plaine, Wit was a foole,
   And could no counsell geue.
His lores—quoth Will—are very sowre,
   His precepts are but colde :
Doe follow mee, then all delights,
   To vse thou mayst bee bolde.
He talkes of Scripture euery hower,
   Unsauery to disgest :
And I will alwayes serue thy turne,
   With that which likes thee best.
Who would not rather rome abroad,
   To seeke some pleasaunt sporte ;
Then to be pend in study fast,
   Like souldier in a forte ?
To hawke, to hunt, to carde, to dice,
   To sing, to daunce, to play :
And can there bee more pleasaunt meanes,
   To driue away the day ?
To tosse the buckler and the blade,

Lewd women to entice
Are not these vertues most esteemde,
  And had in greatest price ?
To lend ech man a friendly looke,
  And vse the gloser's arte ;
In outward shewe to beare good will,
  And hate him with our heart.
Are not such men as flatter best,
  In euery coast esteemde ?
Is not Tom Teltroath euerywhere,
  A busie cockscombe deemde ?
It is a world to see the sotte,
  To haue a checke, hee knowes :
And yet the noddy neuer linnes,[1]
  Men's vices to disclose.
Hee euer telles men of their faultes,
  Such is his rude behauiour,
When hee by speaking nought at all,
  Might purchase greater fauour.
Who countes it not a wiseman's parte,
  To runne with hare and hound ?
To say and vnsay with one breath :
  So winning may bee found.
Wherefore reioyce, set cocke on hoope,
  Let nothing make thee sad,

---

[1] Linne = cease. G.

Bee mery heere : when thou art dead,
   No mirth can then bee had.
Thus wanton Will would euery day
   Still whisper in mine eare :
And Wit, which could not then be heard,
   Who fled I know not where.

Who tries the hazard of the seas,
   By sturdy tempest tost :
If that a drunkard guide their ship,
   Are they not quickly lost ?
How like—I pray you—is hee then,
   To suffer shipwracke still,
Whose wit and wisdome governde is,
   By his vnruly Will ?
This pilot vile, in mee long time,
   Did maister's room supply :
Till Good Aduice did tell mee plaine,
   I ranne my course awry.
Hee spyed a time to breake his minde,
   When Will was gone apart :
And thus to mee he did vnfolde,
The secretes of his heart.
O man, for whome Christ on the crosse,
   His precious blood did spill :
What dost thou meane in mundane toyes
   To spend thy time so ill ?

Dost thou not thinke that God hath eies,
   To see thy vile abuse?
What shew of reason can'st thou bring,
   Thy rashnes to excuse?
Did Christ sustaine most bitter death,
   All sinners to redeeme:
And wilt thou wallow still in lust?
   And not His lawes esteeme?
If He by death and no meanes els,
   Men's sinfull soules could saue,
Doest thou then thinke by wanton life,
   Eternall ioyes to haue?
Too too too[1] much thou art deceaude,
   If so thou doe beleeue
That He to haue men liue in vice,
   Himselfe to death would geue.
With vpright eye peruse His lawes:
   And thou shalt cleerely see,
Into what sinkes of deadly sinne,
   Thy Will hath carried thee.
Thine eyes doe see, thine eares doe heare:
   Thy senses all doe serue thee,
Yet canst thou neyther heare nor see,
   Such thinges as should preserue thee;
In earthly toyes thou canst discerne

---

[1] = the superlative of 'much'. **G.**

That which may best auayle thee,
    But in such thing as touch thy soule,
        Thy eyesight still doeth fayle thee ;
O what a madnesse moues thy minde !
    Thou seest and hast thy senses,
        Yet wilt thou blindly wallow still,
In filth of vile offences,
It better were for one to bee,
    Of sight depriuèd cleere,
Then see to sinne, and not see that
    Which chiefly should be seene.
Take heede therefore, at length repent,
    It better late then neuer :
For Christ, the cockle from the corne,
    At haruest will disseuer ;
At day of doome, the good and bad,
    Shall not alike remayne :
The good shall taste vncessant ioyes,
    The bad eternall payne.
Doste thinke that such as tos-pot-like,
    Set all at sixe and seuen,
Are in a ready way to bring
    Their sinfull soules to heauen ?
And those that in great princes Courtes,
    Doe ruffian-like behaue them ;
Doste deeme that they thereby procure,
    A ready meane to saue them ?

To sweare, to stare, to bib and bowse,[1]
  To flatter, glose and lye ?
Is this—tell me—the stedfast fayth,
  That men are sauèd by?
If white be blacke, if night be day,
  If true pretence, bee treason :
If fire be colde, if senslesse things
  Fulfill the rule of reason :
Then may the pleasures of this worlde,
  Be cause of our saluation ;
For otherwise, thou must confesse,
  They further our damnation :
Take heede therefore, and warnèd thus,
  Let not the worlde beguile thee,
Ne let the lustes of lawlesse flesh,
  With sinfull deedes defile thee.
Let wilfull Will be banisht cleane,
  With all his wanton toyes;
Which filles thy head with vayne delightes,
  Insteade of stedfast ioyes.
Note well my wordes, still serue the Lorde,
  Repent and sinne no more,
Christ hath for true repentaunt heartes,
  Great mercie still in store.

---

[1] *Bib*, to drinke or tipple : *bowse*, over-indulge in drinking. G.

When Good Advice had tolde this tale,
　　Prostrate I downe did fall,
And humbly holding vp my handes,
　　Thus on the Lorde did call.

' O mighty God which for vs men,
　　Didst suffer on the Crosse,
The payneful pangues of bitter death,
　　To saue our soules from losse ;
I yeeld Thee heere most hearty thankes,
　　In that Thou doest vouchsaue,
Of me most vile and sinfull wretch,
　　So great regard to haue.
Alas none euer had more cause,
　　To magnifie Thy name,
Then I, to whom Thy mercies shewde,
　　Doe witnesse well the same.
So many brunts of fretting foes,
　　Who euer could withstand,
If Thou had'st not protected mee,
　　With Thy most holy hand?
A thousand times in shamefull sort,
　　My sinfull life had ended,
If by Thy gratious goodnesse Lorde,
　　I had not byn defended.
In stinking pooles of filthy vice,
　　So deepely was I drownde,

That none there was but Thee alone,
  To set my foote on ground.
Whenas the fiend had led my soule
  Euen to the gates of hell,
Thou caldst mee backe, and doest me choose,
  In heauen with Thee to dwell ;
Let furies now fret on their fill,
  Let Sathan rage and rore,
As long as Thou art on my side,
  What neede I care for more ? '

My prayer sayde : me thought I felt
  Such quiet in my mynde,
As shipmen after tempest past,
  In wishèd harbour finde ;
My Will woulde then no more presume,
  To rule in Reason's place ;
For Good Advice would bee at hand,
  His doyngs to disgrace.
Who tolde me playne that wanton Will
  Did alwayes serve the diuell,
And was his busiest instrument,
  To stirre vp men for euill.
Although the gallant be so braue,
  And sell such pleasures here,
They that best cheape doe buy the same,
  Shall find it all too deere.

Yet they that woulde aduenture there,
    The diuell and all may gayne:
With euery inch of pleasant ioyes,
    He sends ten elles of payne.
If that thou wisely wilt foresee,
    Such winnings to eschew,
Ere Beggery take thee at the back,
    Doe bid the Court adew :
Henceforth exile vile wanton Will,
    Which is thy cheefest foe,
Goe get thee home, live to thy selfe,
    And let all Courting goe.
Experience now should make thee know,
    What vice in Court doth rayne,
And tract of time shoulde teach thee shunne
    Her pleasures mixt with payne :
Though some may dayly there be seene
    That follow vertue still,
Which honour God, obey their prince,
    And flie from dooyng ill,
Yet sure, of them the greatest parte
    Are carried so away,
With vayne delightes, that they ne thinke,
    Nor mynde their soules' decay.
O that I here tolde not a lye,
    O, were it not too true :

That very few theyr Princesse' steppes,[1]
    In godlinesse ensue.
Should I passe on her golden gifts
    And graces to declare ?
The sandes in bottome of the seas,
    More easily numbred are.
If tongue or pen should take in hand,
    Her vertues to vnfolde,
Tongue should not speake, pen would be worne,
    Ere halfe the tale were tolde.
Shee is—next God—the onely spring,
    From which our welfare flowes :
She is a tree, on which nought els,
    But graftes of goodnesse growes :
Shee is a sunne that shines on vs,
    With beames of blissefull happes ;
Shee is a dew that daily drops,
    Great plenty in our lappes.
When angry Neptune shipwracke threats
    Through force of wrestling waues
Shee is a port of safe refuge,
    Which vs from daunger saues.
When duskie clouds of errors blacke,
    Had dimde our ioyfull day,
Through Christ shee causde the Gospell shine,
    Who draue them all away.

---

[1] Elizabeth. G.

Shee worthy statutes hath ordayncd,
　　To keepe men still in awe;
But euery man vnto himselfe,
　　Will now set downe a lawe;
Such as his Will doth fancy best,
　　They neuer care how bad,
Nor far from God or godlinesse,
　　So pleasure may be had.
If lawlesse lust were lawfull loue,
　　If wauering wordes were deedes,
Then would the Court bring foorth more fruite,
　　And not so many weedes.
Thou knowest among the Courting crew,
　　How little fayth is forced :
Sound friendship from the most of them,
　　Is vtterly deuorced.
Who cannot flatter, glozè and lie,
　　And set thereon a face,
Is neuer able for his life,
　　To get a courtly grace.
Who sweates not in his sutes of silke,
　　And is not passing braue,
Amongst them beares no countenance,
　　They deeme him but a slaue :
As long as thou hast store of coyne,
　　And spendst it with the best,
In outward shew great friendlinesse,

To thee shalbe profest.
But if thy wealth begin to weare,
   If pence begin to fayle thee,
Theyr friendship then in time of neede,
   But little shall avayle thee.
For they will shrinke their heads aside,
   And leaue thee poste alone ;
If twenty were thy friendes before,
   Now hardly gettst thou one.
I pray thee let vs scan this case,
   And doe thou sadly tell,
What thing at first, did make thee like,
   And loue the Court so well.
Didst thinke that there a godly life,
   Might soonest be attaynde ;
And motions of the sinfull fleshe
   Most easily be refraynd ?
That cannot be, for all men see,
   How vice is there imbraste,
And vertue with the greatest parte,
   Is utterly defaste.
Did hope of wealth, first pricke thee foorth,
   In Court to spende thy life ?
Or didst thou thinke that liberall gifts,
   With noble men were ryfe?
If ought thou carrie in thy purse,
   Thou quickly there mayst spend it :

But when thy landes and rentes are gone,
　　How canst thou then amend it ?
To begge would greeue thy loftie mynde,
　　That erst had store of wealth,
And hanging is the end of such,
　　As take men's goodes by stealth.
Because thou serust a noble man,
　　Perhaps thou mak'st no doubt,
In hope that he at such a pinche,
　　Will alwayes beare thee out.
Such hope hath hangèd many a one,
　　Whom wilful will did guyde :
By often proofe in these our dayes,
　　Too true it hath beene tried.
For when a halter's sliding knot,
　　Hath stopt their vitall breath,
He was—say they—' a handsome man,
　　Its pittie of his death'.
Thus all too late their pitie comes,
　　But seldome comes their ayde ;
Wherefore do not forget these wordes,
　　That I to thee haue sayde ;
Be not sedewste by wanton Will,
　　Let warnings make thee wise,
And after this, in all thy deedes.
　　Be rulde by Goode Aduise.

This tale beeyng tolde, he heald his peace.
  And I which found it true,
  Did yeeld him thankes and gate me home,
    And bad the Court adew.

[ENDS AND MEANS.]

  We till to sowe, we sow to reape,
  We reape and grind it by and by :
  We grinde to bake, we bake to eate,
  We eate to liue, we liue to die.
  We die with Christ to rest in ioy,
  In heauen made free from all annoy.

Finis.

A PREFACE TO CERTAINE QUESTIONS AND RIDDLES ENSUING, TRANSLATED OUT OF ITALIAN VERSE INTO ENGLISH VERSE, BY H. G.

L yee vnto whome the skanning and
   viewing,
  Shal come of these questions, and riddles
   ensuing :
I let you first know thus much without fayning,
That all of them carry a good and cleane meaning,
If so they be constred aright in their sense,
Thus much may I boldly speake in their defence :
But if in ill part some fortune to take them,
We fayle of the end, to which we did make them.
Which was for the solace of them that can vse
  them :
What thinges can be sound, if men wil abuse
  them ?
To such as are cleane, what can be vnpure ?
Such as are defilde, ill thoughts haue in vre :[1]
If of any riddle badde sense ye pick out,

Gesse at it againe : ye fayle without doubt,
And doe not aright his meaning expound ;
Their true exposition is honest and sound.
And that shall be proued if you will craue tryall,
So truely that no man will stand in deniall.
Committing the sequal to your approbation,
I finish the preface of this my translation.

1.

A father once, as bookes expresse,
Had sonnes twise sixe, nor more nor lesse :
Ech sonne, of children had scores three,
Halfe of them sonnes, halfe daughters bee :
The sonnes are farre more white then snowe,
The daughters blacker then a crow.
Wee see these children dayly die,
And yet they liue continually.

2.

A mightie blacke horse, with gallant white winges,
Within his graund paunch beares many straunge
    things :
Hee oft doth trauayle for mayster's auayle,
And caryes his bridle tyed fast to his taile.
In going he flyes twixt earth and the ayre,
And oft, where they would not, his riders doth
    beare :

431

Hee hath diuers eies, and yet cannot see,
I pray you doe tell mee what may this beast bee?

3.

A certaine thinge liueth in place neere at hande,
Whose nature is straunge, if it bee well scand :
It sees without eyes, it flyes without winges,
It runnes without feete, it workes wondrous thinges:
To places far distant it often doth rome.
Yet neuer departeth, but taryes at home.
If thou doe it couet to feele and to see,
Thy labour is lost for it may not bee.

4.

What am I, that wanting both handes, feete and
        head,
Of all them that see me, being deem̀ed for dead,
Of breath haue great store, and moue to and fro,
Now vp, and now downe, now hye, and now low ?
Alas what hard fortune doth to mee befall,
That guiltlesse am spited of great and of small :
They strike me, and push mee, South, West,
        North and East :
Yet doe I no harme to most, neither least.
When as my breath fayling, I can doe no more,
They then giue mee ouer, but neuer before.

432

5.

I being the daughter of my vncles's brother,
Am now of late become a mother :
And with my milke from my pappes which flowes,
I nourish a sonne, my mother's owne spowse :
Now tell what I am, declare mine estate,
For I giue him sucke, that first me begate.

6.

None liueth more iocound in al the whole land,
Though head doth lye buryed in mucke and in
　　sand :
My beard it is gray, though not very old,
The strong I make weepe, not for heate, not for
　　cold :
Yet such is my state, that the poore loue me well,
And still I am forst with great men to dwell.

7.

From South and West commeth a straunge war-
　　like nation,
Attirde and appareld in wonderful fashion :
In garments milke white, these people are clad :
Which strike and oppresse both good men and bad
But fauour they shew in dealing their blowes,
And saue him from danger, ech on his way goes.
And on his backe caryes dead bodyes great store,

Which with their thicke buffets had beate them
        before ;
Great furies are kindled at end of the fray :
Which makes this straunge nation all vanish away.

8.

Long is it since to the world I came,
Small am I of body, poore, feeble, and lame :
Yet none in this world, nor one neyther other,
In richnesse and substaunce surpasseth my mother.

8.

Not long am I graunted this life to enioy,
So many there are that worke me annoy :
O Lord how they rent mee, it cannot bee told,
What torments I suffer in heate and in cold.
One while am I drowned, such hap doth befal,
Then next doe they rost mee : yet this is not al :
When thus they haue vsde mee, they cannot for-
        beare me,
Ere first being beaten, by peecemeale they teare
        me.
Then serue I the turne of euery estate,
But one kinde of people mee deadly doth hate.

9.

Doe tell me my friends, what crèature is hee,

That two times is borne as all men may see,
And liueth a space, though not very long?
And often is killed, not hauing done wrong?
When y^t his breath fayleth, it liueth no more,
It then is baptisèd, and neuer before.
Though many a one doe euill entreate it,
They loue it right well, and often doe eate it.

10.

A certain dead creature in mine armes I take,
With her back to my bosome, great glee doth shee
    make.
As thus I doe hold her she greatly doth cheere mee,
And wel are they pleasèd, that see me and heare
    me.
While erst it remaynèd in forest and field,
It silent remayning, no speech forth did yeeld.
But since she of life by death was depriued,
With language she speaketh men's sprites are
    reuiued.

11.

A father begat me, yet I haue no mother,
Nor uncle nor aunt, nor sister, nor brother;
Straight when I was born, I began to florish,
For euery estate tooke care me to norish;
Thus many score yeeres, they haue loued me full
    well,

And eke entertaind me, amongst them to dwell ;
All partes of the world I viewed in short space,
And still was bad welcome, in euery place :
Though many by me reape losse, care, and woe,
They neuer will license me from them to goe.

12.

Hard fortun doth haunt me, by nature estranged,
From male vnto female, I often am chaunged,
And where as before I liud well contented,
With prickings and punchings, I now am tor-
      mented :
Now, more to accomplish their greedy desire,
They cruelly beate mee, and scorch me with fire ;
Though badly they vse mee, so milde am I still,
That I yeelde them life that thus doe mee kill.

13.

Amongst the friendships rare,
    Of which old writers tell :
This may be plaste in highest roome,
    And dothe deserue it well :
Whiles Death with gasping throte,
    Did gape for bloody pray,
Life conquered Death, and saude that life,
Which Death did seeke to slay.
    That Life which did this deede,

436

As death would straight haue slaine :
That Life which late by him was saude,
Preserude from Death againe.

14.

Begot without father, in earth I remaine,
And yet I am turnd to my mother againe,
By night and by day, I labour alwaies,
And with my sharp sauor both please and displease ;
Thus heere in this earth my race out I runne,
And neuer have issue, nor daughter, nor sonne.

15.

A female I by name,
   Am sister to a brother :
In all the world may not bee found,
   Our like, nor one nor other.
For hee no sooner dies,
   But I straightwayes doe liue :
And I oft yeelding unto death,
   Still life to him doe giue :
Oft after him I hie,
   And gladly would him stay :
But hee than arow from the bow,
   More swiftly flyes away.
Straightwayes hee folowes me,
   My presence to attaine :

And as hee fled from me before,
   I flye from him againe.
Though straunge our state doth seeme,
   By proofe yee may it try :
That both of vs are still aliue,
   Yet both doe dayly die.
That yee may better know,
   What straungers great wee bee,
Wee day and night doe dine and sup,
   With men of ech degree.

16.

Two are we in name, though in substaunce but one,
First framed by arte then finisht with mone.
Before we are ready, for those that will buy,
Through greatnesse of torment, wee howle and
   wee cry.
Yet feele we no griefe, for all this anoy,
Great numbers by vs have comfort and joy,
Who when for their profits we haue done what
   wee may,
They then do reiect vs, and cast vs away.

17.

Fayre art thou and red, deseruing great praise,
And all men thee reuerence, and honour alwayes ;
Whiles that thy white banner abrode still is spread,

438

For then thou doest comfort both liuing and dead;
But if thy blacke banner bee spread foorth in
    vew,
All honour farewell, all gladnesse adew.
Such woe then thou bringest to more and to lesse,
As pen cannot write it, nor tongue may expresse.

18.

Of thee—O my friend—a thing I doe craue,
Which thou neuer hadst, nor neuer shalt haue:
If that for thy selfe thou purpose to gayne it,
Thy labour is lost, thou mayst not obtayne it.
Although thou shouldst liue a whole thousand
    yeere,
And seeke it, yet should'st thou be nothing the
    neere.
Now if thou doe loue me, euen so as thou sayest,
Doe geue it. For truely, I know that thou mayst.

THE SOLUTIONS OF THE RIDDLES.

1. The father, the yeere: the xii. sonnes, ye xii months: the lx. children, the xxx. dayes, and xxx. nights.

2. A ship.

3. A man's minde.

4. A footeball made of a bladder.

5. An old man being in prison, his daughter comming to visite him, woulde geue him sucke of her breasts and so nourish him,

6. An onion.

7. Men trauelling in the snow are beaten with it, and carry the dead bodies on their garments. vntill they come to a fire, which makes them vanish away.

8. Hempe.

9. A chicken, being first an egge, and then a chicken.

10. A lute.

11. Play at all kinde of games.

12. Wheat being the newter gēder, in Latin is turned into *farinam*, meale, which is the feminine; which is then cōverted into bread, and so nourisheth them that bake it.

13. A man coming to a foūtaine to drinke, saw a serpent climbing vp on a tree, to deuour a neast of young egles; which serpent hee slewe with his sworde, and so saued their liues. Beeing about then to drink of the water, the young birdes, scraping out the filth of their nests fowled it in such sort, that it letted him from drinking: a spaniel that he had there with him, tasting of it, was presently poysoned.

14. Salt.

15. The night and day.

16. A paire of sheares.

17. A good tongue and a bad.

18. A mayde beeing in loue with a young man, desires him to geue her a husbande, which in marrying with her hee might doe.

The End.

MISCELLANIES

OF

The Fuller Worthies' Library.

⊙

THE

SONGS OF SION

OF

DR. WILLIAM LOE,

(1620):

Edited, with Memorial-Introduction and Notes,

BY THE

REV. ALEXANDER B. GROSART,

ST. GEORGE'S, BLACKBURN, LANCASHIRE.

PRINTED FOR PRIVATE CIRCULATION.
1870.
156 COPIES ONLY.

Memorial-Introduction.

ELL-NIGH every-body I should suppose, has heard in one way or another, the pulpit-story of two clergymen preaching in the same church on the same day and as candidates for the same post, their names being respectively '*Adam*' or Adams and '*Loe*'. The latter as the story runs, preached in the morning and took for text—with a tacit gibe at his annnounced successor, '*Adam!* where art thou?'. The former, not to be outdone, responded in the afternoon, with kindred name-play, '*Lo!* here am I'. Who the 'Adam' was, (or Adams : for it is sometimes the one spelling and sometimes the other) tradition hath forgotten. It might have been (if chronology agreed) quaint and audacious-witted THOMAS ADAMS of the immortal ' Sermons': (not the later Adam of the " Private Thoughts ".) LYSONS says the ' Loe ' was our present Worthy, giving as his authority a tractate yclept " Perfect Passages " dated 16th April, 1645—diligently

but fruitlessly sought for by me.[1] THOMAS FULLER
or EDWARD BOTELER or WILLIAM WORSHIP, never
would have hesitated to make the jest, meaning
no harm : and the impression made on myself by
the books and single ' Sermons ' of our Loe, is
that he was of much the same make of intellect
and temperament with these, and perhaps a dash
of SOUTH. So that we may accept the long-told,
variously-fathered anecdote, as really belonging
to him in his younger days. From some ultra-
serious folks the story may fetch a groan, even the
anathema of 'profane ' : but it was'nt so, only o' the
age irrepressibility of a nimble wit. Then what saith
Sir Toby ? " Dost thou think, because thou art
virtuous, there shall be no more cakes and ale " ?
(Twelfth Night, ii. 3) or to paraphrase it, ' Because thou knowest not the bewitchment and in-
evitableness of a pun, is thy genial brother to be
mis-judged ? '. Enter right welcome, then, Dr.
William Loe, with a smile i' thy face and mirth on
thy lips. None the less a true and good and
' *serious* ' man that thou didst ' dearly love thy
jest '.

The name is spelled by himself ' Loe ' and
' Leo ' : for there is no doubt that ANTHONY-A-
WOOD is correct, in regarding the two as one, in

---

[1] Lyson's Environs of London (1st edn.) Vol. I. p 293

the places of their occurring. Twice at least it
is given as ' Leo ' viz : (a) in the Funeral-sermon
—a remarkable one on a remarkable man—of Dr.
Daniel Featley (1645) and the further designation
" sometimes (= sometime) Preacher at Wandsworth in Surrey " (b) in his signature while
Prebendary of Gloucester to certain "chapter-
acts ". From other sources we know—as will
appear in the sequel—our Loe to have been
" Preacher at Wandsworth " and " Prebendary
at Gloucester ". Hence the identification is
certain. His friend Featley had the *alias* of
'Fairclough ' in like manner.[1]

I have not been able to trace either birth-place
or birth-date of our " sweet Singer " and Divine.
Probably he was of Kent : for in his Featley ' sermon ', incidentally naming a ' knight ' (Sir
George Sands) of the county, he speaks of him as
' my countryman of Kent ' (p. 24). The Fasti
Oxonienses (edn. by BLISS I. 275, 285, 335, 381,
382) supplies the *data* of his University career
at Oxford :

---

[1] The funeral-sermon is full of anecdote of rare value
to a biographer of Featley : and besides, Loe has various
allusions to his own travels and experiences : and lovingly
names his own son William as of Trinity College, Cambridge. See page 23 of this Sermon.

Among B. A's, 5th Novr. 1597 : " Will. Loe of
St. Alb. Hall.

Among M. A's, 14th June 1600 : *ibid. ibid.*

Among B. D's, 22, Feby. 1609-1610 "Will.
Loe of St. Alb. Hall did supplicate for the
same degree, but whether he was admitted,
appears not ".

Among B. D's, 8th June 1618 : ' Will. Loe of
Mert. Coll. sometimes of St. Alban's Hall.

Among D. D's 8th June 1618 : ' Will. Loe of
Mert. Coll. a compounder and an accumu-
lator.'

When he took his degree of M. A., ANTHONY-A-
WOOD in his *Athenæ Oxonienses* (edition by Bliss,
III., 183-4) states that " he was much in esteem
for Latin, Greek, and human learning." This
was (as *supra*) in 1600. In the same year he
must have been Vicar of Churcham, Gloucester :
for in its Parish-Register as still preserved, I find
from the present Vicar (Rev. George C. Hall,
M. A.,) record is made that Dr. Loe transcribed
the entries "ex veteri libro cartaceo" in the
42nd year of Elizabeth, *id est,* 1600. Under 1593
there is in his handwriting a note " Finis veteris
libri cartacei " : but the ' Fasti' degree-dates
seem to shew that he could not have been so early
in orders as 1594. Therefore the meaning must

be that an ancient Register was transcribed by him that ended in 1593, while the genuine one commenced from 1594. "Soon after", (1600) he was made Master of the College School in Gloucester: and was instituted " on the 30th September, 1602 " Prebendary of Gloucester [Cathedral 5th Stall]. He was sub-dean in 1605. Probably these offices were held simultaneously as not very onerous pluralities.[1] The Churcham Register further informs us, that he was married while in possession of that 'living', as under 1612 we read: "Sept, 27th, Hester the daughter of William Loe, Vicar, was baptised."[2] The absence of signatures to the successive annual entries prevents our determining the period of his incumbency. Not until 1633 does a signature appear, that of Francis Hathway—another form of the maiden name of MRS. WILLIAM SHAKESPEARE—by which date Loe was most certainly elsewhere.[3] The 'College School' of Gloucester has been very neglectful of its history, as have also been

---

[1] Consult Fosbrooke, and also Rudder's History of Gloucester, (p. 169).

[2] Rev. Samuel Lysons, F. S. A., of Hampstead Court, in a letter to me, from Archdeacon Furney's MSS. in his possession.

[3] I have very cordially to thank the Rev. George C.

the county Historians. There is a tantalizing absence of dates: indeed the Records do not go beyond
the Restoration of Charles II. WOOD mentions
that JOHN LANGLEY succeeded our 'Master' but
not the years of either, while Fosbrooke gives
two Masters between Loe and Langley, viz.,
THOMAS POTTER (1605) and John Clark (1612).[1]
It needed a man of brain to be 'Master' of such
a School as that of Gloucester: and it were
interesting to know the more famous 'boys' of it.
When will our county-Historians understand, that
these are the kind of facts that are of substantive
and abiding value,—not mere 'endless genealogies'
of noble-ignoble nonentities,—pyramid-wise, all

Hall, M. A., of Churcham, for his great kindness in
answering my enquiries.

[1] I must, as in last note, equally thank Dr Washbourne of Gloucester and Rev. Samuel Lysons, as above,
for their like interest and attention. The latter writes me
"Fosbrooke does not give the date of Loe's appointment
to the Cathedral School, but places him between Elias
Wrench who was appointed in 1588, and Thomas Potter
who was appointed in 1605." Perhaps when appointed
sub-dean in 1605 Loe resigned his Mastership. See above
and onward where in the "Merchant Reall" he says under date 1619-20, that he had been "one of the masters
seventeene yeares". This goes back to 1602-3.

too often, broad-based and a 'mere point' at last.

Probably the central thing of our Worthy's life took place in 1618, in which year the Cathedral-Records tell us, he obtained a "testimonial from the Chapter to become Pastor of the English Church at Hamburgh" or as it was spelled 'Hamborough'. This at once links him to the subject-matter of our reprint, the "Songs of Sion"—the manifold dedications of which keep before us the fact that he was the 'Minister' of the 'Merchant-adventurers' of the once and still renowned city. From the Introduction to an exceedingly rare if not uniquely-preserved copy of a book of his, the 'Merchant reall", now in the Public Library of Hamburg, we learn that he let a year and a half pass before he decided to accept the post. These are his words: "I demurred after mine election, a whole yeare and a halfe, and begged of God to resolve me touching my coming unto you". He seems to have been unwilling to leave England: for he continues as follows: "and now being come, I doe protest in the sight of God and His holy angells, that I come not unto you with any Italianated hart of implaccability that cannot be appeased, nor with any Hispanialized hart of Iesuited novelty, nor with a Frenchified hart of singularitie, nor yet

with a **Dutchified** hart of neutrality (all which
I speake not as of any nationall disgrace, for the
finest cambrick may have many fretts and frayes)
but I am come with a good and an honest Englishe ·
hart of orthodox and catholike sincerity." At this
time (1620)[1] the same introduction informs us, he
had been " 22 years a member of the English
church, and 17 years a teacher in the school ".
This is in harmony with the Parish register of
Churcham by which we dated his appointment
there, 1600 or thereby.[2]

The Merchant-adventurers of England to whom
Loe acted as chaplain, were an important company.
Previously to 1618 they moved about a good deal,
according as the ' markets ' for their imports and
exports led them. Thus they are found at Embden,
Middleburgh, Stade, and elsewhere. The second
place ' Middleborough ' will remind the bookish
reader of a number of quaint old title-pages
bearing quaint old Puritan names, and of certain
bibliographical rarities that freely fetch weight
for weight in gold, as SIR JOHN DAVIES' Epigrams
in association with MARLOWE's Ovid's ' Elegies '.
It will also recall silver-tongued Joshua Sylvester

---

[1] Dr. Klose seems to misdate from 1618.
[2] See Note at end of this Memorial-Introduction.

—agent of the 'Merchant-adventurers' there—
who by the way inscribes his "Tobacco Battered"
to our Loe, in the following Sonnet:

"To my reverend and worthy friend, **Mr.** William Loe,
    Batchelor of Divinity.

Lo, what you love and this chimera's hate,
    Care of my friends, compassion of my kin ;
    Zeal of God's glory, horror of this sin ;
    My soveraign's service, honour of our State:
Lo, what all these had pow'r to propagate !
    (Perhaps more hardy then my hope had bin,
    When first this theam YOU GAVE ME TO BEGIN)
    Besides my way, beyond my waining date.
Lo, therefore, whether well or ill I fare;
    Whether the doubtfull field I win or lose;
    In fame, or shame, YOU needs must have a share,
Who on my weakness did this weight impose.
    Like Moses therefore lift your hands on hie,
    That *Joshuah's* hand may have the victory."

(Works, 1641, p. 572).

In 1618 the Hamburg authorities arranged for
the Association settling permanently in their city.
A contract was entered into and 'incorporation,
given. LINGARD, of all our English historians,
slightly notices these 'Merchant-adventurers'. It
were surely worth-while for some Englishman to
get at the facts of these pioneers of England's
now world-embracing commerce.

One of the title-pages bears the date '1620':
so that he was not long in 'imping his wing'
for a poetic flight. The Epistles-Dedicatory bear
witness to the warm, mutual respect of the
'Merchant - adventurers' and their Chaplain.
There were evidently among them 'gentle'
men, in the real and not merely titular sense.
These Epistles also reveal a fine fervour of con-
cern for the spiritual welfare of his 'dear Masters'
and 'table-fellows'.

How long he remained in Hamburg, I have
failed to ascertain: but the probability is,—though
the many dedications of the "Songs of Sion"
give no hint of intended departure,—that he did
not remain very many years subsequent to 1620.

From Lyson's Environs of London[1], under
'Putney', there is a note of 'William Leo
as 'curate' and Preacher in 1624; in which
year his signature occurs as "Preacher at
Putney". This Leo is identified as Wood and
ourselves do, with Loe. Perhaps his Hamburg
residence made him uncertain in his orthography, seeing that Löwe in German means
a Lion i. e. Leo and Loe are just an abbrevi-

---

[1] Vol. I. p 416 : same authority and reference for our
opening anecdote.

ation of Lowe. One of the sermon-books already quoted from, is dedicated " to the right Worship-full Sr Thomas *Lowe*, Knight, Governour," as well as to " the Deputies, assistants and General-tie, of that auncient, much famous, and most worthy companie of Merchants Adventurers, resi-ding at London, Hamborough, Middleborough, &c. &c. There is no claim of relationship made. Let name-enquirers follow up the clue presented.[1] Besides Putney, as we saw, the Funeral-sermon for Featley, bears that the Preacher was 'sometime' of " Wandsworth in Surrey ". I have had most willing helpers there, in the excellent present Incumbent and other friends[2] : but the result of long-continued researches is provokingly meagre. Nevertheless the dates are of importance, albeit they merely authenticate the Incumbency and shew descendants afterwards. At the foot of the page ending 5th March 1636, under Marriages, in Parish Register, there are certain signatures viz : " Wm. Leo, Tho. Ballard, Willi. Ashenden ", the

---

[1] In the Wandsworth Registers, there is a baptism of a Thomas *Lowe's* daughter Rebecca : 13th. June 1645.

[2] I must name Dr. J. T. Harris of Englefield Green, Staines, and the Parish-Clerk of Wandsworth, Mr. Willson, —the latter an intelligent and antiquarianly disposed custodier of the Registers.

first no doubt the Vicar, the other Churchwardens.
The same signatures re-appear in the register of
Baptisms of July, 1636, to November, 1638, with
the substitution of Blagrave for Ballard on two
occasions. The same also in the Burials from
April 1636 to October, 1638. Further: as in the
Register of Burials there is an entry of the inter-
ment of "Mr. Robert Allen, vicar of Wandsworth"
on 16th June 1631, our Loe probably succeeded
him. Under baptisms 16th September 1646 is entered, "Isaack, the sonne of Isaack Loe". Another
Vicar, "Mr. Hugh Roberts" had a son John
baptized 2d Novr. 1645. Probably he succeeded
Loe: and probably Loe held the 'living' until
his death in 1645, though he seems to have been
resident in the City (of London). As "Preacher"
at Putney and as having been appointed "Chaplain to the King"—poor reward of a long-tried
loyalty in 'evil days' (to him)—he would require
to 'abide' in the Metropolis. There at last, in
all likelihood in a ripe old age, he died and was
buried, in no less sacred a sleeping-place than
Westminster. Wood was ignorant of his death-
date: John Walker in his famous (or infa-
mous) "Sufferings of the Clergy" names 1648,
and so Fosbrooke and others. But inasmuch as
Roberts was Vicar at Wandsworth at close of

1645, I had assigned that year for his death independent of an interesting discovery of my friend Colonel Chester—one of many tid-bits that have turned up in the course of his unexampled persistency of research among our national Registers. I will allow him to put the matter before the Reader as he has done in a letter to myself, as follows : " One of the most perplexing entries I found in the Westminster Abbey Registers was this burial " 1645 . Sept. 21. Dr. Lee.—in the South side of the Church, near the Vestry door." I could find nothing of this Dr. Lee. There was no monument and no inscription recorded in any of the printed books. All the Doctors *Lee*, whether of Law, Medicine or Theology or even Music that I could trace, died either before or after that date. And I could find no Will of a Dr. Lee. The man haunted me from December 1866 down to last Spring, when after a great deal of trouble, I got hold of the Wills and Administrations of the Dean and Chapter of Westminster, which had been hid away for a century in a lawyer's office in Doctors Commons, and at last was claimed by and taken to the principal Registry of Probate. Among these, to my great joy, I found that on the 13th of November, 1645, letters of Administration were granted by the

Dean and Chapter on the Estate of "William
Leo, *alias* Loe, S.T.P. "late of the city of Westminster, to Elizabeth Basset, a creditor." The
information was meagre enough : but here was
clearly my troublesome 'Dr. Loe'". I do not
think there can be any doubt as to the identity ;
and the explanation of the later date given by Walker of the "Sufferings"—a book that swarms with
blunders intentional and inadvertent—Le Neve in
his "Fasti", and similar authorities, is, that they
inferred the death-date from the accession of the
new incumbent to his stall : whereas the 'troubles '
of the period kept it vacant for some years.

We have found that at Churcham Loe had a
daughter baptized ' HESTER'. We know not his
wife's name or family. He had at least one other
child, a son, who bore his own name and who appears to have passed a brilliant University career,
being of renowned 'Trinity College, Cambridge',
not of Oxford like his father. In the Funeral-
sermon on Featley preached under the shadow of
his own near-coming death, Dr. Loe makes loving
mention of this son William : and the paternal
regard must have been reciprocated filially : for
in an exquisite specimen of penmanship (were it
no more it should be a literary gem) I happen to
possess, viz, a small MS. volume, antiquely bound,

consisting of 'readings' in Plautus and other of
the classics, together with at least one somewhat
striking original (Latin) poem that I shall
include as a parrallel in my edition of RICHARD
CRASHAW, there is prefixed a very long and
glowing Epistle-dedicatory, to his father. In this
the language labours in setting forth his worth
and genius and among many other things, his
'poetic' fame. It is scarcely worth-while translating this (Latin) Epistle : but as Loe jr. was
a son of 'Trinity' I intend placing the M.S. under
the custody of my friend Mr. W. Aldis Wright,
Librarian of Trinity College, that it may be ac-
cessible to inquirers. The son not the father, was
author of the sets of Latin verses contained in the
" Carmen Natalitium ad cunas illustrissimæ Prin-
cipis Elizabethæ decantatum intra Navitatis Dom.
solennia per humiles Cantabrigiæ Musas " (1635).[1]

---

[1] Colonel Chester sends me the following extract from
the Parish Registers of St. Martins in the Fields : Marriage 5 June 1642: William Loe and Margaret Shipton,
both of Westminster ". Probably Loe *filius*. Further he
writes " in the cloisters of Westminster Abbey was buried
1 Mch. 1676-7, according to the Register " Colonel Hercules Lowe " who in an unofficial Register kept by one
of the Minor Canons, usually more correct than the early

As a contribution to Bibliography I have now to furnish a full and probably complete list of the Writings of our Worthy in chronological order.

1. The Ioy of Ierusalem and Woe of Worldings. A Sermon preached at Paul's Crosse the 18 of Iune 1609. By William Loe, Batchelour of Diuinity, and Prebendarie of the Cathedral Church of Glocester. London, printed by T. Haueland for C. Knight and I. Harrison, and are to be sold in Pauls Churchyard at the signe of the holy Lambe. 1609. [sq. 18mo.] Collation: Title-page, Epistle-dedicatory 2 leaves—Sermon 63 leaves. [Text St. John, xvii. 9.]

2. Come and See, The Blisse of Brightest Beavtie, Shining ovt of Sion in Perfect Glorie. Being the Summe of foure Sermons preached in the Cathedrall Church of Glocester at commandment of Superiours. By William Loe. Imprinted at London by Richard Field and Matthew Law. 1614 [4to.] *⁎* The Epistle-dedicatory is dated " The Colledge of Glow. Febru. 20. 1611 ". Wood misreads " The Bible the brighest beauty &c. and whereas it is ' William Loe ' simply, by

official Register, is given as " Hercules Loe ". It is possible that this may have been of our Loe's line : but nothing seems known of him.

adding "D in divinity, sometime preacher at Wandsworth in Surrey" the foot-note from Wanley, throws the whole chronology of the Life into confusion, as I found on searching at Wandsworth from 1614 onward, instead of the later date of the incumbency. I had not seen "Come and See" at the time, and it is plain Wood had not, and also that Wanley confounded it with the funeral-sermon for Featley.

3. The Mysterie of Mankind, Made into a Manual, or the Protestants Portuize [= Breviary] reduced into Explication, Application, Invocation, tending to Illumination, Sanctification, Devotion, being the sum of seven Sermons. Preached at S. Michaels in Cornehill, London, by William Loe, Doctor of Divinity, Chaplain to his sacred Majesty, and Pastor Elect, and allowed by authority of Superiours, of the English Church at Hamborough in Saxonie. 1 Cor 3. 23. All are yours and yee Christ's, and Christ God's. London, Printed by Bernard Alsop for George Fayerheard, and are to be sold at his shoppe at the South side of the Exchange. 1619 [12mo] Collation: Title-page—299 numbered pages, 49 unnumbered, a blank page, a page of errata, and five blank leaves.

4. The Merchant reall, Preached by Will-

iam ˙ᵂLoe, Doctour of Divinitie, Chaplain of the
King's sacred majestie, and Pastour of the English
church of Merchants-Adventurers residing at
Hamborough in Saxonie. Matth. 16, 26. What
is a man profited if he shall purchase the whole
world and lose his owne soule? or what shall a
man give in exchange for his soule? Printed at
Hamborough by Paule Lang, Ann. Domini, 1620.
[4to] Collation : Title-page— 6 unnumbered and
106 numbered pages.

    5. The Songs of Sion : See our present re-
print, for general title-page and separate titles.

    6. Vox Clamantis : a still voice to the three
thrice honourable estates of Parliament : and in
them to all the soules of this our Nation, of what
state or condition soever they be. By William
Loe, Doctor of Divinitie, and chaplaine to the
king's most excellent Majestie. ⸂Printed by T. ˙S.
for John Teage, and are to be sold at the signe of
the Golden Ball in Paul's Churchyard. [4to.]

    7. A Sermon on Psalm xlv., 3., preached
at Whitehall, with a dedication to the King.
1622. [4to.] *⁎* I find a note of this in my
memoranda, but have mislaid the full title-page.

    8. The King's Shoe Made and Ordained to
tɪample and to treade downe Edomites : to teach
in briefe, what is Edom's doome ; what the care-

full condition of a King; what the loyall
submission of a subiect, and what proiects are
onely to best purpose. Deliuered in a Sermon
before the King at Theobalds, October the ninth,
1622. By William Loe, Doctour of Diuinity,
Chaplaine to his sacred majesty in ordinary.
London, 1623. [4to]. Collation: Title-page—
Epistle-dedicatory 3 leaves and pp. 45. [Text
Psalm lx, 8].

9. A Sermon preached at Lambeth, Apr.
21, 1645 at the Funerall of that learned and
polemical Divine, Dan. Featley, Doctor in Divinity, late preacher there: with a short relation of
his Life and Death, by William Leo, Doctor
in Divinity, sometime Preacher at Wandesworth
in Surrey. Lond. Printed for Richard Royston,
dwelling in Ivie-lane, 1645. [4to]
₊ Prefixed is a singular copper-plate engraving
of Dr. Featley in his shroud, his noble face bare.
2 pp latin verse and pp 32.

The first of this List " The Ioy of Ierusalem "
has escaped all our bibliograpical authorities,
including even the omniverous Anthony a-Wood.
As the text prepares us to expect, it is an exposition of the crown of all Prayers, recorded in the
17th chapter of St. John: and a somewhat
startling request is made as to the time intended

459

to be occupied. Speaking of The Lord's praying,
the Preacher says " whereunto I earnestly desire
you to attend as to one of the Songs of Sion and
the ioy of Ierusalem : and therein I shall pray
you to watch and wait the first houre, to the ioy
of your hearts, who truely seeke and serue the
Lord. As for the second houre, the woe of the
worldlings—His not praying [' I pray not for
them '] shall be denounced, that all flesh may
tremble and all people perceive the glorious
salvation of our God." ' Two hours ' preaching
at a stretch ! Yet judging from the little book
nobly were they occupied. Our modern audiences
have too queasy stomachs to digest such ' strong
meat '. I cull two small morsels from this sermon
worthy of its renowned pulpit— " What was
propositum in God the Father is *depositum* in
Jesus Christ the Son and *repositum* in expectation
of the faithfull " (2 Timothy iv. 8.).   Then
worked out from a Father, this thought seems to
me to lift off the ultra-Calvinistic horror thrown
over the words ' I pray not for the world '—
' Here He prays for His friends not naming His enemies : at the Cross He prayed for His enemies not
naming His friends.'   There surely we have a golden ray shot direct from the Sun of Righteousness.
The 4to ' The Merchant reall ' Anthony a-Wood

states he had never seen, and I do not know of a single copy in any public or private Library of our own Country. I have been fortunate enough to trace it to the Public Library of Hamburg; where it is regarded as one of the rarities of a Library holding many treasures. The ' Merchant Reall ' forms the text of an exceedingly interesting Paper on Loe by Dr. C. R. W. Klose, Secretary to the Public Library, Hamburg, which appeared in " No. 14: July 31st, of the Serapeum " a literary journal published and still publishing at Leipzig. Dr. Klose adds nothing, unfortunately, to the biography of our Worthy, though surely research in the *archives* of the city should have yielded new materials elucidative and illustrative of the " Merchant-adventurers "—but I have to thank him for leading me to a knowledge of (apparently) the one surviving exemplar of a valuable book. To the prompt courtesy of a successor of Dr. Loe—the present British Chaplain of Hamburg, the Rev. C. F. Weidemann, M.A.—I am indebted for copious extracts from the " Merchant Reall " and from No. 3, the " Mysterie of Mankind "—the Bodleian copy of which is unique in England.

I have already given the ' greeting ' of the Epistle-dedicatory of the " Merchant-reall ". The

Epistle itself explains the title and furnishes
certain auto-biographic deails, as follow : "Right
worshipfull and much endeered in the Lord.
Promise is debt, and debt is due. The dutie of
my service, and the debt of my promise, I nowe
make bold to tender unto you all. The promise
which I made unto you at London when I began
this taske, by God's permission I haue finished
at Hambrough, and now tender performance. It
is not many yeares since that a learned Doctour
who is nowe with God, preaching in Court at an
honorable marriage, out of the Proverbs, 'She is
like a merchant shippe that bringeth her mer-
chandize from afarre '. (Prov. 31, 14.) called
his sermon 'The marchant-royall ' : I have termed
this the 'Marchant Reall.' For that royaltie is
is upheld by Realtie. And wise men wishe ever
rather to be Realls than Nominalls ". Further,
as addressing Merchants he has this *bit* on their
' calling ' : "I knowe noe condition of men more
happie then merchants. Their veary youth is
accompanied with many and many fold experienced trialls, both by sea and land, which may make
them prudent. Their mature age is blessed with
a plentifull portion, which may make them thankfull, and their old age affordeth a very surplusage
of marvellous fulness, which may satisfie them ".

In the body of the work we come on these personal *data*, used earlier by us and as there noted
slightly corrective of Dr. Klose : " Mine entrance
unto you here, is and was, both civill and honest.
First by free election of your own fellowshipe.
Secondly by approbation of the State whence I
came. Thirdly by recommendation of his sacred
majestie, under his own hand, who pleased to
grace me, his unworthy servant, with his royall
letters, and of the most reverend archbishop of
Canterbury, who patriarchally tended your peace.
Fourthly with attestation from the famous Uni-
versitie of Oxford under their seale, and from the
Cathedral Church, where I have been a member
two and twenty yeares, and one of the masters,
seventeene yeeres." (pp. 1-2). Take now a few
quaint sentences gleaned here and there from the
" Merchant Reall ". Of man's natural condition
he says " When we come into the world, our
frends cover our shame with raggs, and in the end
when we goe out of the world, they doe the like.
All of us are Mephibosheths, lame on both legs,
both in our love to God and in our charity one to
another. We are all Lazaruses full of sores, and
lie begging at the gate of God's rich mercie"
(p 22). These *characteristics* of various countries
are noticeable : "The sea and the earth, those two

grand caskets of God's treasures are in severall
places diversely furnished. So that one country
seemeth as it were the granary of the world. So
Sicilie was called the granary of the Romane State.
Another, the cellar of the world, as the Canarie
Islands. Another the orchard of the world, as
Lombardy in Ittaly so accompted. Another the
arcenall of the world, as Russia and Norway are
esteemed, espetially for cordage and materialls of
shipping " (pp 23, 24). Here are oddly put antith-
eses, having the Fullerian flavour : "All pretious
stones procede from one and the selfe same matter,
which is the earth, and yet see what great difference there is betweene the vile and the pretious,
between the currant and the counterfaite : even so
among the sonnes of men, all are made of the one
and the same matter : yett what difference there is
betwixt man and man of the same mould, betweene brother and brother of the same bloud,
even as much as betweene Simon Magus and
Simon Peter, Cephas and Caiphas, Judas the traytor
and Jude the apostle, yea what difference is in one
man when God takes him into his hand, as of a
persecuting Saule to make him a preaching
Paule " (p. 37). So too this : " We teach onlie
that good workes have no justifying quality in
themselves before God, but that faith only is like

464

John the divine leaning on Christ's breasts, and good works like St. Peter, that follow after Christ. Faith the bride goeth into the chamber, yea into the bed of her beloued, where the handmaids come not. Faith the bride, good works the handmaids. Faith the roote, good workes the fruite. Faith only necessary to justification, good workes to salvation " (p. 44). Perhaps the truth had been truer put if it had run ' We are saved by faith not by works, but are saved unto or in order to work for the Master '. This, reminds of Bacon : " Be directed therefore to recompence noe man evill for evill, as Joab did Abner, for that's a poore spirit ; much lesse evill for good, as Judas did to Christ, for that's a divell's spirit. Nay, if you doe recompense good with good, as Ahasueresh did Mordicai, it is but common justice ; but to overcome evill with goodnes is more than to preach, or to doe a miracle, or to cast out a divell " (p. 46). Here is a *pat* application : " Our case is as the case of Aaron which had a robe, bells, a tunacle, an ephod, the Urim and Thumim, and blew silke and fine linnen, yet all these were none of his owne, but ornaments ordayned by God, to be put upon him. So have we no pretiousnes in our selves ". (p 74). So this : " Oh what a foolish thing is it to be carefull to keepe the chicken from the kite, the lamb from the wolfe, and the dove from the vermin, and to be carelesse to keepe our-selves from the devill." (p 91).

The " Mysterie of Mankinde " yields kindred quotable things: but we must content ourselves with three in all. First is a small pun in the Preface : " Let us therefore never listen to ' This I say, this thou sayest ' : but let us heare when the Lord sayeth, and let that αυτος εΦα bee our religious ephod to put upon us." Next of the religious hypocrite : " Such are they that have Jacob's voice in prating of godlinesse, but Esau's hands in preachlng unhappinesse. Such are they that professe a linzie woolsey religion, being hatefull to God because they are not reall, hatefull to the world because they are religious, albeit they be but in shew, and hurtfull to themselves, because they are hypocrites and decyve themselves with seeming godlinesse " (p 34). Then this of goodness : " Beleevers see even by the very glimpse of right reason, that nothing but man maketh account of greatnes. God doth not, for with him is no respect of persons ; Nature doth not, for the children of princes are borne naked as well as the cottager's, and death assayleth the Court as well as the cart. Godlines only is that

wherein God delighteth, and good men tender it
as their breath: Godlinesse being the gracious
mother and goodnesse the holy daughter." (p 38).
Finally, the Preacher gives no very favourable
' report' of Church-audiences : "The more vere-
cundious and modest wee are in this our hearing
of God, and in our comming unto Him, the more
bright and beautiful we are in His sacred sight .
. . . . . . But the manner is now with many
to come as Sathan did—for company or custom or
worse—[who] came also when the sons of God
were assembled before him—to the divell's chappell, according to our English proverbe " Where
God hath His Church, the divell hath his chappel."
For even in the great assemblies, while some are
there hearing the Word attentively, others sleep
profoundly, while some reade, others prate, while
some lift up their eyes to heaven, others point out
the finger to note some vanity in the next pue,
while some pray, others scoffe, while some sing
others curse, while some sigh for their sinnes,
others laugh at sinne, and while others sit hark-
ening to the sermon unto the ende, others make
hast to bee gone, and thinke every houre two,
untill they hear the ' Peace of God' which they
will scarce vouchsafe to take with them, nor the
' Grace of God' neither." (pp **231—2**).

It were no hard matter to bring together from these and the other Sermons things worth remembrance. Enough however has been adduced to shew the 'manner of man' our Worthy was. I have intentionally refrained from quoting his vehement and euer-recurring flings at Popery, and equally have passed his fervid and softly-worded, tender prayers. The one reveals the strength of his hatred, the other his charity: and as prayer is a more potential and deep-reaching thing than sermon-making, one may rejoice that his 'Invocations' out-weigh his 'Imprecations'.

Of the "Songs of Sion" now reprinted, it needeth not that I say much. There are sweet, simple, pathetic strokes in these monosyllabled 'Songs' and a quiet, child-like directness that is to me very loveable. I have found them to grow on me, as your child's small words of question and wistful looks, grow and deepen before you. That is, the short, homely, common words, as you dwell on them, dilitate and speak grand things in a modest, most unconscious way. The fact that from beginning to end of the Verse, words of a single syllable alone are used, gives an unique character to the book : and altogether it is a humbly noticeable contribution to the History of the development of our poetic Literature. Our modern travestiers of the 'Pilgrim's Progress' and 'Robinson Crusoe' and other classics, adapted (so-called) for children, might improve their sorry work by turning to Loe's mono-syllables. As a book the 'Songs of Sion' is of extreme rarity. I know only of two exemplars, viz., in the British Museum and in the Bodleian. It is not at Hamburg.

ALEXANDER B. GROSART.

St. George's Blackburn,
   Lancashire.

NOTE.

I embrace the opportunity of this little space, to quote another dated statement from the opening of the Sermon for Featley: "It is not my mind nor meaning, neither was it ever my manner, I having now preached the Gospel seven and forty years, in Court, City, Country and beyond the Seas, to trouble mine auditories with any long or large beginnings" (p 1). 47 years from 1645, carries back to 1598. Cf. our Memorial-Introduction on Churcham. (pp 2—3).

From the encrease of materials while the "Songs of Sion" were being printed, the 22 pages left have proved insufficient: accordingly, I partly page only on one side, in order to keep the pagination continuous. G.

The Poems of Dr. Poe.

Note.

There is a general title-page to Dr. Loe's little volume, which is found only in the British Museum copy, not being in the Bodleian or any other known: "Songs of Sion, Set for the ioy of gods deere ones, who sitt here by the brookes of this worlds Babel, & weepe when they thinke on Hierusalem which is on highe. By W. L." [N. D.] and Mr. Hazlitt in his Hand-Book *s. n.* furnishes another: but it is only a partial enumeration of the separate title-pages: it omits entirely "An hymne or song of seauen straines or strings" &c., and otherwise is imperfect, as our reprint shews. At each division of the little volume, there is a separate title-page and a separate Epistle-dedicatory. These are given in their own places. Collation: title-page and 115 leaves, having throughout, a number of blank pages, as marked. G.

An hymne or song

Of seauen straines, or strings
set to the tone of seauen sobs, and
sighes of a seauen times seauen sad
soule for sinne, and is to be song in
the tune of

I lift mine hart to thee.

Psal. 25. or

Flie soule vnto thy rest.
Seauen times a daie will I praie
to thee o god, and will praie thee
o lord for thy great gifts, and good
graces, both to me,
and mine.

Psalm CXIX.

When the spright of mā doth sighe,
and sob to god, and is lift vp on highe,
the spright of god doth bowe it
selfe to man in ioy,
and peace.

CYPRIAN.`

Epistle-Dedicatory.

To his much esteemed good frend, Mr. JOHN
POWELL, one of the assistants of the worthy
cōpanie of the Marchants Aduenturers, residing
at Hamborough.[1]

Grace, peace, and mercie be multiplied in Christ
Iesu.

ORTHY frend. When Iuliā the Apos-
tate infested the Church of God,[2] sō-
times by barbarous cruelty and somtimes
by deuilish policie, among his other wicked practi-
ses, that was not the least nor the last, when he in-
terdited the Christians all vse of bookes, both
priuatly and publikely, for their children to learne,

---

[1] See our Memorial-introduction for notice of this
Company. G

[2] Usually as in general title-page *supra*, printed with a
small 'g': but I don't repeat this. As usual all the
Divine proper names (but not the pronouns, as they are so
very numerous) and impersonations are given capitals. G.

excepte Poetry. It pleased Almighty God in that
distresse of his Church to stirre vp a learned man,
one Apollinarius, a singular Metaphrast, to put
into heroicall Greeke verse all the psalmes of
Dauid : by which blessing the children of God had
vse and comfort of that booke of the psalme[s]
and the tyrant's decree tooke noe hold of thē,
because nowe it was become deuine poesie ; and
poetry they might read. Which shewes vnto vs
God's especiall and singular providence for his
Church vpon all occasions. And nowe, albeit—
God be blessed—there is noe cause to complaine,
either of any such apostaticall power—for we
haue an apostolicall king—nor of any such wicked
pollicy,—for we haue had kings and queēs,
nursing fathers and nursing mothers of our
Church; yet in these halcyon daies of ours, I
haue presumed to metaphrase some passages of
Dauid['s] psalmes, as an essay to know whether
we might expresse our harts to God in our holy
soliloquies, in mōasillables in our owne mother
tongue or no. It being a receaued opinion
amōgst many of those who seeme rather to be
iuditious than caprichious, that heretofore our
English tongue in the true idiome thereof, con-
sisted altogether of monosillables, vntill it came
to be blended and mingled with the commixture

of exotique languages. And I my selfe haue
seene all the Lord['s] prayer vsed in the tyme of
John Wickleefe to be expressed in words of one sill-
able. And because God's children did reckon seauen
tymes seauen yeares before they could enioy their
yeare of Iubile, I haue made allusion in this
little Essay to tune forth seauē tymes seauen sad
sobbs for sinne, that when we haue spent the
remaynder of our wretched dayes of our pilgrim-
age here, God may in his mercie, wipe away
all teares from our eyes, and bring vs to our
eternall Iubile, in his glorious kingdome. Which
God grant to you, to me, and to all Christian
people for his owne rich mercie['s][1] sake, and the
satisfactory meritts of Iesus Christ our Lord,
Amen.

Written from my studie within the English
house at Hamborough, Jan. 24.

Yours because you are of Christ.

WILL: LOE.

---

[1] In this Epistle I have added the apostrophe : but note
the transition-forms, 'passages of Dauid psalmes' and
'the Lord prayer' and 'rich mercie sake'. Hereafter I
will not make the correction required by present grammatical usage, the more especially as the thing is common
to Spenser and other contemporaries. The Teares of
the Muses says "whom Nature selfe had made (1, 205)

and so elsewhere. Throughout I silently remove mere
misprints, as 'lift' in above title-page is 'life' where however I have left 'tone', which probably ought to be
'tune'. A foreign Press explains such errata. G.

THE FIRST STRAINE.

ORD heare my suite, my plainte,   1
    That my soule makes to thee:
Lord in thy truth one looke of grace
Grant in thy loue to me.

Lord see the moane I make,   2
    Looke on me in thy grace:
Let not my sighes come back in vaine
    But shewe to me thy face,

Loe I was borne in sinne;   3
    My kind, my shape, my all,
My stocke, my flocke, my selfe from birth
    O Lord from thee did fall

And I poore soule am sett   4
    In greefe, in paine, in woe;
My sinnes come on, my soule doth faint,
    O quitt me of my foe.

My sinnes, the haires doe passe   5
    That are set on my head;
My hart doth feare, and faint, and faile
    And I am as one dead.

Thus goe I greeud, and goord,   6
   And frett in hart, and spright:
Thus am I faint with feare and death,
   My sinnes they doe me fright.

The deeds that I haue done   7
   Are sett in vewe of eie;
My faults, my thoughts, my sinne, my shame
   Thy lawes, thy lookes, doe spie.

I. Sighe.

O that my thoughts, words, workes, and
waies, were made so straight and right, that I
might keepe thy lawes O Lord, all the daies and
nights of my whole life: so should I be clere and
cleane from the guilt of sinne and shame.

THE SECOND STRAINE.

GOD if thou shouldst waighe   1
   My waies and take a vewe,
I could not scape thy rod; thy wrath,
   I should in woe it rue.

O iudge me not I pray,   2
   O sheeld me from my fall;

For in thy sight none iust doth liue
 No none I say at all.

Large is thy loue to me,   3
 For it with thee I treate :
O grant me it for Christ, his sake,
 Gainst sinnes so huge, so great.

O Christ what wight doth knowe 4
 His sinne and faults of life ?
O cleanse me from my sinnes at once
 Which are in me most rife.

And keepe me Lord I craue   5
 Least sinnes doe ore me sway :
So shall I then be free, and faine
 To keepe thy lawe for aie.

This Lord of thee I beg,   6
 To thee I hold vp hands ;
And hart and soule, both thirst, and gape,
 As doth the drought in lands.

As maids doe watch and waite,   7
 On queenes, some grace to haue ;
So doe I Lord both day and night
 For grace both beg and craue.

II. Sighte.

O that there were such an hart in me to feare thee, and to keepe all thy lawes that it might goe well with me and mine for aye.

THE THIRD STRAINE.

LORD, turne thee to thy grace   1
  That once thou shewedst to me!
  O saue me not for my good acts :
I seeke, I sue to Thee.

My soule why dost thou faint?   2
  And art with greefe soe prest?
My hart, my mind, why doe you thus
  Fret sore within my brest.

Trust soule to God for aye,   3
  And thou the time shalt see,
When thou shalt thinke, and thanke him still
  For health, and peace to thee.

For why, his wrath doth last,   4
  A space, and then doth slacke :
But in his face, and grace for aye,
  Thou canst not ioy long lacke.

Though gripes, and greefes full sore   5

477

Doe lodge with thee all night
Yet ioy and grace, shal be at hand
Ere that the day be light.

The Lord is kind and meeke   6
When we doe make him greeue ;
He is full slowe his wrath to shew,
Great grace he doth vs giue.

And loe what loue good men   7
To their owne seede doe beare,
Like grace the Lord doth shewe to such
As searue him in his feare.

III. Sighe.

O that I had wings like a doue—my sweete
Loue—that I might fly hence to thee, and so be
at rest both in mind, in thought, in hart, in soule,
and in mine whole.

THE FOURTH STRAINE.

HE Lord that made me knowes   1
My shape, my mould, my lust :
Howe weake, howe vaine, howe fraile,
howe fond,
And that I am but dust.

O God in me set vp   2
   A pure hart in thy sight ;
And eke in all my parts let be
   A good and meeke sweete spright.

With thy sweete spright of power   3
   Cure thou O Lord my sore ;
And I shall teach the good and ill
   To bowe to thy sweete lore.

My soule doth pant and bray,   4
   Mine hart is neere at rest,
But seekes to knowe thy lawe, thy will,
   And what may please thee best.

O would it might thee please   5
   My waies to set in right,
That I might both in hart and deed.
   Thy lawes to keepe in sight.

O Lord I doe tend still   6
   My daies, my time to serue,
That I nor mīe may haue a thought
   From thy lawes once to swerue.

O saue me then O God,   7
   Looke on me with thy health :
For that I rate at such a price
   More thē the wide world's wealth

IV. Sighe.

O let the words of my mouth, the thoughts of my hart, the tune of my voice, and touch of my tongue, be euer in thy sight O Lord as a sweet smell, for Christ, his sake, both at morne, eue, and none daye.

THE FIFT STRAINE.

ITH ioy Lord of the iust   1
     Let my poore soule be fraught :
     That I may liue in peace and glee,
     And free from all that's naught.

Lord keepe me, for in thee   2
     I stay, and stand and feed :
Thou art my God, and of my goods
     O Lord thou hast noe need.

I giue them to the saincts   3
     That in the world doe dwell :
Yea to the folke of faith and loue,
     Whose care is to doe well.

My hart is prest for aye,   4
     And eke my tongue is soe :
I will raise vp my soule in song
     In spight of hell and foe.

To praise my God that hath   5
   Shewd loue and life to me,
And made me scape both bloud and blowe,
   And so did sett me free.

O Lord what shall I pay   6
   To thee for this thy grace :
I vowe to thee, my selfe, my life,
   My loue, and all my race.

Grant Lord, I beg and pray   7
   In thee that we may rest :
So shall our soules sing to thy praise,
   And aye in thee be blest.

V. Sighe.

O my God, why art thou gone from me, and
why dost thou hide thy sweete face from my
prayer, for I seeke thee, and sue to thee, with all
my hart, and that thou knowest full well.

THE SIXT STRAINE.

Y soule giue praise to God,   1
   My spright shall doe the same,
   And all the parts of hart and mind,
Shall praise for aye his name.

Giue thankes for all his gifts   2
   Shew soule thy selfe most kind;
And let not his good deeds to thee
   Once slipp out of thy mind.

He quitt thee of thy faults,   3
   He rid thy life from death :
His good, his grace doth waite on thee,
   His word doth giue thee breath

If thou wert brought to graue,   4
   And turnd to mould and dust,
Yet he will giue thee life in store,
   As he to thee is iust.

Teach me then Lord to knowe   5
   Thy lawe, thy loue, thy lore;
Thy workes, thy words, as signes and seales
   I'le lay them vp in store.

O day of ioy to me   6
   When I learnd first to knowe
Howe for to scape my selfe, my sinne,
   And hell that is soe lowe.

I giue mine all to thee,   7
   My bud, my branch, my fruite :
I beg of thee, O Lord, my God
   To grant to me my suite.

VI. Sighe.

O my God, to thy hands I giue my spright
thou hast bine a pledge for me and that to death,
O God. Thou art the God both of my health,
life, and rest for aye.

THE SEUENTH STRAINE.

 LORD, thou hast me tride, 1
 And day by day dost knowe
My thoughts, my words, my lookes, my
  deeds,
 My sighs, my groans, my woe.

My bones they are not hid, 2
 Thou knewst them all, each one :
For in thy note they were all wrote
 Each ioynt, and bone by bone.

Trie still, and search mine hart, 3
 My thoughts proue day and night
And if the ill doe touch me Lord,
 O leade me to the right.

For thou canst rule my raines 4
 As when I was in wombe ;
O giude me in this life of mine,
 And rest me in my tombe.

D   **483**

Keepe me from men that muse   5
    Of bloud of bane, of ill;
O let me thinke of thee O Lord,
    And howe to doe thy will.

So shall noe shame me taynt   6
    My corps, my goods, my name:
So shall I rest in ioy and peace,
    And touch noe blot of shame.

So shall thy folke for me,   7
    Be glad, and sing thy praise;
So shall my selfe, my seed, my soule,
    Be thine in all my daies.

VII. Sighe.

O let not my suite come in vaine to thee, but
heare O my God, and say to my soule I am, and
will be thy passe from hell, thy port from the sea
of this world, and will bring thee to the bay of
blisse.[1]

----

[1] Following this are two blank leaves or four pages,
with border lines: G.

A months minde.

To Thinke on death, & muse
on the graue, that the feare of death
may not be fierce when Christ shall
call vs out of this world, & is to
be song in the tune

of

1 sayd I will looke to my waie.

PSALM. XXXIX.

*O death I will be thy death (saith
Christ) for he is the death of death, the
death of sinne, the life of man and the
breath of god for man to liue
there in world with
out end.*

HAMBOROUGH.   Januarii 24.

1620.[1]

---

[1] Blank on reverse.   G.

To his much-respected good frend, Mr. THOMAS
   BARKER, one of the assistants of the worthy
   cōpanie of the Marchants Aduenturers, residing
   at Hamborough.

The blessing of both worlds in Christ Iesus.

ELBELOUED, There is nothing more com-
                fortable to a spirituall minded mā then
                to muse and meditate of his departure
hence into the blessed sight of Christ, in the
other life : yet to a worldling that would build
vp a rest for his body here, and sing a requiem
to his soule in this vale of teares, nothing is more
fearefull and hiddeous then for him to heare
death spoken of. We must therefore examine
our selues, whether we can sing a song of Siō in
this exile and banishmēt, whether we can solace
our selues, in hymnes and songs, of our ends and
departure hence : For we must hence : nothing
more sure ; but the tyme when, the place where,
and the manner how, nothing more vnsure. It is
sufficient that God telleth vs, our life is but a flower
that fadeth, an hower that passeth, a shadow that
departeth, a vanity that vexeth, a momēt that warn-

eth, a nothing when we haue done all we can. For our thoughts, our faults, our purposes, our proiects, our loues our liues, when our breath departeth, perisheth in the twinckling of an eie. O then let vs meditate and muse to our selues, and sing and say to our soules, that our end and the last things, are not the least but the best things that we can consider of to mortifie vs and make vs meete for the sauing mercies of God in Christ ; to which I recomend you in my dearest loue, and rest.

Yours in life and death,

W. Loe.

THE FIRST MUSE.

DEARE soule thou hast thought of thy
     end   1
And nowe muse on the way ;
The first part is a life well spent,
     The last is death's doome's day.

Shall I call that the way of woe   2
     By which we passe to blisse ?
O sure there is noe way but that
     To bring me where Christ is.

And what is death nowe dost thou thinke   3
     But downe with all the stickes,
Of which this earth and tent of ours
     Is made, that gainst God kickes.

Death is the farewell of old frends,   4
     Till they meete to be blest;
Death is the iudge to quitt frō iayle,
     The soule that longs for rest.

Death makes the corps of clay to sleepe,   5
     But wakes the soule to see ;

Death payes the debte and teares the bond,
And all to sett thee free.

There is a death of deaths my soule 6
The death of hell and woe ;
But Christ, his death, hath payd for that ;
His word doth tell thee soe.

O Christ, my soule doth thinke on thee, 7
And thankes thee day and night,
That thou hast rid me frō this death,
By thy great power and might.

I. Thought.

Thy Christ, O soule, hath set them free, who
through feare of death were all their life time in
bonds and thrall.
HEB. 2. 15.

THE SECOND MUSE.

MUSE my soule, sith thou art safe, 1
Get home ene to thy rest ;
For God to praise in songs and psalmes,
I hold it for the best.

My soule, howe canst thou feare to goe 2
In stepps where Christ hath bine ;

489

He hath to graue led thee the way
    O then leaue of to sinne.

For hire of sinne is death, and graue   3
    To death are deepe fell wayes ;
There needs no kinues[1], noe cords, noe swords,
    It comes on nights and dayes.

One by a slatt,[2] a flye, a grape,   4
    One by a bit of meate :
One by the ayre, a flower, a thorne,
    Comes to his doome so great.

Why then my soule, feare not this death :   5
    The sting of it is lost :
The bed of graue is sweete, and safe
    Through Christ, his care and cost.

Our sinne made death our foe at last,   6
    Our frend Christ hath it made ;
By death we pass the port of rest,
    When all things else doe fade.

What if this giude[3] doe lead my corps   7
    Through graue both dark and fell ?

---

[1] = knives. G.
[2] =slate or stone (falling from a roof). G.
[3] = guide, as before, and so throughout. G.

Whiles at that tyme my soule doth liue
And with my Christ doth dwell.

II. Thought.

O my soule, ioy and be glad, for thy Christ
hath made thee say to death, O death where is thy
death? O graue where is thy power?

1 COR. 15, 55.

THE THIRD MUSE.

HAT if my frends doe mourne for me   1
     And sobb and sighe in moane ;
  What if my seed doe cry and roare,
     And greeue, and waile, and grone.

This while my soule sees him that was   2
     Once dead but nowe doth liue,
And that for aye my Christ in God,
     My Lord that life doth giue.

What care I who doth shutt mine eies,   3
     Whē death doth make me see
As I am seene of God in Christ,
     And then with him shall be.

What if my life the world doe not   4
     Set out in words of fame!

Whiles I liue with the God of life,
　What care I for the same.

If death showld still be foe to me,　　　　5
　He harmes but my worst part ;
My best part farre out of his reach
　Scornes both his ruth and dart.

And more then this, my corps once dead,　6
　Feeles noe more sting of death ;
But then my soule is free, and liues
　In God, by Christ, his breath.

Nowe then my soule sith thou dost beare　7
　Two things wrapt vp in breast,
Lett each part turne, and goe, and see
　His seate, his scite, his rest.

III. Thought.

O God they that dwelt in a darke place, by thee
haue seene the light, and they that walkt in the
shade of death thou hast brought them to the
light with great ioy and peace.

ESAY. 9. 2.

492

THE FOURTH MUSE.

SHRINKE not deare soule at the sight of
    death   1
    Nor faint thou at God's call;
Howe oft hast thou hard bells to passe
    For frends, for foes, for all.

Howe oft hast thou the sicke bed sene,   2
    Of wights in woe most rife!
Howe oft haue things bine done to death
    And all to giue thee life.

And canst thou hope that some way else   3
    For thee is made in sence?
Whē kings, and prests, and rich, and poore
    Aud all must thus goe hence.

Passe on my soule, and sing, and ioy   4
    In God that makes the graue,
A place for thee to pass to blisse
    And knowes what thou wouldst haue.

Howe oft hast thou seene eies fast closd   5
    And heard by dint of sword,
Howe oft vaine men in field haue fought
    In fence of a vaine word.

What thē nowe dost thou feare my soule?   6
    The stage of death is bed,

And graue, that rests our bones in peace
    That here on earth haue fed.

Let them feare death whose hart and mind   7
    Is more sicke thē their face :
Howe canst thou feare since nowe thy Christ
    Hath shed his bloud for grace ?

Thought.

O giue me light that am set in a dark place,
and shade of death, and giude me by thy good
grace O Christ, to the way of peace.

                    LUCK. 1. 79.

THE FIFT MUSE.

WHAT losse is this sweet soule to loose   1
    This corps, this flesh, this skinn ?
When thou shalt winn thy God in Christ,
    Thy selfe fre'd from thy sinn.

When thou shalt see the soules, the saincts   2
    In ioy, in rest, in blisse :
Whē thou this world a sea of sinne
    A sinke, a stye, shalt misse ?

O change most blest for thee to knowe   3
   To rid thee of these raggs;
And thy selfe clad in robes of state
   In spight of death, his brags.

This skin, this shame, this dust, this dung,   4
   This earth, this mire, this clay,
Shall shine as sunne in raies of rest
   When thou shalt see that day.

Thine eies that were full sad to see   5
   Thine oft and ill done deeds ;
Shall then see Christ still in thy sight
   Where grace and good still feeds.

These eares that heare the ruth and rage   6
   Of tongue, as hott as hell;
Shall then the voice of Christ still heare,
   And saincts, with him that dwell.

And thē this tongue that now doth plaine   7
   Of greefe, of woe, of gall,
Shall tune a part in that sweet quire
   With Christ, with saincts, with all.

V. Thought.

O my soule thy Christ hath tooke part with
flesh and bloud, that by death he might beate
downe him that had the power of death.

HEB. 2. 14.

THE SIXT MUSE.

NOWE what is death the say my soule,   1
    I'st not a sleepe in graue?
They that did feele the worst of it,
    The stile of sleepe it gaue.

And aske thy corps, O my sweete soule,   2
    Whē full with toyle of day,
If it hath not bine glad to rest
    As cloyd with a foule way.

And nowe in this sweete sleepe of death   3
    Thou art sure to be blest,
Why like a child wilt thou not goe
    To this thy bed, thy rest?

Didst thou ere see a bird in cage,   4
    Sitt still within the grate?
That might flie foorth to woods, to groues,
    To meete his loue, his mate?

Did Paule when God his gyues had burst   5
  And rid him out of iayle?
Crie out and say, not yet O Lord
  I doe not like this bayle.

Paule slepte twixt two that did him keepe   6
  But whē that he was free
And rid frō iayle, did he once turne
  To iayle those bonds to see?

O my sweete soule did'st ere thou see   7
  At sea, men sing their songs:
And whē to lād they cāe did greeue
  And tell their frends of wrongs?

VI. Thought.

O heare me O Lord, my God, and giue light to
mine eies least I sleepe the sleepe of death.

PSAL. 30. 3.

THE SEUENTH MUSE.

AST thou O soule, no mind to rest   1
  In all thy paine and toyle?
But wilt thou still goe on and drudge
By lott on sea, on soyle.

Howe oft haue wights in woe and greefe   **2**
     Sought death to ease their paine !
Hath death found thee, and wilt thou not
     To goe from greefe be faine ?

Doth name of death the[e] fright my soule ?   **3**
     What if mē call sleepe death,
Wilt thou be fraid to close thine eies
     Or feare to loose thy breath ?

What hurt will cōe to thee by that ?   **4**
     The first man was in sleepe
Whē God a wife made him for helpe,
     The man in ioy to keepe.

And what if nowe thy God for thee,   **5**
     Whilst thou dost sleepe in graue,
Doth make thy soule a spouse to Christ
     His face, his grace to haue ?

My death, O soule, but parts the frēds   **6**
     That each hath led the way,
And nowe shake hands but for a space
     Till meete in rest they may.

Goe then, my soule, to this sure gaine   **7**
     Part with a frend a space :
The tyme will come when this my dust,
     Shall see thy Christ, his face.

VII. Thought.

The due of sinne, my soule, is death, and graue,
and hell: but the gift of God is life, ioy, and
blisse, by Christ my Lord and God.

Rom. 6. 13.

THE EIGHT MUSE.

ELL me my soule was thou not loth   1
    At first to ioyne with me?
Why nowe art loth to part with that,
    Which much woe letts thee see.

Dost thou not heare the wise to say   2
    The day of death is cheefe;
And is more good then day of birth
    Which brings thee woe and greefe?

Dost thou not trust the wise man's words   3
    On throne, in state, in glee,
That thus did say of death and birth?
    Then hark thou once to me.

The Lord of life that knewe death's force   4
    Doth say that they are blest
That die in God, our Lord, our Christ
    And from their woes haue rest.

O death howe sweete is that thy rest　　5
　　To wights in vale of teares !
Howe sweete is thy grim face to those
　　That liue in woe and feares !

O soule what man is so fell mad,　　6
　　And so in soule cast downe,
To hide himselfe in base things here
　　To loose by them a crowne ?

My soule then see and say in fine　　7
　　With men of God's owne lore ;
For me to die it is more good
　　Then liue on this ville shore.

VIII. 𝔗hought.

O, my soule, if by one man's sinne death did raigne by one, much more they which haue much grace and the gift of faith, shall raigne in life by one Christ, my Lord and God.

Rom. 5. 17.

THE NINGTH[1] MUSE.

HAT ayles thee O my soule, my deare, 1
    Such face, such feare to shewe?
Nowe death doe come to cite thee home
    Is all thy faith, but dewe?

Is death soe fearce, so fell, to eies, 2
    To thoughts, that was soe free?
It is a shame to thee my soule,
    Thou dost noe more Christ see.

Where is thy faith? in words thou could'st 3
    Call oft for death, in life:
Is all but talke? is all but smoke?
    Where is thy hope so rife?

Hath thy sweete Christ now sent for thee 4
    And art thou loth to goe?
Rouze vp thy selfe for shame, O soule
    And doe not serue him soe.

O Lord, raise vp this hart of mine 5
    That faints and droopes in death!
O that I might thy cup once tast,
    And liue in thy sweete breath.

---

[1] Misprinted, ' nigth '.   G.

The spright would come, but flesh is weake 6
   Lord helpe this guest of thine!
And rid her from this flesh of sinne
   Which is a broode of mine.

I come to thee, O Lord I come,   7
   Streach forth thine hand to me!
O death, O graue where is thy sting?
   My crowne, my God I see.

IX. Thought.

They are blest that haue a part in the first life:
for on such, the last death shall haue noe strength,
but they shal be preests of God, and of Christ.

Apoc. 20. 6.

Finis.

Alls Paulls Prayers.

Metaphrased into words of
one syllable of great Brittains
language, & are to be vsed by a devout
Christian soule in his priuate soliloquies,
& holy solaces with his
God.

And are set to the tune of
I loue the lord because my voice.

PSALM CXVI.

O lord my god thou hast brought
vp my soule from out of the graue & thou
didst hold me from those that goe
downe to the pitt.

To his much esteemed good frend Mr. NICHOLAS
BACKHOUSE marchant, one of the assistants of
the worthy companie of the Marchant Aduenturers residing at Hamborough.

The ioy of Ierusalem, and peace of Syon.

MUCH endeered, The cheefest parts of God's
seruice, are either prayer or praise:
prayer for what we want: praise in
thanksgiuing for what we haue receaued.

The sweete singer of Israell in his heauenly
composed hymes vseth both to pray to God and
to praise God. I need not recomend vnto you
prayer. I hope you vse it; as I knowe you doe
publikely soe I doubte not but you vse it also pri-
uately. Preaching is God's speach to you: prayer
is ours to him. Preaching belongs to me; I
preach to you as your pastor, and pray for you
also. Prayer belongs to you, to pray for me,
your selfe, all yours, all God's childrē. For the
manner howe noe better president, noe more per-
fecte patterne, then S. Paull's practice in his
prayers, which I haue here metaphrased for you

in the syllables of your owne mother-tongue. God the father is the obiecte of your prayers and prayses. God the Sonne the presenter of them, as the only Master of Bequests in heauen. God the Holy Ghost the very breath of your prayers, the smile[1] of your soule. Vse this blessed exercise both of prayer and praise. Be in loue with it, and God will loue you. To which loue of his in this modell of my best loue to you, I recomend your well disposed thoughts in the sauing mercies of Christ Iesus your Lord and mine. Resting,

To be required by you, or your frends in Christ's seruice.

W. Loe.

---

[1] Misprinted 'simle' here and so in next piece. G.

505

THE FIRST PRAYER.

CEASE not to giue thankes to thee,   1
   O God, my God most iust,
For all thy gifts of grace and loue,
   To vs that liue in dust.

And Lord I craue a glympse of light   2
   In Christ my Lord, thy sonne :
That so my faith may see that sight,
   And to it still may runne.

That I may knowe thy becke, thy call,   3
   My hope, my helpe, my all :
That I may haue thy power and strength,
   To helpe me when I fall.

For thou O God, hast made vs see   4
   What thou hast wrought in loue :
For thy sweete spouse thy Church, thy wife,
   Thy ioy, thy smile, thy doue.

For thou hast set our Christ, O God,   5
   At thy right hand to shine :
And thou to that place wilt vs bring
   For that deare loue of thine.

O God, thou laidst my Christ full lowe   6
   Within the earth so darke :
But thou didst raise him vp on high
   And settst him as a marke.

On which we fix our eies of faith   7
   Our harts, our minds, our loue :
O bring vs all to him, sweete God,
   That is our deere, our doue.

O God, my hart is fixt on thee, and my tongue
shall sing, and giue praise to thy name for aye.
Psal. 108. 1.

THE SECOND PRAYER.

 DAY by day doe bowe to thee
   And cease not in the night
To seeke thee, Lord, in all my thoughts
   And muse of all thy might.

For of our Christ is made[1] the church   2
   Of vs that liue in clay,
And eke thy guard[2] and saincts on high
   That praise thee day by day.

---

[1] Misprinted 'nāde'.   G.
[2] Misprinted 'gaurd'.   G.

Grant vs, O Lord, that we may knowe   3
    Thy grace, our good, our end :
And that we may feele power and strength,
    And Christ may be our frend.

Let him dwell in our harts, O Lord,   4
    And then we shall thee see,
With all thy saincts in breadth and length
    In depth, in height, in glee.

Then shall we knowe the loue of Christ   5
    That e se is past our skill,
The shalt thou fill vs with thy grace,
    In him to doe thy will.

O Lord for vs this thou can'st dce   6
    And more then all, that is
Of thy good grace to worke in vs,
    In Christ how should we misse.

Praise be to thee in all the world,   7
    Thy church doe sing the same,
And age to age shall eke sett forth
    For aye, to ours, thy name.

O God thou art my God, ere it be day will I
seeke thee : my soule and flesh doe thirst and long
for thee, as drie land which wants raine.

           Psal.   63. 1.

THE THIRD PRAEYR.

Phillippians I. 9.

GRAUNT to vs Lord that loue may dwell 1
　In these poore tents of ours ;
　For we must hence we knowe full [well],[1]
And fade as doe the flowers.

And graūt good Lord that in thy loue　　　2
　It may growe more and more,
That we may knowe what things are ill
　And lead not to thy loue.

So may we in the day of doome　　　3
　In Christ be void of shame,
And fild with his faire fruits of loue
　May scape the rod of blame.

Then shall we sing the praise to thee　　　4
　In midst of all thy sainots,
Then shall our soule[2] be glad, and ioy,
　That nowe is weake, and faints.

I cease not Lord to pray for those　　　5
　That seeke and sue to thee,
That they may knowe howe safe and sure
　In Christ their soules may be.

---

[1] ' Well ', as inadvertently dropped, supplied by us. **G.**
[2] Misprinted 'soules'. **G.**

And that we all may walke and worke   6
   In word, in worth, in all,
As he that hath vs cald to this,
   And rid vs of our thrall.

Who hath vs fre'd from power of death   7
   F.ō foggs and doggs of hell :
And set vs by his chaire of state,
   With Christ for aye to dwell.

Saue vs, O Lord our God, and bring vs from
those that doe not call on thee, that we may
call on thee, and laud and praise thy name for aye.
      PSAL. 106. 47.

THE FOURTH PRAYER.
THESSALONIANS III. 11.

THE Lord our God, our strength and stay 1
   Make vs to loue each one ;
   And make vs knowe howe that we are
Made all of flesh and bone.

That soe we may growe vp in grace   2
   And firme in hart and minde :
That soe to all we may set forth
   Our loue both sure and kind.

Yea not to cease till that our Lord   3
    Doe come in clouds full bright,
To iudge this earth, and all the folke,
    Yea all the world, in sight.

For is it not the loue of Christ   4
    Who did loue vs so deare,
That we through hope of grace in him
    Should liue voyd of base feare.

Lord be thou ioy to all our harts !   5
    Our words, our workes good make,
That we may loue and liue in thee,
    For thy sonne Christ, his sake.

O God of peace, of loue, of life   6
    Grant vs to serue thee still
In spright, in soule, in hart, in mind
    And this of thy good will.

Yea keepe vs Lord frō blame and blott   7
    Till Christ doth come in skey :
So shall we sure be of thy loue,
    To liue, when we shall die.

Heare me O Lord, and that soone, for my soule doth waxe faint: hide not thy face from me, least I be like them that goe downe to the grave.

Psal. 148. 7.

THE FIFT PRAYER.

ʹROMANS. VII. 25.

 THANKE thee Lord, that hast sett nowe   1
    In me a fight, a iarre ;
My mind, my flesh, doe day by day
    In strife sett forth a warre.

My mind to thy sweeteʹlawe giues way,   2
    My flesh in thrall is brought ;
My min would keep thy lawe, thy lore,
    And hath thy will still sought.

But my base flesh is prompt, and seekes   3
    Thy lawe to cast me fro.
O God what shall I doe in this ?
    With me the case is so.

My mind would doe the good full faine,   4
    That thy lawes shewe to me,
But still my flesh doth frett and fume
    Gairst this thy lawe to me.

For I doe not that which I loue   5
    But I doe that I hate,
And all for that my mind is vext
    With this my flesh, my mate.

What shall I doe O Lord my God   6

Ah wretch who setts thee free ?
F ō this fell death of sinne and shame
That I thy grace may see.

I thanke my God who haue me fre'd
For his sonne Christ, his sake ;
To him for aye both night and day,
My hymnes, my songs I make.

O God that thou wouldst beat downe the strong
and ill man, that rules and raignes in my weake
flesh, that I may say to him goe farre from me.

PSAL. 139. 19.

THE SIXT PRAYER.

ROMANS. XVI. 24.

THE grace of God be all my giude.   1
His power be all my staye,
His strength eke be to me a staffe,
By night, and eke by day.

For he it is that hath me taught   2
That which the world nere knewe,
Till Christ our Lord was made to vs
Our Lord, our God in vewe.

To God in hymnes, still will I sing,   3
    His praise in all my mirth :
The world shall sett him forth in praise.
    In all parts of the earth.

If there be wight that liues in life,   4
    And doth not loue our God,
Let him tast of the Lord of hosts
    His curse, his wrath, his rod.

But let the loue of God, and grace   5
    Of Christ, be with you all
That loue and looke, and long for him,
    To rid vs of our thrall.

And let our God that brought from death   6
    Our Christ, our grace, our blisse,
Set vs with sainets in ioy, in light
    Where as our Christ nowe is.

So shall we tūe[1] in that sweete quire   7
    Midst of those sainets in rest ;
And see his sainets in light of lights,
    And so for aye be blest.

O God let them that hate thee flie from thy sight

---

[1] = Tune. G.

as the mist doth from the sunne, but let them
that loue thee be glad and ioy in thee.

PSAL. 68. 1.

THE SEUENTH PRAYER.

HEBREWS. XIII. 20.

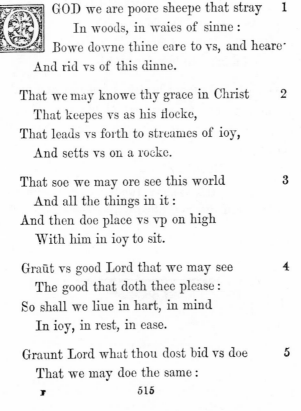 GOD we are poore sheepe that stray   1
     In woods, in waies of sinne :
Bowe downe thine eare to vs, and heare·
     And rid vs of this dinne.

That we may knowe thy grace in Christ   2
     That keepes vs as his flocke,
That leads vs forth to streames of ioy,
     And setts vs on a rocke.

That soe we may ore see this world   3
     And all the things in it :
And then doe place vs vp on high
     With him in ioy to sit.

Graūt vs good Lord that we may see   4
     The good that doth thee please :
So shall we liue in hart, in mind
     In ioy, in rest, in ease.

Graunt Lord what thou dost bid vs doe   5
     That we may doe the same :

Bid what thou wilt and graūt vs grace
  And we will praise thy name.

To Christ our Lord the Lambe of God   6
  That shed his bloud for sinnes,
To rid vs from the feends of hell
  And all their crafts and ginns.

Be praisd of vs all tymes and tyds
  In woe, and eke in wealth :
And let the folke on all the earth
  Giue laud to him for health.

O Lord God of our health, I crie day and night
to thee, let my grones come nigh to thee, and bowe
downe thine eare to my sighes, that I make to
thee.[1]

---

[1] Following this again are two blank leaves, with border lines, and after next title-page, one blank page.   G.

The song of songs

Or the Canticle of Solomon
betweene Christ & his spouse,
the two first chapters, & is set to
the tune of
Blessed are they that perfect are.

Psal. cxix. 1 part.

To his much esteemed good freend Mr. William Christmas, Marchant, one of the deacons of the English Church residing at Hamborough :

Grace here, glory for euer in Christ.

LOUING, and beloued frend, the title of this heauenly hymne sheweth the excellency thereof. For it is called the song of songs, or the Canticles of wise Soloman. The subiecte is most sacred, for it is the nuptiall louesong betweene Christ and his Spouse. Wherein their mutuall loues by sweete resēblāces are mystically and maruelously expressed. What more comfortable song then to sing our hart's loue we beare to Christ, in the blessed vnion by one spirit, wherby we haue euerlasting life. Two of the first chapters of which song I haue metaphrased into monosyllables, which I haue bequethed to your loue as a signe of mine, and to seale both ours. Receaue it as the rest of your colleagues, for I wish you all the happines of both worlds in the sauing mercies of Christ, to which I recommend you and all that looke vpon you with loue, resting,

Yours because of Christ,

W. LOE.[1]

---

[1] Following this is a blank leaf, as before. G.

THE FIRST SONG.

The Spouse speakes to Christ.

O THAT thou wouldst on me so cast   1
  Some lookes of thy sweete loue,
That thou maist make me deere to thee
 My hart with grace to moue.

Thy loue O Christ is farre more deare,   2
 And farre more sweete to me
Then wealth, or wine, or limbe, or life,
 Or ought that I can see.

The sweete that I smell of thy name   3
 Is like an oyle most pure,
And pourd it is on all thy saincts,
 Such is thy loue soe sure.

O drawe me, drawe me, I will runne   4
 To bord, to bed, with thee ;
O pull me, pull me from my sinne,
 O rid me, set me free.

The good are glad in thee ; thy loue   5
 They long and looke for still :

They walke to thee, they talke of thee,
  And all to doe thy will.

Graunt this O Christ, and then we shall   **6**
  Be all in all that is,
And thou shalt find that none of vs
  Of thy grace ought to misse.

O shew me, whom my soule doth loue,   **7**
  Where thou dost feed at noone :
O why should I thus freet, and feele
  The losse of thee so soone.

THE SECOND SONG.

Christ speakes to his Spouse.

 THOU my church, whom I doe loue   **1**
    For whō I shed my bloud,
  If thou knowe not what thou dost craue,
  And hast not seene the good :

Then get thee to those flockes of mine   **2**
  Where as they feed by those
Whom I haue sett as giuds for them
  That I in loue haue chose.

There feed and fatt thy selfe with foode,   **3**
  That saincts doe touch, doe tast ;

And tune their soules in thankes to me
    For loue that aye doth last.

For deere thou art to me my loue,   **4**
    For shape, for strength, for speede:
That none is like to thee my deere
    In thought, in word, in deede.

Those parts of thee where loue doth looke   **5**
    Are set with pearls of grace,
With stones of price, with chaynes of worth :
    I loue to see thy face.

These signes of loue, are seales to thee,   **6**
    What shall be thine else where,
When thou shalt shine in bliss with me
    O spouse, my loue most deere!

There spangs, and specks of gold most pure **7**
    Ile add to all the rest :
There shalt thou loue, and liue with me
    And eke for aye be blest.

THE THIRD SONG.

The Spouse speakes to her mates.

SEE nowe all ye that loue the Lord   1
    Ye nymphes, ye mayds of grace,
Whiles that my Lord and king nowe
    seemes
Farre of from me in place.

And is in midst of troopes of saincts   2
    On highe where he doth dwell;
Where all doe tend on him in loue,
    Where all things sure goes well.

Yet see his grace doth stoope to me,   3
    I feele him with me here;
By power of spright, by gifts of light,
    He comes to me most neere.

And though I be much ioy to him,
    Yet he is all to me;
As bunch of myrrhe twixt both my breasts,
    So sweete to hart is he.

Oh is there ought in the wide world   5
    That smells, that smiles as he?
Ah sweete, ah sweete, my soule doth feele
    His loue a life to me.

523

His loue layd close to my poore hart   6
    To sence giues such a touch,
That for his loue to dye, to dye,
    I would not thinke it much.

Watch then and wayte ye maids that mourne,
    For this my loue will come ;
And iudge he will in truth, and power
    The folke, both all and some.[1]

THE FOURTH SONG.

Christ speakes to his Spouse.

EERE spouse, noe loue is lost on me,   1
    To me thou art most sweete :
    To see thee clad in clothes of grace
      With rings, and roabs most meete.

I ioy, I like, I loue thee deere,   2
    Howe faire, how fresh art thou !
None like to thee in shine of face,
    As I looke on thee nowe.

Howe chast, howe choice art thou my deere ! 3
    Thine eies like doues doe looke.

---

[1] = the race and the individual. **G.**

Thine hart, thy mind, thy thoughts, thy all,
    I write thē in my booke.

The Spouse speakes to Christ.

Nay thou my deere, thou art the cheefe,   4
    The choice, the sunne, the shine !
From thee O Christ, I haue these raies,
    For they are none of mine.

Thou art O Christ, full of this grace,   5
    Thou art the sea, the spring ;
And from thee I doe take these streames
    And to thee thē doe bring

As thankes for all thy loue to me,   6
    And to thy saincts each one ;
Who troope in bands to serue thee still,
    Though here they weepe, and mone.

For they are sure to rest in blisse   7
    When thou shalt call them home
From out this sea of sobs and sighes
    That doth soe frett and fome.

THE FIFT SONG.

Christ speakes to his Spouse.

EERE   spouse, I am both faire and
          sweete :   1
    Of field I am the rose,
And sure all such as liue by me,
    Full choice I am to those.

All thinges else that this world hath, be   2
    Vile weeds, which are most base :
I am the sweet, the sence, the smell,
    That yeald them all the grace.

And thou O loue art mongst the maids   3
    All choice and cheefe in vewe :
Nought in the earth is like to thee.
    In face, in shine, in hue.

The Spouse speakes to Christ.

O thou my deare, that one I loue   4
    Thou art the tree of life ;
Thy shade let sheeld me from all harms
    And I will be thy wife.

Thou with thy spright shalt lead me forth   5
    To the sweete streames of good,

And I shall be fresht with thy loue,
   Wrought to me in thy bloud.

O stay me, stay me, take a care,   6
   O cheare my soule that faints ;
O come for I am sicke of loue
   To liue in midst of saincts.

O put thy left hand to my head   7
   Thy right hand to my side !
O stay me vp both head and hart,
   And still be thou my guide.

THE SIXT SONG.

The Spouse speakes.

 CHARGE ye O you soules of saincts,
   By roes and hindes of loue,
Take heed howe you doe vexe and greeue
   The spright of my sweete doue.

Take heed you wrong not his great name,   2
   With life soe leaud, so vaine,
And doe not dare to moue his ire,
   Who would saue you so fayne.

Loe I doe call, and he doth heare,   3
   And sends to me his voice ;

My moūts of sinnes, and hills of shame
  Haue not soe lowd a noice.

Noe roe, noe hinde, soe swift cā rūne   4
  Nor make such speede as he :
When I doe call, or crie for him,
  He comes, he runnes to me.

The Spouse speakes.

And though this vaile of my base flesh   5
  A full sight bares me fro,
Yet with mine eye of faith, I looke
  On him that loues me soe.

I see him as in a cleare glasse,   6
  I see him shine full bright ;
Through grates of words and gates of life,
  My soule of him hath sight.

And nowe me thinkes I heare him speake   7
  And thus to me doth say :
O church, O spouse, lift vp thy head
  O faire one come thy way.

THE SEUENTH SONG.

Christ speakes.

THE storme is past of greefe and woe,   1
    The spring of ioy is seene :
And all things nowe are fresh and faire
And full, and newe, and greene.

On highe is ioy, on earth is peace,   2
    To men a great good will ;
And all the quire of saincts doe sing
    To shewe their loue, their skill.

Not buds, but figgs and fruits are seene   3
    Of grace, of ioy, of loue ;
O come my deere, shake of thy sleepe,
    Come on my milke white doue.

O let me heare thy voice my deere   4
    O plye me with thy plaints,
O looke thou vp though face be sad
    Ile place thee with my saincts.

O all ye that wishe well to me,   5
    And to my church and name,
Put frō my deere all those that seeke
    Her faith, her loue to blame.

The Spouse speakes.

For he is mine by faith and trust,   6
    And I am his by loue.
We both are one by his great power,
    I long to see my doue.

O come as swift as roe or hind   7
    My loue, my life to me :
Till day doe breake, till sunne doe shine,
    Till shade of death doth flee.[1]

---

[1] Following these are two blank leaves, as before, and so throughout between each piece and reverse of title-pages : not marked further.   G.

A Canticle, or song.

Of the third & fourth chapters
of the song of Solomon being Metaphrased into Monosylables of Great Brittains
language, & is to be vsed by euery deuout
soule in his priuat conference
with his god.

And is set to the tune of
Helpe lord for good, & godly men.

Psal. XII.

To his much esteemed good frend, Mr. Isaac Lee, one of the assistants of the most worthy companie of the Marchant-Adventurers, residing at Hamb.

Encrease of Glory,

MOREthē much beloued, When God brought man forth at the first, he put him not into a wildernes, but into a garden, a paradise and place of pleasure. Wherby I see that his sacred maiestie did not reioyce in the misery, but in the delight and happines of his creatures. Cheerefulnes therefore pleaseth God better then dulnes, dumpishnes, and heauines of hart. Let vs be godly and good in our pleasures, and it will neuer displease our Maker; neither will he grudge or repine at our joy. To this purpose haue I framed certayne hymns for the priuat solace of such as shall take delight there in. One portion whereof I have consecrated to you. Let yt haue acceptance of you by your practice of yt. I expect no other guerdon for my paines. For the Highest knowes with what an honest hart I

composed this and the rest, and what a desire I
had in the framing thereof for the good of many.
I haue euer hated [that] Epicurean resolution :
' Let vs eate and drinke, to morrowe we shall
dye'.   But I haue euer loued entyrely [that]
Christian exhortacion : ' Let vs pray, and praise
God, to morrowe we shall liue '. For to loue, is to
liue, and where we loue, there we liue.   If we
loue God, we shall liue in him by our prayers,
by our prayses, and all by one Spirit.   O then
let vs so loue him, that we may liue in him in our
daylie voices, that they may be hard to his glory,
our comfort, and good example of our brethren.
The God of heauen ioy your hart in all your life,
and in your death, that we may all meete to sing
together in the quire of heauen with the angells
in the sauing mercies of our Sauiour Christ.

Yours much more then mine owne,

W. Loe.

THE FIRST SPEACH.

The Spouse speakes to Christ.

N bed I sought my loue by night,   1
    But could not find him there,
I sought him, but he was farre off,
    And did not come me neere.

I rose, and walkt the streates to see   2
    If my soule could him find
Whom I did want, yet found I not
    The day-starre of my mind.

Thē rā I straight to those that teach   3
    And watch and waite for me,
And sayd to thē, cā ye shewe nowe
    Where I my loue might see.

And thus halfe spent with care and cost,   4
    My soule gan faint and faile:
Loe then my loue did shewe himselfe:
    And would not let me quaile.

So that by a newe acte of faith   5
    I sawe where he was not.

We misse him in our beds of rest,
   The world is not his lott.

The streets are strayts of cost and care   6
   Where we doe lose him quite ;
But in the Word, and soule of man
   We feele him in his might.

But whē I found him, hold I tooke   7
   Fast hold on him I layd,
Noe more to part with him at all :
   Then he to me thus sayd.

THE SECOND SPEACH

Christ speakes to his Spouse.

OWE that my spouse hath toyld all night
   And lokt and longd for me,
   I charge you all that are my frends,
   And looke to liue in glee.

Stirre her not vp, nor wake my deere   2
   With toyes, or tales of yore,
But let her rest in peace and ioy,
   And vexe her nowe noe more.

Oh who is this that comes so faire   3
   From out the foule world's lane,

And hath shakt of[f] her slough of sinne
    That would haue beene her bane ?

It is my Church, my chaire of state   4
    Where I doe loue to be :
It is my doue, my stay, my deere,
    It glads me her to see :

That is so quitt from world of woe,   5
    From sinke of sinne and shame ;
She seekes to me for all her wants,
    Shee trusts to my great name :

She smells as myrrh and spice of cost   6
    Gracd with my chaines of loue ;
She is my spouse, no spott she hath,
    She is my milke-whit doue.

All faire and full of grace most bright   7
    She comes, she rūns to me :
Come on my deere, make thou noe stay,
    Thy loue, thy life to see.

THE THIRD SPEACH.

The Spouse speakes.

 NOWE my soule thou hast a glymse   1
    Of ioy that is on high !
O blest are they that vewe it all,
    Or doe that place come nighe.

The courts on earth of kings most greate   2
    Are rich and rare to vewe ;
But this, where my Christ rules and raignes,
    For aye is fame and newe.

The gard of this great court of state   3
    Are sainctes and sprightes of might,
That doe his will at all his beckes,
    And dwell with him in light.

The courts of kings are made with hands   4
    Their care, their cost is vaine ;
But here's a Court not made by mē
    Where my sweete Christ doe raigne.

The Spouses speaketh. [*sic*]

He in him selfe is all the state,   5
    He giues his Court the grace ;
He is the light, the hight, the all,
    That is still in that place.

Come forth ye saincts of God in Christ,   6
     And see this court of rayes :
O take a vewe of this your life,
     O seeke it all your dayes.

Christ is your Bride groome, and you are,   7
     To him a spouse most bright ;
He hath you bought with bloud most deere
     And gaynd you with his might.

THE FOURTH SPEACH.

Christ speakes to his Spouse.

HOWE faire art thou my deare, my spouse   1
     With out, and eke with in !
Howe voyd of filth or spotts of shame,
     Of sinke or stinch of sinne !

For I doe purge thee of the same,   2
     My word doth make thee free,
And they that teach to thee my lore
     Are all most sweet to thee.

Their speach is full of grace and loue,   3
     To those that heare the same ;
Their words are impt[1] with zeale of loue
     To keepe thee frō all blame.

---

[1] An 'imp' is a graft or shoot inserted into a tree :

Those that doe rule and giude the stearne   **4**
    Are as the necke to head :
They are both strong and stout to gard
    The soules that they haue fed.

The two sweet bookes of league most **newe** **5**
    Are breasts full fraught with milke,
And all that sucke the ioyes of tℏē
    Are clad in robes of silke.

That is the grace of saincts, and such
    Shall shine in rayes of rest :
Till day doth dawne, and shad[e] doth fade,
    And they for aye be blest.

Thus art thou faire, my loue in me,
    In thee there is noe spott :
I will in blisse sett thee my deere,
    Cleane voyd of sinne or blott

---

hence to ' engraft ' and hence, as here,' to add and so to strengthen. So SHAKESPEARE " imp out our drooping country's broken wings " (Richard II. ii. 1) and MILTON "her broken league to *imp* her serpent wings" (Sonnets X. 8.) These two quotations remind us that the term was originally used of the Falconer's repairing of the hawk's wing by adding feathers. G.

THE FIFT SPEACH.

Christ speakes still.

NOWE my loue I hauc thee sought,   1
  And brought thee frō the lands;
I haue the[e] led in bands of grace
  From out the curse and bands.

To me from all parts of the earth   2
  I will the[e] guide and call;
And quite[1] thou shalt be frō the bands
  Of them that did thee thrall:

Who once did vexe and greeue thee sore,   3
  In bane, in bloud, in woe;
But I will saue thee safe from them,
  And rid thee from thy foe.

For thou my hart hast caught with loue,   4
  One cast of thy faire eie,
Of faith I meane, doth wound my hart,
  Which made me faint and die.

Christ speakes still.

All sweets the world can yeald to me   5
  Are banes to thy sweet smell;

---

[1] = quit, released.   G.

Thou art my spouse, in life and death,
  The graue shall not thee quell.

The words which from thy lipps doe droppe 6
  When thou dost pray or praise,
Are farre more sweet to me then sweets
  That sunne doth see by dayes.

Thou art a spring to me shutt vp, 7
  A well seald by my ring :
Frō whēce doth flowe pure streames of loue,
  To me thy lord and king.

THE SIXT SPEACH.

Christ speakes.

THOU art closd vp my spouse, my deere 1
  That none might doe thee ill ;
  That force of foes, nor rage of fēds,[1]
On thee might doe their will.

That noe wild boore of wood, so fell, 2
  Thy rootes, thy plants might marre :
For I looke on thee with mine eies,
  And vewe their ire a farre.

= fiends. G.

Thy plants are like sweet fruits of choice   3
 My deere ones all they are,
Of thee and them, as of mine eies
 I watch and haue a care.

Sweet sent as myrrhe and cane ye yeald,   4
 As all cheefe spice of choice :
So are thy plants O deere, to me,
 For they doe heare my voice.

For tast, for touch, for smell, for hewe,   5
 Thy fruits are all most pure,
I ioy to see them in this plight,
 And in my loue so sure.

From thee O spouse doth flowe full farre   6
 Thy streames to dales and hills,
And I the spring doe flowe to thee
 To fill thy spouts, thy rills.

Who so of thee doth drink is drencht,   7
 And thirsts no more for aie :
Thou art the streames of God, to flowe,
 To soules that faint in waye.

THE SEUENTH SPEACH.

The Church speakes to Christ.

F I be then so sweet my deere   1
    My Christ, my God, my Loue,
  The̅ breathe on me with thy sweet breath,
    That it my hart may moue.

O all ye powers of my sweete God
    Blowe on me North and South,
That these my plants of my poore soule
    May blest be by his mouth.

And make the̅ sweet to him, as are   3
    The plants of loue and grace :
So shall my loue ioy still to come,
    And glad him in this place.

Yea he will come to me, his owne   4
    Which he hath bought full deere,
And will take of the fruit that he
    Hath made to him so neere.

Christ speakes.

I come my loue to thee, myne own   5
    As thou hast cald to me :
And as thou wilt, so will I take
    These fruits, a part of thee.

I see thy workes, thy words, thy thoughts 6
 They all to me are sweet,
For they are mine, I gaue thē thee,
 And all else that is meete.

Nowe all ye blest of me, and sainets 7
 Cheere vp and glad your mind,
That yett in this deere loue of mine
 Such grace and loue doe find.

A Canticle, or song

Betweene Christ, & his church
of the fift, and sixt chapters of the Song of
Solomon, metaphrased into Monosyl-
labls of Great Brittains language, & is to
be vsed by every deuout soule in his
priuat conference with
his god.

And is set to the tune of
Lord be my iudge, and thou shalt see.
Psal. cxxvi.

To his much esteemed good frend Mr. WALTER
PELL, one of the assistants of the most worthy
cōpanie of the marchants-Adventurers, residing at Hamb :

Ioy of both worlds,

OUING frend, If you would die well,
you must endeuour to liue well.   Then
let your death be neuer so suddaine, it
will not come vnexpected, neither will you be
vnprepared.   The daies and houers of daies that
you haue spent in Gods seruice, either in praying
or praysing him shalbe so many cordialls of comforts and consciences of well led purposes, and
will so take vp your hart in ioye and solace, that
noe terrour of death, or darkenes shall appale yt.
Who would not then be busie in this so serious, so
sacred a busines?   Let vs neuer thinke to be
soundly merry, if this be not our musique.   Reason and Religion guides vs here vnto.   For veary
Reason sheweth vnto vs that we must all die, and
Religion enlighteneth vs howe we may die well.
Fooles iudge actions by euents, but the wise forsee
by iudgmēt of reason and faith, what will inevi-

tably ensue. To this purpose all this is sayd, that as I haue in myne endeered loue, sent you an introduction herevnto in this paper-token, so you would accept and practize it. So shall I euer rest your votary, praying to God for your eternal happines in Christ Iesus, his sauing mercies.

Your perpetuall votary,

W. Loe.

THE FIRST SPEACH.

Christ speakes to his Spouse.

 AM come downe O spouse most deere, 1
To take those fruites of thine,
Which thou with hart and grace of loue,
Dost knowe of erst were mine.

I haue thought well of all thy workes, 2
As well of will as deede.
I dranke thy wine with millke so sweet,
With loue they doe me feede.

O you my frēds and saincts most blest, 3
Cheere vp yourselues with me,
And ioy your harts with this my spouse,
Whose cates of love you see.

The Church speakes.

When once this world had luld in sleepe 4
Of sinne, my selfe, my sēce,
Yet wakt mine hart to Christ my Deere,
And thou didst drawe me thence.

547

Christ speakes to his Spouse.

Thou camst to me, and knockst full oft   5
   At doore of my poore hart :
Thou knockst I say full oft my deere,
   And pearst me with thy dart.

And saidst Ile come and lodge with thee,   6
   And dwell with thee in grace.
Shut out the world, thy sinns, thy shame,
   And let me come in place.

For all the night I wayte for thee,   7
   My lockes with dropps of paine
Are wett, and all to stay for thee
   That I thy loue might gaine.

THE SECOND SPEACH.

The Church speakes.

 HAUE put of my coate sayd I,   1
   Howe shall I put it on ?
My feete I washt, shall I them file ?
Oh noe, my loue be gone.

Thus did I plead for my long stay :   2
   For who so loues my deere

Must care, and carke, and strang[e] things
    tast,
  Of woe, him to come neere.

For cleane of soyle, of woe and ill   3
  Who liues that seekes my deere?
No, no, the world will plague thē all
  That serues our God in feare.

But whē my loue these words did heare   4
  He shrunke, and went me fro,
And hid him selfe, and spake noe more
  That I had searud him so.

And then I rouzd my hart, I yearnd   5
  That had him lost so sone :
I rose, and lokt, and chid my selfe
  For that which I had done.

I sought him, but he hid him selfe,   6
  And would not me come nigh :
I roard and cride, and vsd all meanes,
  I card not for to die.

For that I had lost him my deere   7
  That sought me for his doue,
But yet I foūd him not, nor knewe
  He hard my voice in loue.

THE THIRD SPEACH.

The Church speakes still.

HE men that should haue had a care　1
　　They smote, and did me wound ;
With words most false and vaine, they
　　sought,
To ding[1] me to the ground.

I charge you all that loue the Lord　2
　　If that you shall him find,
Tell him howe sicke I am of loue
　　In hart, in soule, in mind.

O what—say they—is this thy deere　3
　　More then the sonnes of men
That thou art thus farre gō in loue,
　　And aye doe not him ken ?

My loue sayd I is white and red,　4
　　His face is pure and bright :
He is the cheefe and choice of all,
　　In him is all the light.

For God in him is full and faire,　5
　　In grace, in face, in all.

---

[1] A living word in Scotland still = cast.　G.

His head fine gold, his lockes faire flockes,
    In him there is no gall.

His eies like doues, full of pure loue   6
    His cheeks are beds of spice ;
His lips are sweet as flowers in May,
    To me he is most[1] nice.

His hāds are sett with port[2] and price,   7
    Pure myrrhe doth dropp him fro :
His will is rule of truth and faith :
    This is most true I knowe.

THE FOURTH SPEACH.

The Spouses speaketh. [*sic*]

EA all his acts are firme and strong   1
        As sett in gold most sure :
    No shewe of change, but streight and
        cleere
    Both sound, and safe, and pure.

---

¹ Misprinted ' not'. **G.**

² port = state or splendor. So Shakespeare, Taming
of the Shrew (i. 1)
        " Thou shalt be master, Tranio in my stead :
    Keep house, and *port*, and servants as I should" :
et alibi. See onward for ' port' again. **G.**

His mouth is as sweet things of choice,   2
   Frō whēce doth flowe my blysse :
He is all sweet, in part, in whole,
   And I poore soule am his.

A forraigne congregatio speakes.

Since then O deere such is thy loue,   3
   Shewe vs where he is found,
And we will seeke this loue with thee,
   In all the world so round.

For nōe, but thee O church cā'st him   4
   Make knowne, in word, in deed :
O tell vs then, and we will ioyne,
   And he shall be our meede.

Thē sayd I to those that him sought   5
   He is gone downe to be
In beds of spice, with soules and saincts:
   That is my loue, that's he.

Yea I am his in his sweet loue,   6
   And he is mine by faith :
In spight of hell, or sinne, or shame
   His word to me so saith.

And both of vs are one in God,
    And knitt in soule and spright,   7
By loue most sweete and ioy of hart
    I liue still in his sight.

THE FIFT SPEACH.

Christ speakes to his Church.

THOU thou my Church did'st me not
       seeke,   1
    But putts me farre thee fro,
Yet nowe thou dost looke back to me,
    I will not serue thee so.

But I will come and dwell with thee   2
    In grace, in loue, in awe.
I will thee ioy, in mirth and glee,
    And teach to thee my lawe.

Turne backe thine eies fṝo me my deere   3
    That art thus fixt on me,
Thy strength of faith doth ioy me so,
    That I mind none but thee.

The men that feede thy soule with foode   4
    Haue all one hart, one tongue,
They tune all like a quire of saincts,
    They sound forth all one songe.

So that their paines are not in vaine,   5
   They bring to me much fruit :
They cry and call to me for helpe,
   And I doe heare their suite.

Thy locks, thy lookes, are seene so faire   6
   Thy blush, thy smile so sweet,
That I doe ioy in them that teach
   Those things that are so meete.

Though kings and queens, and all folk else   7
   My name and loue doe vse,
Yet on thee, on thee loue, I looke,
   On thee, I thinke, I muse.

THE SIXT SPEACH.

Christ speakes to his Spouse.

THOU art my spouse, most chast, most
      pure   1
   Whom all the world doth loue :
Thou art my deere, my peere, my ioy,
   Noe spott in thee my doue.

Those that doe looke and see thy face   2
   Do praise and plaud thee still,
And bless thee that hast God thy Lord,
   And didst yeald to his will.

And thus they say, rapt with thy state　　　3
　　What's shee, so faire as morne ?
So pure as sūne, so bright as mone,
　　Of what state is shee borne ?

Her face is faire through force of faith,　　4
　　She is most bright in heue :
Yea in her looks is feare and dread
　　To cause her foes to rue.

The Spouse speakes to Christ.

And thus all gast[1] and rapt with sight
　　Of thy sweet port[2] and state,
They stand in stond all pale and wan,
　　For thee they can not mate.

Noe more then glympse of starr cā dashe　　6
　　The sūne in height of skye,
Or light on earth, the mone at full
　　Can darke, or once come nigh.

Cheare vp thy selfe my loue I say,　　　7
　　For though thou didst me miss,
I meane not thee my loue to leaue,
　　For all the world that is.

---

[1] Transition-form of 'aghast'. G.
[2] = carriage, or behaviour. See former note. G.

THE SEUENTH SPEACH.

Christ speakes to his Spouse.

DID but go to see my vine   1
  Howe it did bud and sprout,
 To see what fruits my plants did yeald
  And howe they were come out.

And nowe I see they bud and blooe,   2
  And yeald me fruit good store :
Ile care for them, and they for me,
  That they may haue the more.

The soules that came to me of late,   4
  I prune, I plash,[1] I purge,
That they may bring forth farre more fruite
  With this my rod, and scourge.

And nowe they are well growne my deere,   5
  I hast, I runne to thee ;
With speed at need I hast, I post,
  With wings of wind to see.

What thou dost want, or wouldst nowe haue 6
  Speake loue, I'le giue thee it.

---

[1] Qy = to water, and hence as in Shakespeare, ' a shallow *plash* ' (Taming of Shrew 1. i.) but THOMAS WRIGHT says 'To interweave branches of a tree : to cut and lay a hedge '. G.

Thou shalt not feare my loue to thee,
In rest by thee I'le sitt.

Come then my loue to me full fast,   6
Let all saincts ioy and sing :
To house of God I'le safe and sound
My deere shall my loue bring.[1]

Nowe all ye saincts and soules on high   7
Looke, see, fixe fast your eie,
On this my loue ; marke well her grace,
No fault in her I spie.

---

[1] The meaning is clear, though here and elsewhere, the grammatical structure be faulty.   G.

A Canticle, or Song.

Of the seuenth, & eight chapters of the song of Solomon being
Metaphrased into Monosylabls of great
Brittains language, & is to be vsed by
euery deuout soule in his priuat

conference with
his god

And is sett to the tune of
Giue thanks vnto the lord our god.

PSAL CVII.

To his much esteemed good frend, Mr. WILLIAM
WALCOT, marchant, one of the most worthie
cōpanie of Marchant Adventurers, residing at
Hamborough.

Happiness for euer.

IND frend, Forced fauours were euer
sleighted and thankles. But voluntary
respects had euer with the best and
most noble minds, courteous acceptāce, howe
small and meane soeuer the thing was. For a
ma to giue his soule to his Creator when he sees
he must dye, and his goods to the poore, when he
sees he must part with them; and to forgoe our
sinne, whē we can noe longer followe yt, are cold,
yea vnkind obediences. But for a young man to
remember his creator in the daies of his youth,
and in his best and strongest age to bequeath
himself euery day to God in prayer and praise, is
that reasonable and seasonable sacrifice where
with the Most High is most pleased. To this
purpose, and noe other, God knoweth, I haue
tendered these voluntary Essaies to diuerse of my

masters and table-brothers. Let me not seeme to be officious, while I desire to doe good, and expresse my loue. For as vnto the rest so vnto you, Beloued,[1] haue I sent this parcell Receaue yt, as I meane yt, both with hand and hart, and then I am assured, it · will neuer repent you of your acceptation, nor me of my dedication. The great Lord keeper of heauen and earth keepe you in his feare all the daies of your life, and preserve you for his sauving mercies in Christ Jesus in the end of your life and for euer.

Yours in Christ to be required,

W. Loe.

---

[1] An unintelligible word follows here, viz ' Gā-naunt '. G.

THE FIRST SPEACH.

Christ speaketh.

HER feet are sweet, her gate a grace,   1
    All shod with Peace and Truth,
    Of God's owne spell to runne the race
Frō bane, and woe, and ruth.

Her loynes are girt fast with the same,   2
    The price of it is rare,
The skill is framd with hand of might,
    All full of cost and care.

Her wombe like a round cup that wants   3
    Noe wine to cheere her plants;
As heaps of wheate set all with flowers,
    Pure graynes to helpe our wāts.

Her breast the two sweet leagues of grace   4
    Are as to twins of birth,
Whose milke doth feede the babs of God
    Which dwell here on the earth.

Those that doe rule, aud guide her folke   5
    Like necke doth beare vp head:

So those doe stay as tower of strength
   Till they at full are fed.

Her eies are like two fonts most cleare
   In which we may well see   **6**
Our selues in face, in fact, in faith,
   And drawe thence life and glee.

Her nose from whence we sent[1] the good   **7**
   Is as some tower of state,
For she can iudg and find it out
   From tyme to tyme past date.

THE SECOND SPEACH.

Christ speakes still.

ER tire of head is full of grace   **1**
   To all that doe it see;
And I am tyde by mine owne will
   O loue to be with thee.

O loue howe full in all thy parts   **2**
   Dwells loue and life by me:
Howe sweet and faire art thou in all
   When I doe looke on thee.

Thy growth is like a palme tree tall,   **3**
   For prest, thou dost rise more:

---

1 Scent. **G.**

Thy teats are full of milke and mirth,
   And yeald thy babes great store.

I said I will goe to my tree   4
   And ioyne me to my palme,
And make it yeald all salues for sores
   To cure all wounds, as balme.

Christ speach still.

And I will cause her for to yeald   5
   Good workes of faith and life;
And with her power to driue frō her
   The sinnes that are so rife.

The soules that thirsts shall haue their fill,   6
   Her words shall spring as wine:
By mouthes of those that teach my lore,
   And preach those lawes of mine.

Yea they shall cause the lipps of him
   That sleeps and snorts in sinne   7
To speake, and praise the God of life
   That rouzd him from that din.

THE THIRD SPEACH.

The Church speakes.

SUCH as I am, I am not mine,　　　1
　　　But his that loud me deere,
　　In none but him will I be glad,
　None but him will I feare.

For he once gaue him selfe for me,　　2
　　And made of me his choyce.
Him will I heare, he is my deere,
　　It's life to heare his voice.

O come my loue, letts lodg all night　3
　　In fields ; in townes, letts goe,
And see how all our flockes doe feede
　　Letts runne as swift as roe.

Vp to the vines letts hast in morne,　4
　　And vewe howe they doe bud,
And see the signes of fruits and grace,
　　And looke if they be good.

For hence we shall knowe full our tyme　5
　　When we shall ioyne in one,
In all the blisse that I haue made
　　To quitt thee of thy mone.

See loue thy plants both in them selues　6
　　Doe bud and bloome most fresh,

And yeald a sent to mōe them by
　　That are but young, and neshe.[1]

All plants that growe in vs I keepe,　　7
　　Both old and young I loue;
And all for thee O Christ my God
　　Thy grace and lookes to moue.

THE FOURTH SPEACH.

The old Jewish Church speaketh.

THAT I might my Christ once see　　1
　　Clad in this flesh of mine,
And find him here on earth to dwell
　　Made once, once of my line.

Thē would I kisse and cull my deere　　2
　　The world could not me touch;
But if it did I would not passe,
　　Nor think of it too much.

Then would I bring thee to the light　　3
　　Though nowe pent vp in darke,
And then thou shouldst me teach to know
　　My Christ, my God, by marke.

---

*[1] = tender : query, transition-form of nice?'　G.

Then would I feast thee with the best   4
    With cupps of loue and grace,
Thē would the soules in Christ be glad
    To vewe our rest and place.

The old Jewish Church speaketh.

His left hand then should stay my head,   5
    His right hand stay my hart,
And thē I would not feare the world
    Nor hell nor death, his dart.

His heat would giue me life halfe dead,
    And raise me vp cleane gone ;
His light would make me shine like pearle :
    O like him there is none.

I charge ye O ye saincts that loue   7
    Dare not to greeue my deere,
Nor once to stirre him vp in ire,
    But lerne his wrath to feare.

THE FIFT SPEACH.

Christ speaketh.

WHO is this that from denns of sinne
    From lusts and life most leaud,
    Doth band her selfe gainst all the ill,
And shewes her wrath and feud.

I'st not my church ? O it is shee   2
    Whom I haue loud of old !
And did her take from powers of hell
    When she was bought and sold.

And her fiō ire of sinne and shame   3
    Where shee had falne from me,
I raisd to life from depth of hell
    I quitt, I sett her free.

For there by faith she leand on me,   4
    And I to her gaue way.
Then shee to me did ope her hart,
    And thus to me did say.

The Jewisch [sic] Church speaketh.

O sett me as a signe, a seale   5
    On hart, on arme, on all.
O hold me deere, my loue, my Christ
    For I to thee doe call.

Let naught me moue from my sweet loue
    Lest greefe me gore, and woe,
For the least shade when thou art gone
    Doth shew to me my foe.

The zeale where with I loue my deere   7
    Is like the graue most fell,

And burnes me vp like coles of fire,
To saue my soule from hell.

THE SIXT SPEACH.

The Jewish Church speaketh.

EA more then fire or flame it is   1
    Noe source can quench this loue,
   Noe paines, noe gaines, or loss, or crosse
From him my hart can moue.

Noe wealth, noe peelfe, noe feare, no force   2
    All this I scorne should me
Once moue, to thinke, or ioy in ought
    But in his grace and glee.

We haue a plant, deere loue thou knowst   3
    The church that thou hast chose,
From out the iles so farre frō hēce :
    O we would not her lose.

She is but smale of growth as yet,   4
    For want of thy good grace ;
But if thou cast a looke on her,
    And let her see thy face.

Howe fresh, howe faire will she come forth, 5
    And growe, and beare to thee

Her buds, her bloomes, her fruites of faith
   All good, and faire to see.

Christ speaketh.

If she be firme and fast to me,   6
   As wall, as tower of strength
I'le make her pure and sure in league
   By word and deed at length.

And if she will giue way to me,   7
   And to my words giue eare,
I'le make her safe in league of peace,
   And she shall be my deere.

THE SEUENTH SPEACH.

The Jewish Church speaketh.

THE faith and loue that thou dost seeke   1
   In her, thou findst in me,
   My plea of faith found grace and peace,
And I was ioynd to thee.

The want of words to feed thy saincts   2
   Which thou in her dost craue
Is not in me to doe thy will,
   Howe then should she it haue.

Grāt thee to her thy grace in good,　　3
　　And shee will to thee bend ;
She will thee serue in word and deede
　　If thou thy grace her send.

Christ speaketh.

My spouse is as a vine to me,　　4
　　She flowers and fruits doth yeald,
She is the corne that brings me thrift
　　And growes faire in my feild.

The Jewish church speaketh

My vine shall aye be in my sight,　　5
　　Yea till the world haue end
I will it dress, and keepe my selfe,
　　And grace and peace it lend.

Sith thus I care for thee my deere　　6
　　Shew thou thy loue in praise,
And teach my name, my fame to all,
　　So long as last thy daies.

The Spouse speaketh.

If thou my deere wouldst haue me doe　　7
　　As thou hast bid to me,

Then grāt me grace to act the same
And thou it sone shalt see.[1]

---

[1] Following this are two blank 'leaves, as before: and on this page (164) the pagination ends.   G.

A METAPHRASE.

Of the first, and second chapters of Jeremies Lamentations for
the sacking and burning of Jerusalem, and
the temple, by Nebuchadnezer king of
Babell, and by Nebuzaradan the captaine
of his gard, put into monsyl-
lables of great Brittains
language.

And is set to the tune of
I lift mine hart to thee.

Psal. XXV.

To his much esteemed good frend, Mr. EDWARD
MEEDE, one of the assistants of the most worthy companie of Merchants-Aduenturers, residing at Hamborough.

Grace in this world, and ioy in the other.

LL happines in the Lord Iesus, I present
vnto you a part of Ieremie's Lamentations
metaphrased. You may see herein my
true heart unto you all. In the midst of lament-
table discōtents I tuned my soule, tongue and pen,
to the laud of God : and the rather in these Lamentations, for that they sorted some what to my
retired meditations. One tyme or other all men
are not as they would be. It is the condition of
God's children. Happie is that man that can vse
God's scourge to his amendment. The great
Moderator of all things, knowes his children fittest
to be made palmes, to be spread with burthens
and waights, and not to be oliues. That so we
might more think of our victorie, then of our rest.
It is enoughe for vs that we shall once triumph
in heauen and rest for all. To this holy rest and

eternall tranquillity, God giude vs all, into whose blessed keeping I recommend you in Christ sauing mercies, and rest,

Yours much deuoted,

W. Loe.

THE FIRST DEPTH.

Frō dumps and doomes of woe
   From depth of wrath and ire,
We call, we crie, we roare O Lord,   Aleph.
   With zeale as hot as fire.

The State where once thy name
   Was great in light of grace,
Is led a slaue by force of warre :   Beth.
   A curse is in the place.

Our streeats that flockt with folke
   Most rich, in cloths most gay,
Are nowe made void, and laid full wast   Gimel.
   By night, and eke by day.

We that did rule and raigne,
   And brusd the world with might,
Doe nowe pay taxe, and tole, and disme[1]
   By force of armes, in spight.

---

[1] Tithe or tenth. Once used by Shakespeare, " many thousand *dismes* " (Troilus and Cress., ii, 2.) G.

We weepe full sore all night,
 By day our teares doe fall :   He.
Our eies are sore, our cheekes are wett,
 Yet on the Lord we call.

They that did loue vs once,
 And were our frends in shewe,
Are turnd to gall, and doe vs kill Van.
 As ferce as doth our foe.

THE SECOND DEPTH.

UR prince is made a slaue
 To sitt with folke most base ;
We find noe rest but woe and moane, Zain
And shame doth fill our face.

Our sinne, our sinne hath greeud
 The Lord of hosts full sore.
Our shame, our shame for that doth come, Heth.
 On vs nowe more and more.

Our things of worth the foe
 Hath seizd all to his hand,
They staine the church of thy great
  name   Teth
 We cā them not with stand.

The facts that we haue done
  Are all filths in his sight,
He pluckes vs downe, and none doth build,   Jod.
  Not one will doe vs right.

We sighe for bread in want
  We giue our wealth for yt :
O helpe sweete Lord for we are vile,   Caph.
  O drawe vs from this pitt.

O let all those that passe
  Looke on my woe, and see
If ere they sawe the like of this   Lamed.
  That nowe is done to me.

THE THIRD DEPTH.

N all my bones is fire,
    A net my feete hath caught :
  God turnes his face, and makes me
      faynt,   Mem.
    His wrath it hath me taught.

His hand is on my necke,
  His yoke hath bound me sore,
He beares his hãd so hard on me   Nun.
  That I can rise noe more.

My men of force are gone,
　　My young men crusht with might,
My maids and babes are trod to dust　Samech.
　　And all this in my sight.

For these things, weeps myne eies,
　　My soule is farre from glee :
The foe doth force me to this woe,　　　　Ain.
　　And none doth care for me.

We stretch our hands for helpe,
　　And none doth take a care,
We are as is the filth of all,　　　　　　Pe.
　　They looke not howe we fare.

Yet thou art iust O Lord,
　　For we haue gone from thee :
Thou wilt vs helpe for this at last :　　Zade.
　　O shewe thy face to me.

THE FOURTH DEPT. [sic]

Y preests gaue vp the ghost
　　While they did seeke for meate, Koph.
The old men eke gave vp their breath :
O Lord our woe is great.

579

I am in greefe O Lord,
  Mine hart is fild with woe :
The sword doth kill, and Death doth
    rage,   Resch.
  For that thou art my foe.

When I doe sigh and grone
  Noe eie doth care for me :
My foes doe ioy, and glad themselues,   Shin.
  My woe and moane to see.

O let my sighes O Lord,
  Loud crie make in thine eares :
I haue done ill, cleãse me of that   Thau.
  And rid mine eies frō teares.

O Lord why with a cloud,
  So black of wrath and ire,   Aleph.
Hast thou vs clad, and cast vs downe :
  Why are we burnt with fire ?

The Lord doth raze our race,
  Our stocke, our flocke, our all ;
Downe to the ground, he dings[1] vs fast : Beth.
  Our prince, our peeres doe fall.

---

[1] See a former foot-note. G.

THE FIFT DEPTH.

HE strength of all our house   Gimel.
    Is spent, yea all is gone :
The Lord's ferce wrath hath cut vs of,
    To helpe vs there is none.

He bends his bowe at vs   Daleth.
    He shootes vs through full sore :
He kills the choice of all our flocke :
    O Lord what wilt thou more?

Our forts of fence and strength,
    Our fields so fresh, so full,   He.
Are all laid wast ; our goods, our babes,
    Our foes from vs doe pull.

The king and preest at once   Van.
    The Church and State doe waile,
The daies of feasts are turnd to fasts,
    The Lord he doth vs quaile.

The Lord hath cast downe all,   Zain.
    They roare, and make a noice,
With in thy house O God our king,
    Where once was hard our voice.

Our wall, our wealth, our state,   Heth.
    Our God will lay full lowe :

His hand is bent to stricke vs all :
Thy will O Lord is so.

THE SIXT DEPTH.

THE lawe, and all is gone,   Teth.
  Noe preest, noe peere of light :
 The Lord hath rid vs of them all,
Not one doth come in sight.

The graue men of our State   Iod.
 The sage, and such as giude,
Doe sitt on groūd in dust and clay,
 With sacke they cloth their side.

Mine eies to see this, faile.   Caph.
 With teares they drope and melt :
The babes doe sowne[1] in midst of street,
 Such woe, and want they felt.

They crie for bread, for drinke Lamed.
 To all that stand them nighe :
And in their lapps that gaue thē sucke
 They faint, and faile, and die.

What woe is like to ours?   Mem.
 Our breach as seas doe roare :

---

[1] = swoon G

There's none can helpe or heale our wound
   O Lord our greefe is sore.

They that should see and say,   Nun.
   And tell vs of our sinne,
Haue taught vs things both vile and vaine,
   Noe good we find there in.

All such as pass vs by   Samech.
   Do scoffe at vs and mocke :
Is this the place say they of strength ?
   Is this the whole Earth's rocke.

THE SEVENTH DEPTH.

OUR foes doe hisse and gnash   Am.
   Their teeth, and thus doe saye :
This is the day we haue sought for
   To bring thee downe for aye.

But Lord this is thine acte   Pe.
   To throwe vs downe each one :
In days of old it was thy will
   To bruise vs bone by bone.

Our teares doe shower on vs   Zade.
   To thee our harts doe cry,
By day and night we take noe rest
   Our soules doe faint and dye.

We crye out in the night   Koph.
   Like babes we hold vp hands :
We faint for want of bread, O Lord
   O rid vs of these bands!

O see sweet Lord the babes   Resh.
   That are but a span long,
We eate for foode ; our preests are slayne
   And cast out as the donge.

The young and old on ground   Shin.
   Are cast, and faint, and die :
Ourmaids so fresh, so faire in hewe
   Are kild, and cast them by.

Naught else but feares O Lord   Thau.
   Doe wake vs day and night :
It is the day of thy ferce wrath
   Of foes, of warre, of spight.

A Metaphrase.

OF THE THIRD Chap-
ter of Jeremies Lamentations for
the sacking and burning of Jerusalem, and
the temple, by Nebuchadnezer king of
Babell, and by Nebuzaradan the captaine
of his gard, put into monosyllables of great Brittains
language.

And is set to the tune of
I lift mine hart to thee.

PSAL. XXV.

To his much esteemed good frend, Mr. JOHN
GREENWELL, on[e] of the Assistants of the
most worthy companie of marchants-Aduentu-
rers residing at Hamb :

All ioy, and happines in Christ.

WELBELOUED in the Lord, we are
all strangers here in the Earth; our
home is aboue in heauen.   It was a
great greefe to God's Israel to tune the songs of
Sion in a strange country.   Howe then is it with
vs, that we like so well of the things here, and
thinke not of the blessings aboue.   Hierusalem
was once the mistresse of the world, the metropolis
of the earth, and yet when the world's darling
forgatt God she was layd in the dust.   That is the
cause of the prophett's lamentation.   Indeed who
would not shower downe teares to see the holy
place defiled, and Jerusalē made an heape of stones ?
But wee see noe place be it neuer so glorious in
our eies, noe persons be they neuer so gratious in
the sight of men, that can escape God's hand whē
he will scourge.   The Turkes haue encroched into

Christendome, and made that citty of Constanti-
tinople which was once the glory of the East, a
veary cage of vncleane Mahumetans. What Christian's hart doth nót bleed to see yt? to heare of
yt? We haue cause to lament this. The prophet
had reason to condole that. O that our harts
were touched with remorse for the poore distressed
Christians that liue tributaries to the misbeleeuing
Turke. Consider in these hymnes the condition of
God's people so subjecte to moane and misery.
God directe all our harts toward him in wealth,
in woe, in all. And so I cōmending you to God
with the rest, in the sauing mercies of Jesus
Christ, am,

Yours because of Christ.

W. Loe.

THE FIRST DEPTH.

I AM the man O Lord   1
     Haue felt thy wrath, thy rod :
O send me helpe in this my woe
     My Lord, my Christ, my God.

Thy stormes and clouds of ire   2
     Doe beate me day and night :
Thou shewst me woe, and wast, and warre
     And hid'st from me the light.

All the day long O Lord   3
     Thine hand is turnd gainst me :
Noe helpe, noe hope, noe ioy, noe mirth
     That I poore wretch can see.

My flesh and skin are vile,   4
     And parcht as in a drought ;
My bones, my hart are broke in twayne,
     This Lord thy wrath hath wrought.

O Lord thou mak'st a fort,   5
     With me to warre and fight
With gall and greefe thou dost me fill
     And none will doe me right.

As they that long are dead,　　　　　　6
　　And cleane cast out of mind,
So am I sett in night of death
　　With woe and greefe all pind.[1]

THE SECOND DEPTH.

N hedge is pight[2] me round　　　　1
　　To close me in this woe :
I can not stirre, thy chaines me bind :
　　O Lord what shall I doe ?

And when I cry and roare,　　　　　　2
　　In all my greefe and gall
He shutts me out, and will not heare
　　Ne cares he for my call.

He ramzes[3] me in so fast,　　　　　3
　　With stones, and clay full thicke,
My pathes he crokes, and giues noe ease,
　　My soule is faint and sicke.

As beares doe teare their pray,　　　　4
　　And waite more bloud to spill,

---

[1] Misnumbered 3, 5, onward, dropping 4, and so making seven stanzas (apparently) : corrected.　G.

[2] Pitched, placed.　G.

[3] Query—rammes = rams ?　G.

So hath my foes me rent and torne
  As if it were thy will.

I peece by peece, am hald,   5
  And puld by hand to raggs :
I by my selfe do sitt and weepe,
  While my foe sitts and braggs.

Thy bowe O Lord is bent,   6
  To shoote at my pale face :
I am a marke for shafts to hitt,
  O yett shewe me some grace !

THE THIRD DEPTH.

OR see the shafts doe sticke,   1
  In all my raynes through out :
I am the butt, and none but I
  At which shootes all the rout.

My foes make me their iest   2
  And song by night and day ;
Where is thy God, thy Lord, thy helpe
  Thus they to me doe say.

Mine hart is fraught with gall,   3
  My bloud is drunke vp still :
With shame and greefe I waile and wast,
  Make hast me Lord to kill.

My strength is dasht, my teeth   4
   Are broke with in my head :
Thou laist a¹ loade on me, poore soule,
   I wish I were cleane dead.

My soule doth not once heare   5
   Of peace, of grace, of light :
I can not call to mind my state
   That once I had in sight.

O Lord my strength, my hope,   6
   My helpe I looke from thee,
But all is gone, and there is none
   That cares, nor lookes to me.

THE FOURTH DEPTH.

CALL to mind sweet God,   1
   This moane, this woe of mine,
This gall, this greefe, this plaint, this
      cry,
   For I O Lord am thine.

My soule is faint, and failes,   2
   When I to mind doe call :
My greefe hath made me cry and roare
   To see my woe and fall.

---

¹ Misprinted 'on'.   G.

Yet haue I hope in thee 3
    That thou wilt helpe at last,
And wilt not quite my soule for aye
    From thy sweet sight out cast.

It is thy loue O Lord, 4
    That I am not quite sold,
And rid from earth, both braunch and roote,
    And closd vp in the mold.

Thou failst me not in morne, 5
    All night I feele thy stay;
Thy hand is great, and in thy truth
    Thou hearst what I doe say.

For thou O Lord art mine, 6
    My soule doth hope in thee:
Thou art my lot, my land, my rent:
    Once more, Lord sett me free.

THE FIFT DEPTH.

THOU art good, O Lord 1
    To them that wayte and tend :
To soules that seeke and sue to thee
Thou dost thy grace downe send.

It is right good O Lord   2
  To hope for helpe from thee :
For of thee Lord is all man's good :
  O shewe thy smile to me.

It is full good for man   3
  In youth to beare thy rod ;
For he shall learne there by to knowe
  The Lord to be his God.

Then sitts he pale and wan,   4
  And mute without a peeare :
He will take heed all tymes that he
  Doe searue the Lord in feare.

And if he see there's hope   5
  His mouth from dust will cry ;
And to the Lord make plaint, and moane
  To day that he doth dye.

He giues his cheeke to such   6
  As smite him, and doe taunt :
He will not giue his eare to those
  That vaine and vile things chaunt.

THE SIXT DEPTH.

T HE Lord doth not for aye   1
    Cast of his choice of men,
But though they greeue, yet in his tyme
    He brings them from that den.

For by his will the Lord   2
    Greeues not his flocke at all :
Nor doth he crush the sonnes of mē
    When they on him doe call.

He rights men in their ill :   3
    The face of the Most High
Is sett to helpe the flocke of Christ,
    Yea he will drawe them nigh.

Out of God's owne sweet mouth   4
    Comes forth not good and ill :
When we are plagued it is our sinne
    That doth our deare soules kill.

Let vs then search our waies,   5
    And turne to our good God :
So shall he quite put farre from vs
    His scourge, his plague, his rod.

Lift vp both hand and hart   6
    To him that dwells on highe,

And shewe our sinns, our shame to him
Least that for him we dye.

THE SEUENTH DEPTH.

THOU hast vs slayne O Lord 1
And hid'st vs with a cloud,
So that our sute comes not to thee,
Though we doe cry full loud.

We are as drosse and doung, 2
Our foes doe on vs rage :
A feare and snare is come on vs,
And that from age to age.

Mine eies cease not to weepe 3
But day by daye we moane :
Till thou O Lord dost looke from high,
And ease vs of our grone.

My eies and hart doe ake, 4
The one with teares doth runne,
My hart it sobbs, and sighes full sore
For that which I haue done.

Men chase me like a bird, 5
They haue cut of my life
They cast great stones to keepe me downe
They kill me in their strife.

Yet from these depths O Lord
   I haue cald on thy name :
Thou to my voice wilt giue an eare
   And ease me of the same.

THE EIGHTH MUSE.

THOU wont'st to say, Feare not,   1
   Thou wont'st my cause to plead :
And to the streames of love and life
   Thou wast wont me to lead.

O Lord my wronge thou seest   2
   Judge thou my cause with those
That gape, and hope to eate me vp :
   With rage they doe me close.

Thou Lord hast heard their cries   3
   Howe they doe rage and roare :
Howe they doe spite and spitt at me,
   And raue still more and more.

They make their songs on me   4
   They iest, and gibe, and mocke :
When they sitt downe, or rise, or walke
   They flout, they feare thy flocke.

Giue them their lott O Lord,   5
   Looke on the worke they wrought :

Giue them thy curse with greefe of hart,
   That haue my woe thus sought.

Cast them all cleane from thee   6
   Let not the Earth them beare,
For that they doe not seeke to thee
   But rage with out all feare.

A METAPHRASE.

Of the fourth, and fift Chapters of Ieremies Lamentations for
the sacking, & burning of Ierusalem, and
the temple, by Nebuchadnezer king of
Babell, and by Nebuzaradan the captaine
of his gard, pnt into monosyl-
labeles of great Brittains
language.

And is set to the tune of
Ilift mine hart to thee.

PSALM XXV.

THE FIRST DEPTH.

HOWE is our gold so dymme?
　　The fine gold howe is't lost?
　The stones of the Lord's house are wast,
　　This is our case, our cost.

Our sonnes that were so strong　　　**2**
　Are trod as clay in streete,
And as the potts so are they broke,
　They crush them with their feete.

The formes of fish in sea,.
　That are most strange to see,
Yea they to young ones yeald their breasts :
　With vs this may not bee.

The babe that suckes is drye,　　　**4**
　For bread the young ones cry,
But bread and breast they can haue none
　And so they faint and dye.

They that did feede most fine　　　**5**
　The crusts most course would haue ;

To his much esteemed good frend Mr. IOHN
STAMPE, marchant, one of the cōpanie of the
Marchants - Adventurers, residing at Ham-
borough.

Eternall blisse in Christ Jesus.

MINE unfained loue in Christ vnto you :
Noe wise man would sell his thoughts
for all the world. For as they are
much pleasing to a man's selfe so are they benefi-
ciall vnto others. I little thought whē I began
to make an Essay into this businesse that it would
haue enlarged it selfe into eleuen branches.
What it is, and as it is ; euen the all of it, I
devote to all my table-brothers ; wherein your
selfe haue a part. I shall desire your acceptance
with the rest. And euen so herein I commēd
my loue to you, my lines to the world's censure,
and the vse of thē to God's children ; for whose
sake I haue endeuored this. Thus with my prayers for your successfull prosperity in all things
I leaue you to God's sauing grace. *Remay[n]ing*
Your affectionate,
W. LOE.

They that put on their robs of silke,
    The pigs coote[1] seekes, and craue.

The woe that we doe bere   6
    Is farre more great then when
our God did rayne fell fire fröskey,
    And burnt the sonnes of men.

THE SECOND DEPTH.

HEY that were pure as snowe,   1
    And white as is the milke,
And lookt so red, so fresh, so faire,
    And clad them selues with silke,

They are as blacke as cole,   2
    By face they are not knowne;
Their skin is parcht, and cleaues to bones,
    They waile, they weepe, they moane.

They whom the sword doth kill   3
    We connt in a good case;
For they that liue doe pine for want,
    Both they and all their race.

The babes that sucke the breast   4
    We seeth for meat in pott,

---

[1] = cot or stye. **G.**

Or else we pine for want of meate,
   Our limbs doe fade and rott.

The Lord is wrath with vs,   5
   On vs he shoures his ire,
And we are cleane put out of sight,
   He burnes vs vp with fire.

The kings of all the earth   6
   Doe stand in maze to see :
Our foes march in our streats with routs,
   And we poore soules to flee.

THE THIRD DEPTH.

UT this is come to vs   1
   For that we shed the bloud
Of such as were most neere to God,
   And shewd vs all the good.

The bloud I say of them   2
   Doth cry gainst vs to God,
And nowe we feele his hand of ire,
   His scourge his whipe, his rod.

This bloud of men so iust,   3
   Hath bine our bane, our woe,
And made vs turne our backes frō such
   As made them selues our foe.

For we car'd not for preeste,   4
   Nor those that did vs good,
But were both ferce and fell to them,
   We stroue to sheed their bloud.

For this our eies doe watch   5
   And waite, and still doe faile,
No helpe, no hand is stretcht to vs,
   And so we fainte and quaile.

The foe doth hunt our stepps   6
   As we goe in the streete :
They kill, they cry, they roare on vs,
   They tread vs with their feete.

THE FOURTH DEPTH.

HEY hunt vs in the feilds,   1
   On hills, in dales they kill ;
   We dare not once loke out of dore,
   Our streats with dead they fill.

The breath of all our liues   3
   Is caught fast in their snare,
And left he is in plight full ill,
   Both base, and poore, and bare.

Let these be glad that dwell   3
   Farre of[f] out of this place :

Take heede least you doe moue the Lord,
  Gainst you to turne his face.

For he hath plagued vs sore   4
  For all our sinnes and ill,
And yet we hope he will loke back
  And cease our folke to kill.

THE V. CAP.

O Lord call thou to mind
  What is come on vs all:
Take heede to vs that in our woe
  To none but thee doe call.

Our lands, our rents, our all   6
  The foe from vs doe take.
The folke that are to vs most strang [e],
  A prey of vs doe make.

THE FIFT DEPTH.

OUR babes doe know noe sires,   1
    And they that gaue the breast
     Doe sitt, and sighe, and roare, and cry,
  Ne can they like their rest.

Our drinke to vs is sold,   2
  Our wood we buy full deare;

And all this ill is come on vs,
    For thee we did not feare.

Our neckes are prest with yokes,   3
    On vs they lie full sore :
We moile, and toyle, and haue noe rest :
    O Lord what wilt thou more.

To those that be our foes,   4
    For bread we giue our hands :
They tire on vs, and make a prey,
    They breake in to our lands.

They that are dead, and gone,   5
    O Lord haue done the sinne,
And wee poore soules doe pay the price,
    These take vs in their gin.

Base slaues whom we did beate,   6
    Ore vs now rule and tire ;
And there is none that doth vs helpe,
    Our feete stickes in the mire.

THE SIXT DEPTH.

OUR bread we gett with dread,   1
    It costs vs halfe our life :
    We waile in midst of woe, and waste
All night, all day in strife.

Our skin, like to a moore   2
    Is blacke for want of meate :
Our parts are parcht to skin and bone :
    Thy wrath O Lord is great.

Our maids they make a prey   3
    To serue their minds and lusts :
Our wiues they wrong in all our sights,
    Yet Lord thy hand is iust.

By hand our prince they hang,   4
    The old men they doe scorne :
Our greefe doth last till it be night,
    And eke till it be morne.

They make our young ones grind   4
    And toyle like horse in mill :
Their backes they load with batts[1] of wood
    Till that they doe them kill.

The old men sitt noe more   5
    To iudg the cause in gate :
The young mē wai le that wont to sing :
    Oh when will be our date.

---

[1] Loads. G.

Our ioy of hart is gone, 6
   Our daunce is turnd to moane :
Our minds doe muse of nought but woe,
   We sitt, and sighe, and grone.

THE SEAUENTH DEPTH.

THE crowne is gone from vs, 1
   And all the rule is fled ;
   What shall we doe O Lord our God,
Our sinne hath struck vs dead.

For sinne our hart is faynt, 2
   For sinne our eies are dymme ;
For sinne our foes doe warre on vs,
   And rend vs limbe by limbe.

Our hills and dales are waste, 3
   The foxe doe roome and range ;
These things to see our harts doe bleed,
   To vs it is most strange.

Yet Lord thou art for aye, 4
   Thy throne is sett full sure :
Thou can'st vs helpe, when hope is gone,
   O Lord nowe doe vs cure.

Why then dost hide thy face, 5
   And wilt not on vs looke ?

Thou wilt at last thy grace vs giue,
   That is wrote in thy booke.

Turne to vs Lord we praye,   6
   And then we shall see grace :
O giue to vs the daies of old,
   Thy name sett in this place.

What shall thy wrath like fire   7
   Still last, and burne, and kill :
O cease sweet Lord we doe thee pray
   So shalt thou find noe ill.

Seauen Dumpes.

ON THE SEAUEN WORDS
that Christ spake on the crosse
which shewe the seauen depthes of the
lawes curse, which our lord did
feele for our sinnes.

*And is set to the tune of
I lift mine hart to thee.*

PSALM **XXV.**

To his much esteemed good frend Mr. GEORGE
FRANKLYN, on[e] of the Assistants of the most
worthy companie of marchants-Adventurers
residing at Hamb :

Grace here, Glory hereafter, in Christ.

LOUING and beloued, The words of a
dying father, or of a dying frend are
wont to take deepe impression in the
minds and memories of good natures. Whose
words shall pearce, if the words of our Christ,
our dying Christ, and that for vs, and his last
also : Whose I say if not his ? To you I send the
last words of Christ, in the last place, yet you
are not the least in my loue. The first in intention is last in execution. And nothing is conveayed
to the intellectuall powers that is not first in the
sensible parts. It was God's purpose of our
Christ, euen in the creatiō, that he should be thus
vpon the crosse. See then your Christ at his last.
Tune your dolefull dumps to a sad soule, and ioy
in sobbs. For he prayes, cries, yells, promiseth,
perfecteth all, that we may be all in all with God.

What can be more? Christ passion is the modell of our profession, yea the medall of our perfection. For God's strength is perfected in our weakenes.

We may sowe in teares, we shall reape in ioy. Let my Spring be wett so that I may haue a plentifull Autume I care not. *Vir dolorum* can best tune his voice to dolours. If God will haue it so, His will be done. He did so with his owne. We cannot imagine our condition free. God giude vs through all by his sauing. grace, to which I shall euer recommend you, and rest,

Your more then much affectionate,

W. LOE.

THE VEWE.

GOD my soule lift vp,   1
    And stretch mine hart in twaine,
That it may feele, and faile, and die,
    For life is in this paine.

My poore heart is so full   2
    And fraught with thought of thee,
That it's nighe rent to see thy loue
    So much, so maine for me.

O take thy crosse and nailes,   2
    And straine my hart at length,
That thy deere loue may not be pent,
    But shewe my soule my strength.

And nowe my thoughts are free   3
    Thy loue to vewe in sight,
My hart doth pant, for that noe more
    It feeles here of thy might.

O fill my hart once more,
    And stretch and straine it still,

That I may lothe and loue no more
My sinne that brought this ill.

But I want space in hart, 6
    And grace in all my life,
To end my smart in sight of this,
    And sinnes that are so rife.

But since my hart O God 7
    Holds not a sight of thee,
O doe thou Lord hold fast my hart
    And shewe thy loue to me.

THE FIRST DUMPE: ON THE FIRST WORD.

Father forgiue them for they knowe not what they doe.—
Luck. 23. Verse 34.

WHAT voice is this so shrill 1
    That soūds thus in mine eare?
O put from them their sinns O God
    That knowes not what's thy feare.

Is't not thy voice O Christ, 2
    On crosse when thou didst hang?
And eke for those that did thee kill,
    Is't not thy voice that sang?

A tune to God on highe   3
  With which his eare was pleasd,
To see thy deere loue stretch so farre,
  And made the world so eas'd.

They knewe not what they did :   4
  Was ere such a thing seene?
To pray for those that made a prey
  In woes so sharp so keene.

O soule full oft thou hast   5
  Not knowen what thou hast done :
Noe way for helpe to cure that greefe
  But in thy Christ, God's sonne.

O pray my soule for them   6
  That hate thee to the graue,
And let not wrath lodg with thee once,
  It's Christ that must thee saue.

When foes doe curse, blesse them   7
  For Christ hath taught thee so;
Who prayd for such as did him kill
  And brought to curse and woe.

THE NEXT DUMPE : ON THE NEXT WORD.

Verily I say vnto thee, This day shalt thou be with me in
paradice.—LUCK 23. v. 43.

SOULE looke vp to this,   1
    And harke what voice thou hear'st ;
Thy Christ in midst of gripes of death
    Doth heare, what is't thou fearst ?

Then sure he will thee heare,   2
    Aud giue eare to thy crye,
Nowe that he sitts on throne in state
    And is thy God so nighe.

A theefe doth cry and call,   3
    Christ heares him by and by :
O soule thy Christ will heare thee sure
    If thou dost call and cry.

O learne it is but one   4
    To whom Christ grants an eare,
That sued to him in death at last,
    And sought him in his feare.

Yet it is one my soule   5
    Least thou shouldst faynt and dye,
And that thy Christ would not thee heare
    In death when thou shalt cry.

And yet it is but one,   6
  Least soule thou shouldst be proud,
And thinke that God would heare thee still
  When that thy cry is loud.

O learne sweet soule by this   7
  To sue to God in life,
And driue not of[f] till death doe come
  To die in iarre and strife.

THE THIRD DUMPE: ON THE THIRD WORD.

Behold thy mother, Behold thy sonne.
JOHN 19. v. 26, 27.

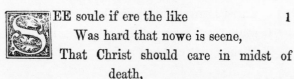

SEE soule if ere the like   1
  Was hard that nowe is seene,
That Christ should care in midst of
    death,
  And greefes that were so keene

For those that could not helpe,   2
  But sawe him in that plight,
Burst soule and die, to see his loue
  To her that bare his might.

And eke to him whose loue   3
  Was fixt sure in his breast:

616

That Christ should care in midst of greefe
    That he should liue in rest.

She that whose seede did bruse,   4
    The head of hell and death,
Hath hart all prest with woe and greefe
    To see Christ lose his breath.

O child see that thou loue,   5
    And loke, and long for good,
To those that haue thee borne and bred,
    And are thee nighe in bloud.

Shall not our Christ loue those   6
    Thinke you that searue him still,
And haue a care of all such folke
    That seeke to doe his will.

My soule they are all deare   7
    He cares for all their seede,
Ne shall there one that serues our God
    Be void of his full meede.

THE FOURTH DUMPE: ON THE FOURTH WORD.

My God, my god, why hast thou forsaken me ?
MAT. 27. vers. 46.

 NOWE my soule giue eare   1
    To this great cry and yell,
That shakes the heauens and moues the
    earth
    And teares the powers of hell.

My God, my God cries Christ   2
    Why putts thou me thee fro,
And why dost hide thy face frō me
    As if I were thy foe.

O soule he cries for thee,   3
    That thou maist haue God's light,
And nere be cast in pit full lowe,
    And hid out of his sight.

This cry did darke the sunne   4
    In full smyle of his beames :
O soule doth not it dymme thy sight,
    And cause of teares full streames ?

My soule great is our sinnes   5
    That causd these groanes and cries :

My eares that heare, are dull and deafe,
　My hart it faynts, and dies.

What paine didst thou O Christ　　　　6
　For me base wretch then beare,
That thou didst yell, and cry, and roare
　In such great greefe and feare.

Wast not that I might nere　　　　　7
　Feele God goe from my hart?
Wast not O Christ that I might not
　Of hell once feele the smart.

THE FIFT DUMPE: ON THE FIFT WORD.

I thirst.—John 19. v. 28.

HAT thirst was this O Christ　　1
　　That thou di'st feele so fell?
　　　That made thee call for drinke in
　　　　drought,
　　　That causd thee thus to yell?

Wast not for my poore soule　　　　2
　Thou didst cry in thy thirst?
That I might tast these streames of ioy
　That man had at the first.

And nere to thirst for aye,   3
   But haue the streames full glad,
That ioy the hart, and soule, and all,
   And blesse the mind that's sad.

Thou art the rocke O Christ   4
   From whence the source doth flowe
That makes vs feele no thirst at all
   But vp wards for to growe.

Come to this source my soule,   5
   And drench thy deepe sad mind,
Thou cāst not chuse but here thou must,
   A well of blisse sure find.

For Christ didst thirst for thee   6
   That thou mights[t] drinke I say,
The streames that flowe from throne of God
   Where Christ doth dwell for aye.

All soules doe thirst for this   7
   All saincts for this doe crye,
And bray as harts doe for the flouds,
   And so to faynt and dye.

THE SIXT DUMPE.

It is finished.—JOHAN. 19. VERS. 30.

OWE all is done my soule   **1**
    T hat can be done for the
The houres of death and powers of hell
    Are all put farre from me.

Christ nowe hath paid the debt,   **2**
    The bond in two is rent,
The lawe, the curse, the woe, the crosse
    Is laid on him that's sent.

Loe Christ hath tane for thee   **3**
    Thy sinne, thy shame, thy crosse,
And rid thee from the hags of hell
    That would haue wrought thy losse.

Nowe is the world all iudged :   **4**
    All powers of death and hell
Haue done their worst, and nowe in woe
    Doe cry, and roare, and yell.

It's done, it's done, saith Christ !   **5**
    Ye[a] all is past and cleare,
That thou my soule maist liue in blisse
    And be to God most deare.

Is this the way O Christ,   6
  That we tast woe with thee,
That so we may once rule and raigne,
  And thy sweete face still see.

O lett thy will O Lord,   7
  Be done of vs in fine,
And by vs let thy will be done
  That still we may be thine.

THE SEUENTH DUMPE: ON THE SEVENTH WORD.

Father into thy hands doe I commend my spirit.
Luck. 23. vers. 46.

 COME ioy of mine hart,   1
  And seaze my soule with this;
What is there ought in the wide world
  That cā be more to blisse

Then for my soule to heare
  My Christ his soule to giue,
Into the hands of God my Lord
  There still for aye to liue?

Nowe soule, thou seest thy blisse,   2
  And where thou maist be sure,

622

To haue thy rest, thy ioy, thy stay
  Thy loue, thy life, thy cure.

O blest are they that dye,   4
  They rest from all their care;
When once the Lord doth sett them free,
  What Death or Hell can dare?

In his, O soule, thy Christ   5
  For thine made suite to God
Thou need'st not feare the day of death
  Nor graue, nor hell, his rod.

For thou art safe in him   6
  That keepes thy life in store,
And it is hid in Christ, thy Lord,
  What can'st thou wishe nowe more?

O soule die in these words,   7
  Giue vp thy selfe in fine
To God in Christ, and feare no ill
  For he saies ' Thou art mine '.

TO HIM THAT MADE THESE HYMNS.

WHEN with my thoughts I vewe thy saynct
like Muse

How on[e] while drencht in sobs, and
sighs for sinne;

And yet more low, the paths of death doth vse;

There seisd with greef, yet prayes: then sours[1]
euen in

Heauen's gate it self: and there true loue doth
find,

And then it's Christ doth see, and vew: his payne,

His cross: his speare-pearst side, his greef of
mind

Thence dumpt twixt ioy and greef: as on[e] half
slayne

I muse, euen at thy muse, how well, how fit it
lymms

It's greef, sobs, sighs and tears, in tunes, in songs,
and hymns.

J. P.

---

1 = soars.   G.

TO HIM THAT MADE THESE HYMNS.

HER'S but one God, that this world one
     hath made
       One Christ, one Truth, one faith, one
        hope, one loue;
To serve this one, in hymns of ones, dost shade
Thy zeale, to teach vs that in one we moue.
Loe, as thy hymns be ones, so is thy name but odd,
How fitt? both name and hymns doe ioyne to
     praise one God.
Thus ten and one, in one thou hast nowe framd,
That we in one should keep the lawe of ten;
Thus by seauen and seauen thou hast them so
     namd
For seauen tymes seauen, day by day, we break
     them.
Loe, your hymns, of one, ten and one, and seauen
     by seauen
Learns, God to laud, his lawe to keepe, the way
     to heauen.

                   G. F.[1]

---

[1] Query—Dr. Giles Fletcher, (*pater*)? G.

Finis.